DAY HIKES IN THE SANTA FE AREA

Founded in 1892, the Sierra Club works in the United States and other countries to restore the quality of the natural environment and to maintain the integrity of ecosystems. Educating the public to understand and support these objectives is a basic part of the Club's program. All are invited to participate in its activities, which include programs to study, explore and enjoy wildlands.

DAY HIKES

IN THE

SANTA FE AREA

Fifth Edition

Enlarged and Revised

SIERRA
CLUB

FOUNDED 1892

By
The Santa Fe Group
Of
The Sierra Club

ISBN: 0-9616458-3-0

Library of Congress Catalog Card Number: 99-75609

First edition, first printing - 1981
First edition, second printing - 1982
Second edition - 1986
Third edition - 1990
Fourth edition - 1995
Fifth edition - 1999

Published by the Santa Fe Group
of the Sierra Club
621 Old Santa Fe Trail, Suite 10
Santa Fe, NM 87501

Produced by Courier Company

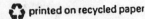 printed on recycled paper

TABLE OF CONTENTS

Acknowledgments vii

Background of Sierra Club Outings viii

Introduction ix

How to Use this Book x

Safety Tips for Hikers xiii

Hike Locations Map xviii

Map Legend xix

Summary of Hikes (table of key data for each hike) xx

Hike Descriptions .... 3 - 247

Glossary 248

Useful Addresses and Phone Numbers 251

Suggested Reading 253

Index of Hikes 259

Sierra Club Application Forms.................................. End

ACKNOWLEDGMENTS

Beginning with the first edition in 1981 *Day Hikes in the Santa Fe Area* has been a team effort by hiking enthusiasts and leaders in the Santa Fe Group. Authorship credits are given to the original writers, even though each new edition has involved revisions based on the changed condition of trails and roads.

Special thanks for their contribution to Edition Five go first to the book committee: Eleanor Eisenmenger, Norma McCallan, Tobin Oruch, Lionel Soracco, Norbert Sperlich and Ned Sudborough.

Next we thank those who added new hikes to our book: Eleanor Eisenmenger, Matt Gervase, Norma McCallan, Lionel Soracco, Norbert Sperlich and Ned Sudborough.

Re-hiking and reviewing the old hikes were: Dave Bryant, Matt Gervase, Carolyn Glick, John Jasper, Norma McCallan, Bob McKee, Lionel Soracco, Gordon Spencer, Norbert Sperlich, Ned Sudborough and Lee Sullivan.

Special thanks to Dorothy Grossman for the cover design, to Wes Horner for the maps and to Robin Bond for the line drawings. Tobin Oruch designed the greatly expanded summary chart of hikes. We especially thank Roger Peterson for expert advice. Lionel Soracco had overall responsibility for editing and preparation for publication.

The idea of a trail guide for the Santa Fe area was first promoted by Ann Young. She, Betsy Fuller and Bill Chudd, joined by Ingrid Vollnhofer, Linda Zwick, Jana Oyler, Norbert Sperlich and others were the driving forces behind earlier editions. This Fifth Edition would not exist without their earlier labors of love.

BACKGROUND OF SIERRA CLUB OUTINGS

by
Kenneth D. Adam

In 1892 a group of concerned and dedicated people met in San Francisco to form an organization, the Sierra Club, of those interested in mountain exploration. The first president was John Muir, and there were 182 charter members. The club's purposes included the publication of information about the mountains and the enlistment of support and cooperation by the public and government in preserving the forests and natural features of the Sierra Nevada. It almost immediately took the lead in the successful battle to preserve Yosemite Valley and its high country as a National Park. The club held its first outing in 1901.

The Rio Grande Chapter came into being in 1963 with 52 members, and initially included not only New Mexico, but all of Texas and the eastern part of Arizona. Almost immediately most of Texas and all of Arizona formed their own chapters, leaving in the Rio Grande Chapter the state of New Mexico and the El Paso area of Texas. In the early 1970s the Santa Fe Group was formed, and soon had an active outings program.

Every weekend visitors to Santa Fe, as well as newly arrived and long-time residents, take advantage of our local Sierra Club hikes, backpacks and cross-country ski trips, which are open to the public without charge. For a complete list of Sierra Club outings and public meetings throughout New Mexico pick up a copy of the Rio Grande Sierran in a box outside our office at Plaza de Desira, 621 Old Santa Fe Trail, Suite 10, or call us at 505-983-2703 and leave your address and a request for a mailed copy. Better yet, become a Sierra Club member and receive all local and national mailings. There's an application at the end of the book.

INTRODUCTION

by
Betsy Fuller

The area around Santa Fe contains a wealth of varied hikes perhaps unequaled by any other place in the state. Access to the 12,000 foot peaks of the Sangre de Cristo Mountains is within an hour's drive of the plaza. Winter walks at elevations of less than 6,000 feet are within easy reach when the mountains are too deep in snow to be walked. There are several nationally designated wilderness areas nearby, and the Santa Fe National Forest contains over a million and a half acres of land. Within an hour's drive of Santa Fe you can find five of the seven life zones.

The Santa Fe Group of the Sierra Club has felt the need for a guide to this wealth of wilderness, and this volume describes some of the typical walks that are so close. We have included walks that are classed as easy as well as more difficult ones, and we have tried to give fair representation to the many varied types of terrain that are within reasonable driving distance of Santa Fe. There are other excellent hikes in the Santa Fe area. For further information we refer you to the publications listed in the "Suggested Reading" section at the back of this book.

The fourth edition of this guide has sold out and, rather than reprint it, the editors decided to issue a new, fifth edition. All hikes carried forward from edition IV have been re-hiked and revised wherever necessary. A few of the old hikes have been dropped due to area closures or route changes which rendered the hike less interesting. In addition seven new hikes have been added. Each hike has accompanying maps.

The money earned from the sale of this book has been used in a variety of environmental campaigns including efforts to save old timber stands from logging, to save pristine wilderness areas from mining operations, to protect the foothills east of the city and the National Forest near the ski basin from development, to have the East Fork of the Jemez declared a National Recreation Area, to dedicate the Baca Ranch (Valles Caldera) to public ownership, to pass New Mexico's hard rock mining bill, to help publish the mining manual, "Avoiding the Shaft" (a mining activist handbook), as well as to contribute to the support of other environmental groups furthering congenial aims. Little of this would have been possible were it not for "Day Hikes in the Santa Fe Area."

HOW TO USE THIS BOOK

The hikes in this book are arranged according to geographical area. The map on page xviii shows the approximate starting location of the hikes, and the chart on pages xx - xxiii summarizes key facts about each hike so you can quickly gauge its difficulty, appropriate season, road condition, roundtrip driving distance from the downtown Santa Fe Plaza, and more.

Hikes are graded as "easy," "moderate," and "strenuous." These terms are somewhat loose and mean different things to different hikers. It would be wise for a hiker new to the area to attempt one of the shorter hikes first to see how his or her rating compares with the editor's. In general we call a hike **easy** if it is under six miles in length and involves relatively little elevation change. A **moderate** hike is usually between six and ten miles, involves more uphill climbing and may be over less well maintained trails. A **strenuous** hike is over ten miles in length, usually involves substantial changes in elevation, is often at high elevations and sometimes is over very rough trails.

Of course, any hike can be partially completed, thereby reducing the difficulty while still providing a rewarding experience. Hikes which, in our view, are particularly rewarding even when partially completed are given a double rating. For example, "Easy to moderate" (or "E-M") would designate a hike which is moderate if completed, but has an easy but rewarding first part. Some hike descriptions are of two hikes; for example, the Apache Canyon Loop (page 66), which also includes a trail to Glorieta Baldy via Apache Canyon. In such a case the difficulty levels are separated by a "/". Thus "Easy-Moderate/Strenuous" would mean the first hike (Apache Canyon Loop) is moderate if completed, but contains a rewarding, easy first part. The "Strenuous" after the slash means than the second hike (to Glorieta Baldy) is strenuous.

The term "cumulative uphill hiking" under ALTITUDE RANGE in each hike description is the estimated total number of feet you must walk uphill during that hike. Merely subtracting the lowest elevation point from the highest does not accurately describe a trail that involves a great deal of up and down hiking.

Before you start on the hike, read through the preliminary material and the hiking directions to be sure that it's the kind of outing you have in mind. You might want to take a camera along or a wildflower field guide or binoculars for birding.

The sketch maps at the beginning of each hike description give a general idea of the length, direction and "shape" of the walk. For greater detail we urge you to purchase the U.S. Geological Survey topographical map ("topo") that covers the area of your hike---available at many sporting goods stores in Santa Fe. The pertinent topos are listed at the beginning of each hike. If you are not familiar with these maps, spend some time studying them so that you'll recognize what the contour lines mean, which way is uphill or downhill, what the scale is and what the symbols mean. A topo map and a compass (plus the skills in using them) might save the day in case you get lost or disoriented.

In addition to the topo map, it will be helpful to have a New Mexico road map and also maps of the Santa Fe, Carson and Cibola National Forests, where most of these hikes are located. These maps are available in Santa Fe at the Public Lands Information Center in the BLM office, 1474 Rodeo Road (505-983-7542). Recently excellent maps of some of the wilderness areas have been published. These allow you to picture the entire region your trail is in, and they contain contour lines, too.

Every effort has been made to make the directions, both driving and hiking, easy to understand and accurate. However, this book should not be considered a step-by-step, do-it-yourself hike book for beginners. Because of changes in the routes of trails, vandalism of signs, destruction of landmarks, as well as the possibility of human error, the accuracy of every detail cannot be guaranteed. Mileages given are necessarily approximate.

One final word: wilderness is destructible, so when you are in it, respect it, love it and take care of it. Stay on the trails and don't take shortcuts. Pack out your trash to the last gum wrapper; even pack out somebody else's trash. Be careful with matches. Admire the flowers and rocks, but leave them there for the next passerby to admire, too. And remember that you are only visiting where other animals live, so treat them and their environment with the respect you'd like to receive where you live.

Happy hiking!

SAFETY TIPS FOR HIKERS

by
Herb Kincey, St. John's College Search and Rescue Team

Certain safety procedures should be followed by anyone going into wild country. Failure to observe these rules can lead to accidents or even death. Chances of becoming a statistic in the records of a search and rescue team will be greatly reduced by following these safety rules.

DO NOT GO ALONE: Unless you are experienced and prefer solitude, a party of at least four persons is recommended so that if one person is injured, one can remain with the victim while the other two go for help. Try never to leave an injured hiker alone.

Instead of going solo, find an experienced hiker to accompany you or join one of the Sierra Club weekend outings, lead by experienced hikers who are willing to share their knowledge with you. An outing schedule is available in a box outside our office at Plaza de Desira, 621 Old Santa Fe Trail, Suite 10.

PLAN YOUR ROUTE CAREFULLY: Know the escape routes. Plan a route ahead of time using U.S. Geological Survey and U.S. Forest Service maps. When traveling on foot allow about one hour for each two miles covered plus an additional hour for each 1000 feet of altitude gained. At all times know where you are on the map and the best way out to civilization.

GET WEATHER REPORTS AND BE PREPARED FOR EMERGENCIES: Fast-moving frontal systems can bring sudden and violent changes in New Mexico weather. Try to obtain an extended weather forecast before setting out. The highest peaks in New Mexico are above timberline and remote. On hikes above timberline the safe policy is to start for the summit at

xiii

dawn and turn back about noon, the time when storms begin to form. Storms at high elevations provide two life-threats: hypothermia (from wind and rain) and electrocution (from lightning).

CHECK WITH AUTHORITIES: Most of the New Mexico high country lies within National Forests. Forest rangers know their districts and can offer valuable advice on trails, campsites and potential problems. Many desert lands are administered by the Bureau of Land Management (BLM), whose officials will be glad to help. The New Mexico Department of Game and Fish will make recommendations about where to hike during hunting seasons. Booklets from this department describe the areas open to hunters along with season dates. These are useful publications for hikers wishing to avoid hunting areas. Bright clothing is appropriate for safety during big game hunting season.

GO PROPERLY EQUIPPED: As a rule the most serious dangers in the wilderness are WIND, COLD and WETNESS. Even during July it can snow on the higher peaks, and hard summer rains occur almost daily in the mountain range. It is quite possible to die from "exposure" (hypothermia: a disastrous drop in body temperature) at any time of the year, especially above timberline (about 11,800 feet). Having warm clothing, even during the summer, is vital. A shirt, sweater, socks, mittens and cap (all of wool or polypropylene) should always be carried. Even when wet, wool is warm against the skin. For protection against wind and wetness carry a weatherproof parka or poncho. One of the first signs of hypothermia is shivering. This may be followed by difficulty walking and speaking, confusion, drowsiness and coma. Steps should be taken to restore and maintain body temperature as soon as signs of hypothermia appear. These steps may include locating shelter from the elements, use of warm clothing or blankets, replacing cold wet clothing, providing warm, non-alcoholic drinks and body-to-body transfer of heat. If symptoms intensify, medical help should be obtained as soon as possible.

Always carry these items with you when going into the back country: map, compass, flashlight, sunglasses, candle, waterproof matches, whistle, pocket knife, protective clothing, minimum first aid, extra food and water. Water is very scarce in some areas; carry plenty, at least a quart per person. Water purification is recommended for water from streams or lakes. Giardia is now a common problem in wilderness areas.

ALLOW TIME FOR ACCLIMATIZATION: Persons going into high mountains from low altitudes should beware of trying to climb any of the major peaks until they have had a few days to acclimatize. Many people who go too high too fast suffer "mountain sickness." The symptoms are vomiting, diarrhea, and feeling very ill. Pulmonary edema, a major medical emergency, also can occur above the 8000 foot level. The symptoms include extreme fatigue or collapse, shortness of breath, a racking cough, bubbling noises in the chest, and bloody sputum. Unless transported to a much lower altitude immediately the victim may die within a matter of hours. If available, administer oxygen until reaching a hospital. Several other procedures may help prevent the "mountain miseries": arrive in good physical condition, get plenty of rest and sleep and avoid alcohol and smoking.

LEAVE INFORMATION WITH RELATIVES OR FRIENDS: An itinerary of your trip, along with the names and addresses of each member, description and license numbers of vehicles used, and expected time of return should be left with a reliable person. Once under way, stick to your planned route and schedule. Any time a group is seriously overdue or an accident has occurred, the New Mexico State Police should be called in order to obtain assistance (505-827-9000).

LEARN THE LIMITATIONS OF EACH MEMBER: Assess the strengths and weaknesses of each member of the party. Do not try anything beyond the ability of the weakest hiker. Set the pace to that of the slowest hiker. <u>Be willing to turn back when conditions warrant doing so.</u>

KEEP THE PARTY TOGETHER: Individual members of a group should not be allowed to fall behind the main party or go ahead of it. Many wilderness fatalities have resulted from disregarding this rule. If the group is large, select one person to set the pace, another to bring up the rear. If hiking in the dark for some reason, assign each hiker a number and count off periodically.

WATCH FOR FLASH FLOODS: Most New Mexico streams are shallow and present few fording problems. However, flash floods occur in the steep arid canyons and arroyos around the perimeter of the mountains and in desert areas. Be especially careful in these hazardous areas and do not camp or leave vehicles parked there.

BEWARE OF LOOSE ROCK: In some places loose rock can be a serious hazard. Keep your group bunched together when going up or down this type of terrain. Never roll rocks down a mountainside. Another party may be below you.

GET OFF EXPOSED RIDGES DURING STORMS: Summer storms move in fast and will bring rain or hail, high winds, low visibility and lightning. Try not to allow your group to be caught on a peak or exposed ridge. If you are unable to get down in a lightning storm, have the group spread out with about 30 feet between each person. Stay away from lone trees or rocks. Avoid shallow caves or depressions, for ground currents may jump from the edge to your body. Insulate yourself from the ground (with pack, rope, clothing) and squat down, allowing only your feet to touch the ground or the improvised insulation.

Do not lie down.

EMERGENCY SIGNALS: The following signals are considered standard by many search and rescue groups. <u>Distress</u> - 3 evenly spaced signals given within 30 seconds. Repeat as required. <u>Acknowledgment</u> - 2 signals given in quick succession. <u>Return to camp</u> - 4 evenly spaced signals given within 30 seconds. Repeat as required.

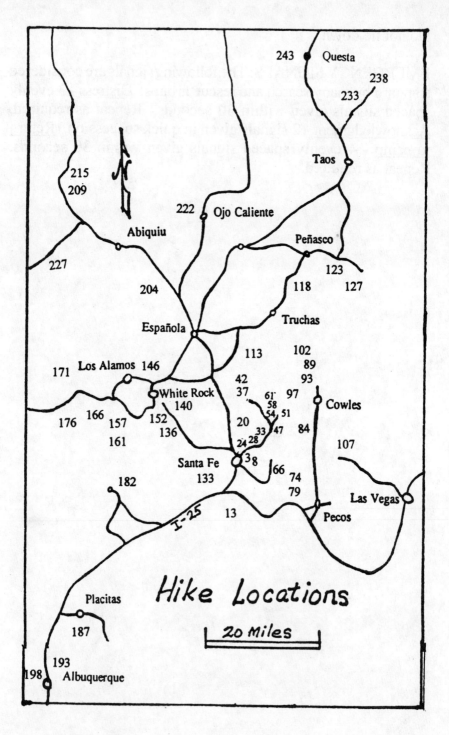

Hike Locations

20 Miles

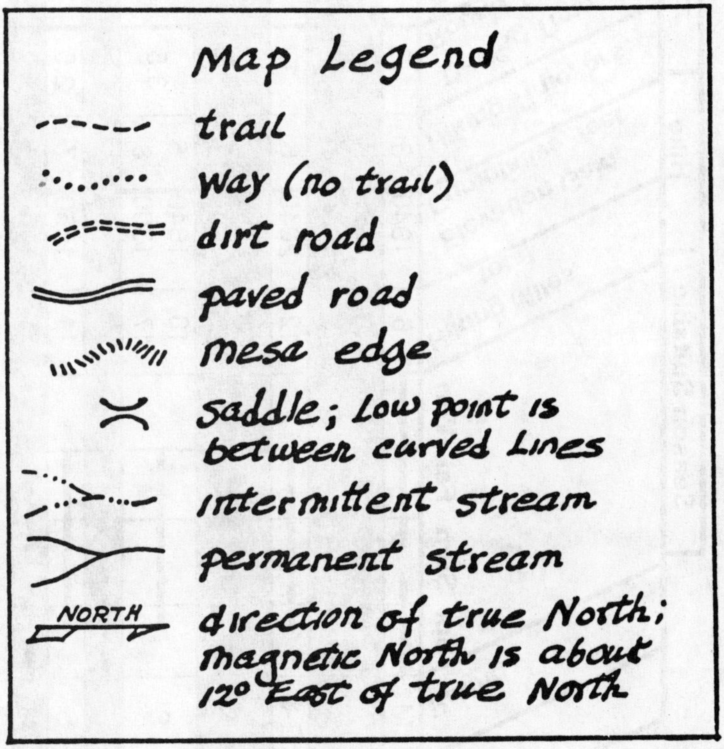

Map Legend

- - - - - - trail
:······· way (no trail)
======= dirt road
~~~~~ paved road
"""""""" mesa edge
✕ saddle; low point is between curved lines
-·-·-·- intermittent stream
⟩⟩⟩ permanent stream
NORTH direction of true North; magnetic North is about 12° East of true North

SUMMARY OF HIKES

Hike (Options)	Page	Rating	Spr	Sum	Fal	Win	Hiking Miles, total	Elevation Gain, feet	Cumulative	Hiking Time, hrs	Driving Time, Round Trip, hrs	Driving Miles, RT, from Plaza	Comments *
Ancho Rapids	152	M					6	1040	3	1.5		74	s
Apache Canyon Lp	66	M					6	800	4	1.5		29	s,u
+Glorieta Baldy		S					13	2900	7				
Aspen Vista	47	E-S					12	2040	6	1		27	
Atalaya: •St. Johns	8	M					7	1800	4	0.5		5	l,s
•Ponderosa Ridge							5.5	1590	3			7	
Beatty's Cabin;	89	S					10	1640	5	3.5		94	f,h,w
Pecos Falls							17	1300	8				
Borrego/BearWallow	33	E					4	760	2	0.8		18	w
Brazos Cabin	113	S					11	1550	7	2.5		78	h,w
Buckman Mesa	140	M					5.5	1100	4	2		42	h,l,s

Season Suitable: Spr, Sum, Fal, Win (suitability indicated by bars)

Trail	Page	Diff		Miles	Elev	Hours			Comments*
Cañada Bonita +Guaje/Caballo Mtn	171	E / S		4 / 14	650 / 3300	3 / 9	2	86	s
Chamisa Trail	24	E		5	1240	2.5-3	0.5	12	l
Diablo Canyon	136	E		6	400	3	1.7	36	u
Dockwiller Trail	93	M		8	1700	5	3	91	s,w
East Fork Trl/Box	176	E-M		9/8	7/800	4-5	3	110	s,w
Glorieta Baldy	74	S		11	2800	6	1	40	l,s
Glor. Ghost Town	79	E		6.5	950	3.5	1	40	w
Gold Hill (Taos)	233	S		10	3420	6	4.5	184	
Hermit Peak +Porvenir Canyon	107	S		8 / 14	2700 / 2800	5 / 7	3.5	170	s / w
Holy Ghost/Spirit	84	S		14	2750	9	3	81	w
Hyde Park Circle	28	E		5	1000	3	0.7	16	f,l,s
Jicarita Peak	127	S		11	2440	6-9	4	151	s,u
Kitchen Mesa	209	M		5	600	2.5	2.8	122	c,s,u
La Junta Circuit	42	S		13	2800	8	2	34	h,w
Lake Katherine	61	S		14.5	3300	7-8	1.3	30	w

* Comments

c = cliff (no dogs) d = dogs prohibited f = fee area

h = high clearance vehicle recommended l = loose footing

s = steep terrain u = unpaved access w = water plentiful (dogs)

SUMMARY OF HIKES, CONTINUED

Hike (Options)	Page	Rating	Season Suitable Spr	Sum	Fal	Win	Hiking Miles, total	Elevation Gain, Cumulative, feet	Hiking Time, hrs	Driving Time, hrs	Round Trip Driving Miles, RT, from Plaza	Comments*
La Luz/Sandia Crest	193	S					14/16	3800	8/10	2	115	f,l,s
La Vega	54	M					7	1500	3-4	1.3	30	w
Nambé Lake	51	M					7	2100	5	1.3	30	l,s,w
Ojo Caliente (2)	222	E/M					3/6	700	1.5/4	2	100	c,s
Otowi Ruins/Bayo	146	M					8	900	5	1.5	57	c,s
Painted Cave	166	S					15	2400	7-8	3.3	97	d,f,h
Pecos Baldy Lake	102	S					15	2600	7.5	3.5	102	f,w
+East P.B. Peak							17	3800	9			
Pedernal	227	S					9	1870	6-7	3.5	146	c,l,s,u
Petroglyphs (3)	198	E					1/3/2	100	1/2/2	2.5	140	d,f
Rail Trail (3)	13	E/M					4-10	200	2-3	.5/.8/1	13-31	d,f
Rancho Viejo	37	S					11.5	2300	6.5	2	34	h,w

Rim Vista/Salazar	215	E/M		5/8	1700	3/5	3+	130+	u
St. John's Area:									
• Dorothy Stewart	3	E		3	440	2	0.3	5	
• Monte Luna/Sol				2	7-800	1.5			l,s
Santa Barbara	123	S		12	1100	7	2.5-3	143	u,w
Santa Fe Baldy	58	S		13-14	3600	8	1.3	30	l,s
Stewart Lake	97	S		10.5	2500	6.5	2.8	90	w
Stone Lions Shrine	161	S		12.8	2700	8	2-2.5	92	d,f
Tent Rocks	182	E		2	350	1.5	2	80	c,f,l,u
Tesuque Creek	20	E		3	500	2	0.5	8	u,w
Tetilla Peak	133	E		2.5	950	2-3	2	36	h,l,s
Trampas Lakes	118	S		11.5	2450	6	3	108	u,w
+Hidden Lake				13.5	2700	7.5			
Tunnel Spring (2)	187	S		14-16	3240	8-10	2.5	108	f,s,u
Upper Crossing	157	S		13	1600	7	2-2.5	92	d,f
Wheeler Peak (2)	238	S		14	4310	7/8	4.5	184	s
Wild Rivers (3)	243	M		2-9	1500	5-6	5	220	f,s,w
Window Rock	204	M		8	1000	5	1.5	70	

* Comments

c = cliff (no dogs) d = dogs prohibited f = fee area
h = high clearance vehicle recommended l = loose footing
s = steep terrain u = unpaved access w = water plentiful (dogs)

DAY HIKES IN THE SANTA FE AREA

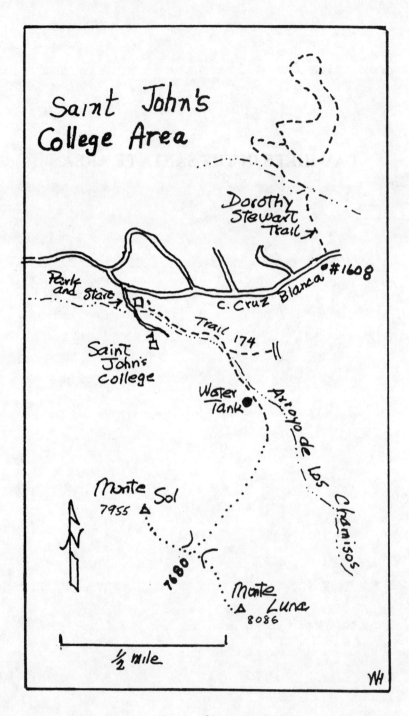

Saint John's
College Area

Dorothy
Stewart
Trail

Park
and gate

C. Cruz Blanca °#1608

Trail 174

Saint
John's
College

Water
Tank

Arroyo de Los Chamisos

Monte Sol
7955 △

7680

Monte
Luna
△ 8086

N

½ mile

YH

SAINT JOHN'S COLLEGE AREA

by
Lionel Soracco

U.S. GEOLOGICAL SURVEY MAP REQUIRED: Santa Fe - 7.5 minute series.

SALIENT FEATURES: The two hikes described in this section are within Santa Fe and easily accessible from the St. John's College parking lot. Neither takes more than two hours, both are easy, both take you out of development and both afford sweeping views of the Santa Fe landscape.

RATING: Easy

ROUND TRIP DRIVING: 5 miles.

SEASONAL CONSIDERATIONS: Can be hiked year round. A few inches of snow could be on the ground in winter.

DRIVING DIRECTIONS: From the northeast corner of the plaza, drive east (towards the mountains) on Palace Avenue one mile, crossing Paseo de Peralta and continuing to the intersection of Palace and Alameda. Turn left onto Alameda. A few hundred yards past Smith Park, Alameda veers right (south) to become Camino Cabra. Continue south on Camino Cabra past Cristo Rey Church. About 0.7 miles past Cristo Rey, you'll pass the Los Miradores condominium development on your left. Turn left onto Camino Cruz Blanca at the St. John's College sign. Turn right off Cruz Blanca into St. John's College, then immediately left into the Visitor's Parking Lot and park at the far (east) end.

Dorothy Stewart Trail

ROUND TRIP HIKING DISTANCE: Approximately 3 miles.

ROUND TRIP HIKING TIME: Between 1 ½ and 2 hours.

ALTITUDE RANGE: Highest point, 7550 feet; lowest point, 7320 feet; cumulative uphill hiking, 440 feet.

HIKING INSTRUCTIONS: The trailhead is on Cruz Blanca east of St. John's, where 3 parking spaces are planned but not developed as of 1999, so we're starting at St. John's. Walk to the east end of the parking lot, turn left, cross over to Cruz Blanca and turn right. Now walk about a half mile towards the mountains, passing Calle Picacho, Ocaso del Sol development and Joaquin Lane. Just past street address 1608 look for a small boulder about ten feet to the left (north) of the road. This marks the beginning of the trail. As of late 1999 there was no sign at the trailhead. So far you have walked about 15 minutes.

The trail leads northwards along the east edge of an arroyo on a trail easement donated to the Forest Trust by Irene von Horvath. You are soon beyond any homes and into the characteristic piñon-juniper forest. After a quarter mile you descend a few switchbacks. A little further and you reach Arroyo Mora and a trail sign announcing "Dorothy Stewart Trail" with due credits to the builders, The Forest Trust.

Continue northward past this sign. You'll reach a streambed and, about 20 yards further, a trail leading off to the left. Don't take this (for the adventurous, it takes you across the hills to Camino Militar and on to Upper Canyon road). Keep going north. After rising slowly for 200 yards the trail turns right and starts uphill. Hiking about 100 yards more brings you to a fork. You are about to enter a loop which circles the hill you're on. The loop takes a half hour to complete. We prefer the clock-

4

wise route, so turn left. After a pleasant walk around the hill, you'll again be at this point.

The trail is clearly marked so no special instructions are required. After a ten minute walk along the north side you'll find a rustic bench just off the trail to your left, where you can rest and get a great view of the Santa Fe River valley, Cerro Gordo (the hill bordering it on the north), and, looking westward across the Rio Grande valley, the Jemez Mountains and Los Alamos. Continuing clockwise on the loop you'll pass an unofficial trail leading off to the left. On the east side of the loop there's another bench with views of nearby Picacho Peak due east, and, to the northwest, the distant Tesuque Peak, top of the Santa Fe Ski Area. Returning on the south side of the hill brings you back to the beginning of the loop. Retrace your steps down the hill, turn left and follow the trail south to Cruz Blanca, then turn right (west) to reach St. John's and your vehicle.

NOTE: As of 1999 only the Dorothy Stewart segment of a large, proposed network of trails on the east side of Santa Fe has been completed. Check with the City of Santa Fe Parks and Recreation Department, 505-473-7228, for an update on this.

Monte Sol and Monte Luna (Sun Mountain and Moon Mountain)

ROUND TRIP HIKING DISTANCE: Approximately 2 miles.

ALTITUDE RANGE: Highest points, 8086 feet (Monte Luna) and 7956 (Monte Sol); lowest point, 7300 feet (Arroyo Chamisa); cumulative uphill hiking, 800 feet for Monte Luna, 670 for Monte Sol.

HIKING INSTRUCTIONS: As you stand in the St. John's parking lot, look south and above the college buildings and you'll see two sizeable hills. The nearer one is Monte Sol.

Joined to it by a saddle to the south is Monte Luna. You'll hike to the saddle, then climb the hill of your choice.

Walk to the east end of the parking lot and follow Trail 174 down into Arroyo Chamisa. Turn left at the arroyo and follow it as it curves around a bend. Continue in the arroyo past Trail 174 (which leaves the arroyo eastwards towards Atalaya Mountain). After a few minutes you'll reach a road on your right leading up from the arroyo bottom to a large, green water-storage tank. Walk up the road past the tank, then look to your right and note the saddle between Monte Sol and Monte Luna. That saddle is your next destination. Although many trails have been worn in over the years by meandering hikers there's no "official" one. Perhaps the simplest way to get to the saddle is to drop down into the small arroyo just to your right and follow it up to the saddle. Along the way you'll find some of those "unofficial" trails. Take them if you like; just keep the arroyo in sight and head towards the saddle.

Once at the saddle you can look across the southern half of Santa Fe towards Albuquerque, the Ortiz Mountains and, to the east, the Sandia Mountains. For a better view climb Monte Sol (north of you) or Monte Luna. Monte Sol is the easier climb. To get back to the parking lot just reverse directions.

Take a two-mile walk every morning before breakfast.
–Harry S. Truman

6

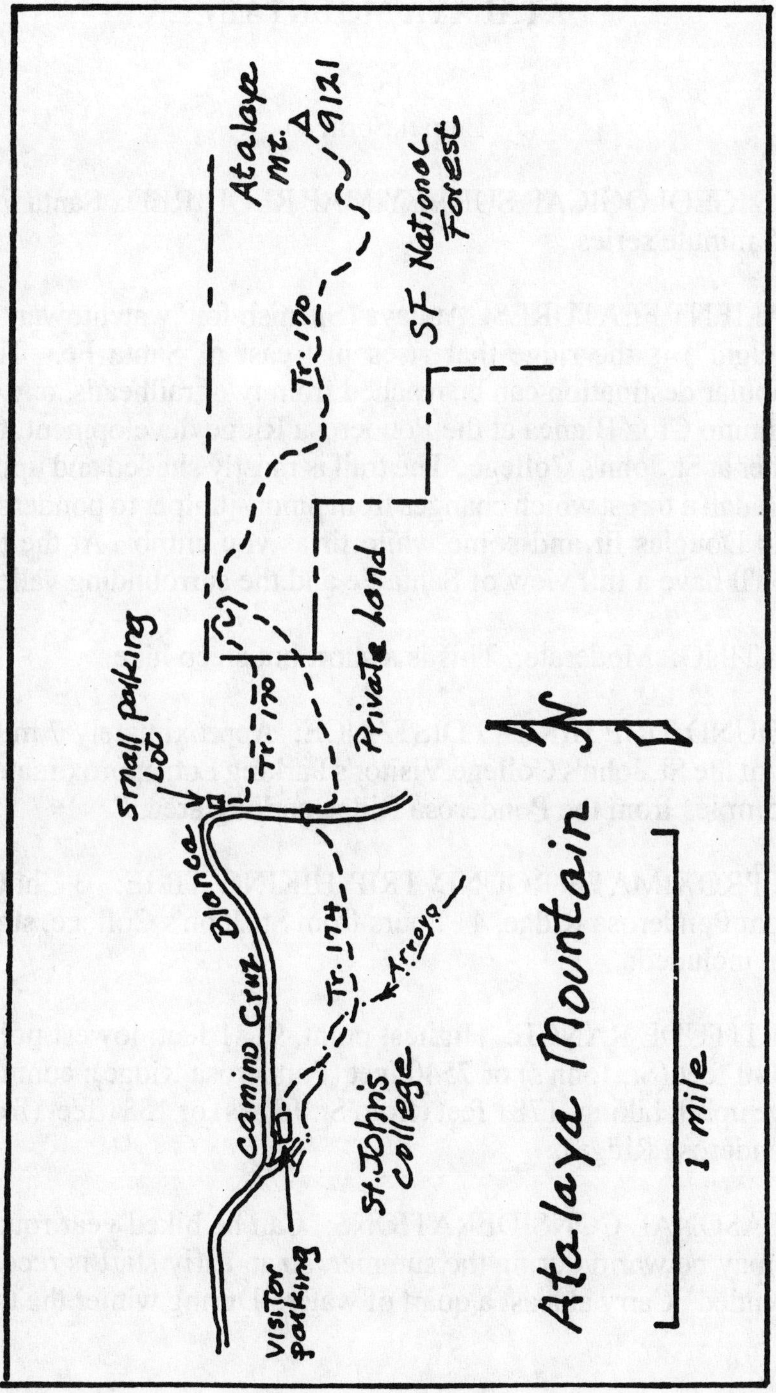

Atalaya Mt.
△ 9121
Tr. 170
SF National Forest

Small parking Lot
Tr. 170
Private land

Camino Cruz Blanca
Tr. 174
Arroyo

Visitor parking
St. John's College

Atalaya Mountain

1 mile

ATALAYA MOUNTAIN

by
Lionel Soracco

U.S. GEOLOGICAL SURVEY MAP REQUIRED: Santa Fe - 7.5 minute series.

SALIENT FEATURES: Atalaya (Spanish for "watchtower" or "height") is the ridge that rises just east of Santa Fe. This popular destination can be reached from two trailheads, one on Camino Cruz Blanca at the Ponderosa Ridge development, the other at St. John's College. The trail is mostly shaded and uphill through a forest which changes from piñon-juniper to ponderosa and Douglas fir and some white fir as you climb. At the top you'll have a full view of Santa Fe and the surrounding valley.

RATING: Moderate. This is a short but steep hike.

ROUND TRIP HIKING DISTANCE: Approximately 7 miles from the St. John's College Visitor's Parking Lot; approximately 5.5 miles from the Ponderosa Ridge parking area.

APPROXIMATE ROUND TRIP HIKING TIME: 3+ hours from Ponderosa Ridge, 4+ hours from St. John's College, stops not included.

ALTITUDE RANGE: Highest point, 9121 feet; lowest point, 7340 feet (St. John's) or 7540 feet (Ponderosa Ridge); cumulative uphill hiking, 1781 feet (from St. John's) or 1581 feet (from Ponderosa Ridge).

SEASONAL CONSIDERATIONS: Can be hiked year round. It may be warm during the summer, so an early start is recommended. Carry at least a quart of water. During winter the trail is usually accessible, although there may be several inches of snow at the higher elevations and a foot or more at the top.

ROUND TRIP DRIVING: 5 miles to St. John's College, 6.5 miles to the Ponderosa Ridge/Camino Cruz Blanca trailhead; about 30 minutes.

DRIVING DIRECTIONS: From the northeast corner of the plaza, drive east (towards the mountains) on Palace Avenue one mile, crossing Paseo de Peralta and continuing to the intersection of Palace and Alameda. Turn left onto Alameda. A few hundred yards past Smith Park, Alameda veers right (south) to become Camino Cabra. Continue south on Camino Cabra past Cristo Rey Church. About 0.7 miles past Cristo Rey, you'll pass the Los Miradores condominium development on your left. Turn left onto Camino Cruz Blanca at the St. John's College sign. If you're starting the hike at St. John's (Trail 174), turn right off Cruz Blanca into St. John's College, then immediately left into the Visitor's Parking Lot. The trailhead is at the far end of the lot.

If you're starting at the Ponderosa Ridge residential development (Trail 170), continue eastward on Camino Cruz Blanca 0.8 miles to where the road turns right (south). After turning, you'll be facing the entry gate to the Ponderosa Ridge-Wilderness Gate residential development. To your left is a small parking area with a large informational sign regarding Trail 170. Park here, not along the roadside. If the lot is full park at St. John's and begin the hike there.

HIKING INSTRUCTIONS: Trail 174 (St. John's trailhead) and Trail 170 (Ponderosa Ridge trailhead) intersect a short way up the mountain; from there to the top the trail is 170.

First I'll describe Trail 174 to that intersection. Looking eastward from the St. John's parking lot, you'll see your

9

destination, a long ridge rising gradually as it proceeds north-wards. Starting at the far end of the parking lot, Trail 174 quickly winds down to the Arroyo de los Chamisos (dry except for a few weeks early in spring), crosses the arroyo, rises to traverse a field of chamisa bushes skirting St. John's new dormitory complex, recrosses the arroyo, and starts eastward up a narrow creek bed. Signs will guide you.

After entering the small arroyo of the creek, you'll pass through a log maze built to discourage equestrians and cyclists. For the next quarter mile, the trail follows the arroyo, with numerous "Stay on Trail" signs at creek crossings. A sign indicates where you leave the creek and head to the right and steeply upward to the Wilderness Gate Road.

Cross the road -- careful, there's occasional traffic here -- climb the steps and continue another quarter mile through woods to the log fence marking the entrance to the Santa Fe National Forest. Overhead are power lines running north-south across the foothills. A trail marker indicates that Atalaya is 2 miles distant. Climb up from the fence 40 yards, then turn left to follow Trail 174 another quarter mile to its intersection with Trail 170.

If you start the hike at the Ponderosa Ridge parking area (Trail 170), follow the wall south 50 yards to a gate. Turn left, through the gate, and continue uphill on the dirt road. You'll spot a house with a red metal roof. Just past that house the road veers right, but you continue straight ahead, passing under some powerlines and climbing wooden steps which lead to a log fence marking the Santa Fe National Forest boundary. Passing through the gate, follow the trail as it winds steeply uphill to its intersection with Trail 174.

Note: Both Trail 174 and Trail 170, from trailheads to log fences, pass through private property. Rights-of-way were negotiated over a period of years by the Sierra Club, Friends of Atalaya, Forest Trust, private landowners and representatives of the Santa Fe National Forest. Respect this arrangement by keeping to the trails.

From the intersection to the top, you'll be on Trail170. As this is a much-used trail, there are several alternate trail choices along the way. If they are signed "Trail Closed for Rehabilitation" don't use them.

The rest of Trail 170 is a well-worn shaded ascent through the forest. Notice the tree population gradually changing from piñon and juniper to ponderosa pine, Rocky Mountain juniper, and Douglas and white fir. Hiking in the summer, you'll experience gentle breezes and temperatures cooler than in the city below.

You'll reach the ridge a few hundred yards south of the summit. Turn left and follow the trail to the highest point, where you will be rewarded with a sweeping view of the city. Relax in the shade of the many trees and amuse yourself by identifying landmarks in Santa Fe. Can you spot your residence or hotel?

To return, reverse your course, but be careful: walking downhill, though easier, makes you potentially more prone to falls.

Most wild animals get into the world and out of it without being noticed.
–John Muir

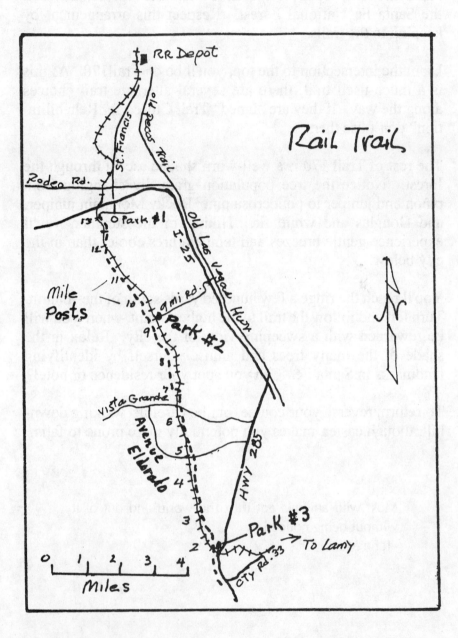

Rail Trail

RR Depot

St. Francis

Pecos Trail

Rodeo Rd.

13 0 Park #1

I-25

Old Las Vegas Hwy

Mile
Posts

11½

10

9 mi Rd.

9

Park #2

8

7½

Vista Grande

6

5

Avenue
Eldorado

4

HWY 285

3

Park #3

2

→ To Lamy

Cty Rd. 33

0   1   2   3   4

Miles

N

RAIL TRAIL

by
Norma McCallan

U. S. GEOLOGICAL SURVEY MAPS REQUIRED: Not necessary, but if you are curious, the trail overlaps these three: Santa Fe, Seton Village and Galisteo, all 7.5 series.

SALIENT FEATURES: Little driving, ideal for a short hike along an historic railroad route. Great vistas. Can be done in sections, with various options possible. Almost impossible to get lost. Minimal elevation change. No water available. You are likely to see hikers, bicyclists and an occasional horse. I'll describe 3 routes, allowing walks from the beginning, the end and the midway Nine Mile Road.

Note: The Santa Fe Southern is a working railroad, which is one of the charms of this hike. You are quite likely to see either the regular run or a chartered trip pass by. The train moves slowly and whistles a lot, but observe caution when crossing the tracks.

Soon after the Atchison, Topeka & Santa Fe established the first rail line in New Mexico, starting at Raton Pass in December 1878, it abandoned plans to route its main line through Santa Fe and ran the tracks from Las Vegas to Galisteo Junction (now Lamy) and on down through the Galisteo Basin to the Rio Grande and Albuquerque.

A station was established at Galisteo Junction and a branch line completed to Santa Fe in February, 1880. The AT&SF ran passenger service along this branch line until 1936 and continued freight service until March, 1992, when the line was purchased by the Santa Fe Southern RR. It started out as a freight operation, but soon allowed riders in its caboose and added the first of several coaches in 1993. Besides its scheduled 3 days a week run to Lamy with freight and passengers, special entertainment trains run regularly.

Through a joint endeavor between the Santa Fe Conservation Trust and Santa Fe County, an easement was purchased from the Santa Fe Southern Railway in 1998 to create a public trail next to the tracks between Rabbit Road and the intersection of the tracks and Highway 285. It is anticipated that some day the trail will be extended north to the railroad depot on Guadalupe Street.

RATING: Easy to moderate. Strenuous if you do the entire distance.

ROUND TRIP HIKING DISTANCE: Length of the official Rail Trail is 11.5 miles one way. It is not recommended to do that as a round trip, but rather to hike various segments, so the distance is variable.

APPROXIMATE ROUND TRIP HIKING TIME: Depends on length traveled. Segments recommended here would be 2 - 3 hours each.

ALTITUDE RANGE: Highest point is 6880 feet, lowest point is 6600 feet.

SEASONAL CONSIDERATIONS: Best fall through spring. Hot in summer.

ROUND TRIP DRIVING: Depends on route. Approximately 13 miles from Plaza for Route #1, 19 miles for Route #2, 31 miles for Route #3.

DRIVING DIRECTIONS: For all 3 routes go south on Old Pecos Trail to the intersection with Rodeo Road (about 3.6

miles from the Plaza), reset odometer to zero, then proceed as follows:

Route #1 Trailhead: Continue south on Old Pecos Trail across the interstate overpass. Turn right at 0.45 miles onto Rabbit Road and continue past the southern end of St. Francis Drive. At 2.9 miles the road crosses the railroad tracks. Turn left here, just before the tracks, and park in the flat area, where you can see the marks of many vehicles.

Route #2 Trailhead: From the Rodeo Road intersection, turn left off Old Pecos Trail onto the Old Las Vegas Highway, which parallels I-25. Pass the exits to Arroyo Hondo and Seton Village, and at 2.8 miles turn right onto Santa Fe County Road 660, "Timberwick & Nine Mile Road." The road veers left after passing over the interstate. Stay· on Nine Mile Road (Timberwick soon takes off to the right) as it ambles generally south. At 5.9 miles the pavement ends at a turnaround. Park here. Nine Mile Road apparently bears that name because it accesses the 9 mile marker of the railroad tracks.

Route #3 Trailhead: Cross the interstate overpass and take the Las Vegas entrance to I-25. At 6.7 miles take the exit to Clines Corners, Highway 285. At 11.9 miles, shortly before County Road 33 heads left for Lamy, the railroad tracks cross the highway. Turn off to the right onto the dirt parking area just before the tracks and park.

HIKING INSTRUCTIONS: Mileage numbers indicate RR mileposts ("milepost 13"), or a mile-indicator painted on a trestle or tunnel ("mile 12.6"), not hiking miles traveled.

Route #1 - Rabbit Road. Proceed south along the tracks. About 0.1 miles in you will pass milepost 13. At mile 12.6 the trail dips down to cross Arroyo Hondo, which is spanned by the longest trestle of the line. Arroyo Hondo, by the way, is the site

15

of a large Indian pueblo which was excavated in the 1970's by the School of American Research, then re-buried.

Once past the trestle, the single hiking trail on the left of the tracks is joined by a trail on the right. The double-trail continues for the remainder of the way, but only one is the designated trail. See map for the official route. Houses are now very sparse and generally at some distance from the trail. Soon you pass a dirt road on the left, which accesses the subdivision of Arroyo Hondo. Just before this intersection, high on the right bank, is a small white wooden cross, a *descanso*, inscribed "en memoria de Conzalo Valdez de 1888 a 1966."

Enjoy the vistas of the often snowy Sangre de Cristo Mountains to the east and the Jemez Mountains to the west. In the spring there are lots of wildflowers such as lupine and verbena among the grasses and the many large piñon and juniper trees. You may be lucky and see a flock of Mountain Bluebirds.

The next landmark, shortly before milepost 11, is a large, dark-green water tank, built in the 1980s - another sign of the burgeoning growth in the county. You have come about two miles. If you only wanted a short walk this is a good spot to turn around. If you're dying to check out the water tower you can easily hike north to it from the next trailhead.

Route #2 - Nine Mile Road. This trailhead has an official sign, "Santa Fe Rail Trail, 11.5 miles unimproved trail," by the stile which gives you access through the fence and down to the tracks.

<u>North Route.</u> If you want to check out the 1.8 miles of track between here and the green water tank mentioned above, turn right (north). Note the fine stonework in the double tunnels under the tracks at mile 9.5 and the trestle at milepost 10. Another tunnel with a handsome arch, this one so large you

could walk through it, appears at mile 10.4, and makes a good spot for a break. A weathered old RR crossing sign marks an abandoned dirt road coming in from the east and a large trestle shows up at mile 10.8. At milepost 11.0 you can see the water tank which was your destination.

South Route. To cover the next section of track, turn left (south) and almost immediately you will pass a trestle at mile 9.4. Note the two old windmills near the house on the left, most probably what the topo identifies as "9 Mile Ranch." To the southwest there are great views of the Ortiz, San Pedro and Sandia Mountains as well as the closer Cerrillos Hills. The faint blue silhouette to the south is the Manzano Mountains. At mile 8.1 a trestle is passed and at 7.4 there is a tunnel, with a handsome stone arch.

Soon the official trail crosses to the east side of the tracks and you pass a low wooden trestle at milepost 7.1. Ahead you can see the many houses of the Eldorado subdivision. At 6.7 is a small electric substation on the east side. Shortly you come to a paved road, Vista Grande, one of the two main roads travers-ing this popular subdivision.

This intersection, approximately mile 6.5 on the tracks, is a good spot to turn around on this segment. On your way back you will enjoy views of Tetilla Peak to the west, the Jemez Mountains to the northwest and the Sangre de Cristo Mountains to the east.

Route #3 - Highway 285 Northward. A new sign where the tracks cross the highway announces "Santa Fe Trail, 11.5 miles unimproved trail." There is, by the way, no easement for the last 1.5 miles of tracks to Lamy east of the highway. The private landowners along there will not like you hiking that section, and, indeed, another sign at this southern end of the Rail Trail announces "End of Trail, Hazardous Conditions

Beyond this Point - No Trespassing!" So, turn right (west) and start hiking.

There is a different feel to the southern end of the Rail Trail. Here you'll find sweeping vistas of the broad Galisteo Basin, San Pedro and Ortiz Mountains, Cerrillos Hills, and far to the south, the faint blue outline of the Manzano Mountains. Stop at milepost 2 to admire the view before the tracks turn northwards. There is a handsome wooden trestle over a small arroyo at mile 2.2, a good spot for a brief break. Now you start getting great views of the Jemez Mountains to the northwest, the Sangre de Cristo Mountains to the east and Glorieta Baldy and Thompson Peak prominent on the horizon. A dirt road appears at milepost 3 and a trestle at mile 3.2. Another dirt road at 3.3 has mail-boxes. You pass a good-sized trestle at mile 3.9 and another at mile 4.8. Shortly you arrive at the paved Avenida Eldorado, the other major road through Eldorado. You can turn around here, or brave the urban ambiance and continue on to the Vista Grande intersection at mile 6.5, where you turned around on the last segment.

> How many hearts with warm red blood in them are beating under cover of the woods, and how many teeth and eyes are shining! A multitude of animal people, intimately related to us, but of whose lives we know almost nothing, are as busy about their own affairs as we are about ours.
> –John Muir

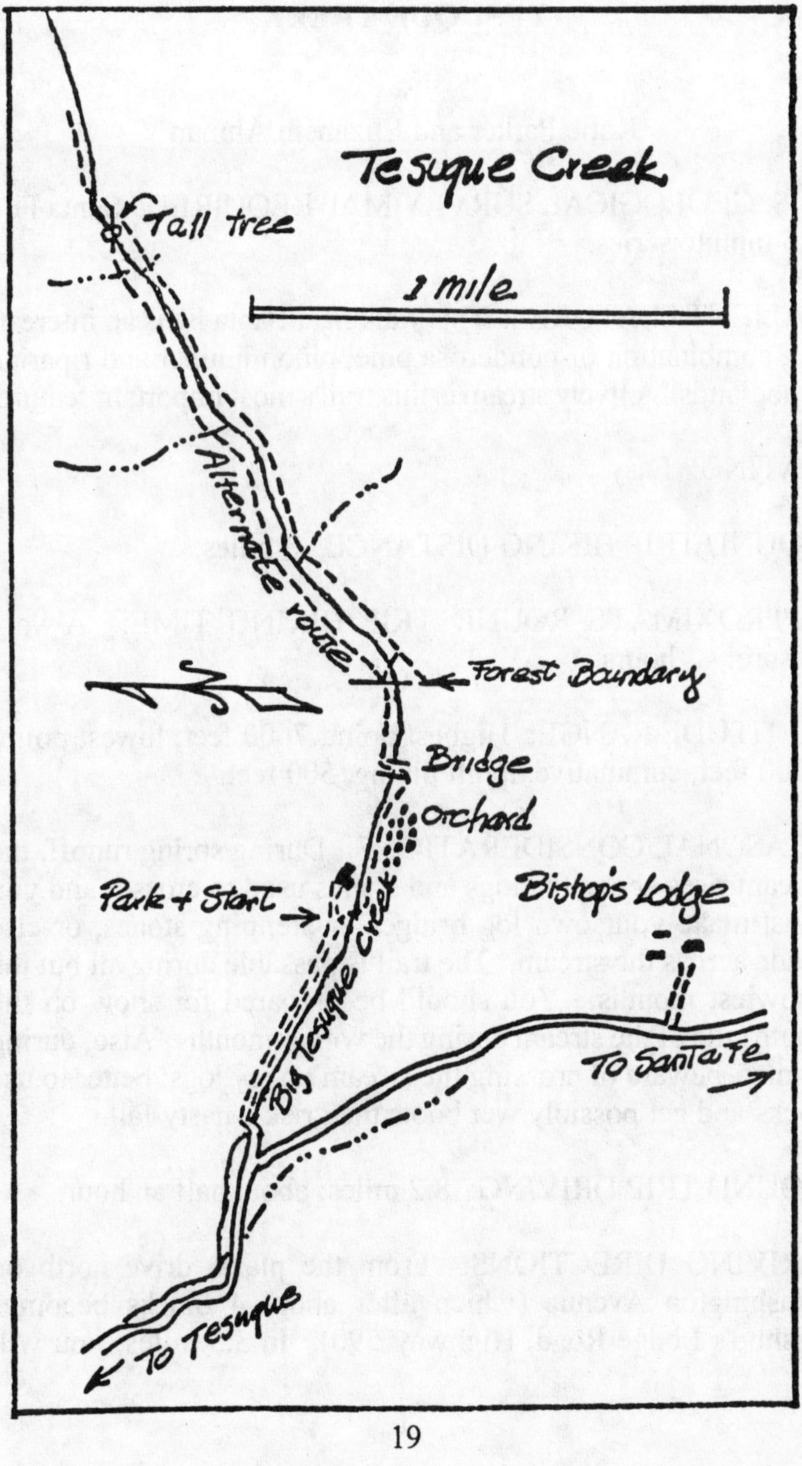

Tesque Creek.

Tall tree

1 mile

Alternate route

Forest Boundary

Bridge

Orchard

Park + Start

Bishop's Lodge

Big Tesque Creek

To Santa Fe

To Tesque

19

TESUQUE CREEK

by
Katie Parker and Elizabeth Altman

U.S. GEOLOGICAL SURVEY MAP REQUIRED: Santa Fe - 7.5 minute series.

SALIENT FEATURES: This walk near Santa Fe is an interesting combination of ponderosa pine, piñon/juniper and riparian woodlands. A lively stream is this trail's most important feature.

RATING: Easy.

ROUND TRIP HIKING DISTANCE: 3 miles.

APPROXIMATE ROUND TRIP HIKING TIME: A very leisurely 2 hours.

ALTITUDE RANGE: Highest point, 7600 feet; lowest point, 7100 feet; cumulative uphill hiking, 500 feet.

SEASONAL CONSIDERATIONS: During spring runoff, the stream rises above the logs and stones used to cross it and you must make your own log bridges or stepping stones, or else wade across the stream. The trail is passable during all but the snowiest months. You should be prepared for snow on the south side of the stream during the winter months. Also, during winter, beware of crossing the stream on icy logs: better to use rocks and get possibly wet boots than risk a nasty fall.

ROUND TRIP DRIVING: 8.2 miles; about half an hour.

DRIVING DIRECTIONS: From the plaza, drive north on Washington Avenue (which after about 4 blocks becomes Bishop's Lodge Road, Highway 590). In 3.5 miles, you will pass the entrance to Bishop's Lodge; almost exactly 1 mile beyond this entrance the paved road takes a 90-degree turn to the left, marked by a large yellow highway sign with an arrow pointing left. Don't take this left turn. Take instead the dirt road to the right, Santa Fe County Road 72A, at the blue street sign saying "Big Tesuque Canyon." Drive a short distance down this road until you come to a parking space in one of the two areas on the right identified as trail parking. The second sign says, "No Parking Beyond This Point." Respect the admonition, for if the parking privilege is abused by hikers then access to the trail along an easement over private land may be closed.

HIKING INSTRUCTIONS: Walk a short way up the road to a rock pillar and three 5-foot wooden posts to your right. Pass through the posts. The trail begins immediately beyond the posts, although there is no sign. Stay on the trail to avoid encroaching on private land. You will immediately cross Big Tesuque Creek on a wooden bridge. The trail follows the river upstream and passes an old abandoned vineyard and orchard on your right. After about 5 minutes you come out onto a dirt road. Note the sign on the left marking the trail back toward Tesuque that you just walked along. Go left over the car bridge and then turn right up the river, where a sign says "Winsor Trail–>." The trail follows the fence line. Look for woodpeckers in the cottonwood trees along the river bottom here and for a little pond on the left, indicated by runoff crossing the trail.

In another 8 to 10 minutes the fence ends and you will go through a Forest Service gate (more like an obstruction) to enter the Santa Fe National Forest. There is a sign here giving the distances to Tesuque, Hyde State Park and the Ski Basin. Be alert for bicyclists along this popular trail. About 100 yards past the gate and just before reaching the stream the trail forks. Keep to the right and follow Trail 254 across the stream to the south side. (You will return on the left fork.)

As you climb upward along a trail that parallels the creek, you will see signs of washes and trails leading off from the main trail. Keep to the main trail that leads upward to a rubble-covered hill where the trail splits. Take the left fork, where a sign will confirm that you are on the Winsor Trail. Continue along as the trail rises 20-50 feet above the creek. The trail here is quite wide, looking like an old road.

About thirty minutes into the hike, you will come to another stream crossing; you have just passed the return trail. The Winsor Trail continues on for many miles, with numerous stream crossings. For this hike, go back on the trail you came on for about 30 yards from the stream and you will notice a side trail heading down toward the river past a huge ponderosa pine. This is your return trail and involves another stream crossing. Cross to the north side of the creek and follow the trail back, until it joins the other trail at the fork near the Forest Service gate, mentioned earlier, to make a walk of about 3 miles.

Stop occasionally to look back up the canyon; at one point you will be able to see the radio towers above the Ski Basin. When you reach the large wooden bridge, cross the bridge and turn right onto the trail that you came in on. It goes alongside the old orchard, past various private properties.

These beautiful days...do not exist as mere pictures—maps hung upon the walls of memory to brighten at times when touched by association or will...They saturate themselves into every part of the body and live always.
–John Muir

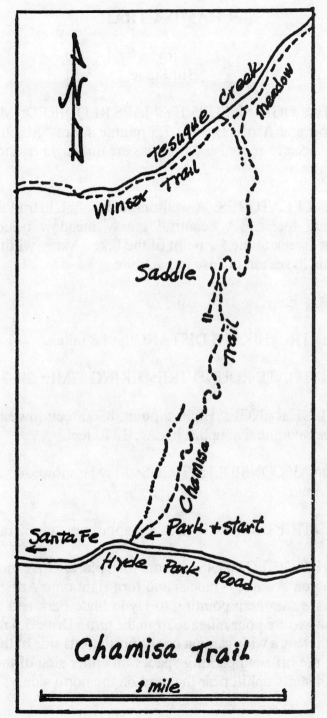

Chamisa Trail

1 mile

CHAMISA TRAIL

by
Bill Stone

U.S. GEOLOGICAL SURVEY MAPS REQUIRED: McClure Reservoir and Aspen Basin - 7.5 minute series. Much of the trail has been re-routed and portions are no longer as shown on these maps.

SALIENT FEATURES: A well-defined mountain trail through evergreen forest. A beautiful grassy meadow beside Big Tesuque Creek at the far point of the hike. Many wildflowers and birds in season. Close to Santa Fe.

RATING: Easy.

ROUND TRIP HIKING DISTANCE: 4.8 miles.

APPROXIMATE ROUND TRIP HIKING TIME: 2½-3 hours.

ALTITUDE RANGE: Highest point, 8500 feet; lowest point, 7800 feet; cumulative uphill hiking, 1240 feet.

SEASONAL CONSIDERATIONS: May be snowed-in and icy in midwinter.

ROUND TRIP DRIVING: 12 miles; approximately 30 minutes.

DRIVING DIRECTIONS: From the plaza, drive north on Washington Avenue 6 blocks and turn right onto Artist Road. There is a sign here pointing to Hyde State Park and the Ski Basin. Measure your mileage from the turn. Drive 5.6 miles to where there is a wide canyon on the north (left) side of the road. Park in the off-road parking spaces on either side of the road. The trail starts uphill near the road on the north side. There is

24

a U.S. Forest Service sign saying "Chamisa Trail 183 - Tesuque Creek 2¼." This is the Chamisa Trail.

HIKING INSTRUCTIONS: The trail goes due east for a few hundred feet and climbs sharply. It then turns due north. It is deeply forested, with piñon, two species of juniper, and ponderosa pine at the start. There are many switchbacks and as you climb higher there are views of the canyon and Hyde Park Road. Gambel oak and Douglas fir now appear. White (limber) pine and white fir appear at higher elevations. The trail is narrow and at some places proceeds along a steep dugway, with little room to pass another person. The footing here is loose and sandy.

After you have walked a mile and a quarter and climbed 700 feet, you will come to the crest of the trail (altitude 8500 feet). A trail coming up the canyon from the left meets Trail 183 here. This is a good place for a break.

The trail now goes downhill. It turns sharply southeast, to your right, then, after a few hundred feet, toward the northeast (left) and continues in a northerly direction for the rest of the hike. It proceeds down a dry stream bed (very wet in spring). The footing is rocky in places. Aspen is found here as well as the trees mentioned above.

After one mile you come to a small grassy meadow. Continue about a quarter of a mile and you will see two sign posts. This is the junction with the Winsor Trail 254. The Chamisa Trail ends here. There is a grassy meadow northeast (upstream) of the junction and the Big Tesuque Creek is on its western border. The meadow is a beautiful, quiet spot and a good place to have your lunch. There is a large granite boulder in the middle of the meadow. The altitude is 7960 feet. This is the furthest point of the hike.

Return the way you came. Be sure to get back on the same trail (Chamisa), by turning left (south) at the two posts. The Chamisa Trail is level at this point. (The Winsor Trail follows the Big Tesuque downstream.) The 540-foot climb back to the saddle is moderate in most places, but very steep in two. On reaching the saddle again (8500 feet) the trail divides. The trail to the left, which is level here, is the trail you came up on. The other trail goes steeply down into the canyon and will eventually return you to the parking area. Proceed to the trailhead on the latter trail.

Many wildflowers and plants may be seen along this trail. Among the predominant ones are Oregon grape, yucca, scarlet gilia, red penstemon, lupine (slopes near the crest are covered with its blooms in the late spring) and many Compositae. In addition, you may see mullein, yellow evening primrose, yarrow, wild iris, salsify and coneflower in the meadows.

I have seen 42 species of birds along the Chamisa Trail. Among them were hawks, hummingbirds, woodpeckers, flycatchers, swallows, jays, ravens, nuthatches, chickadees, thrushes, warblers, vireos and the sparrow types.

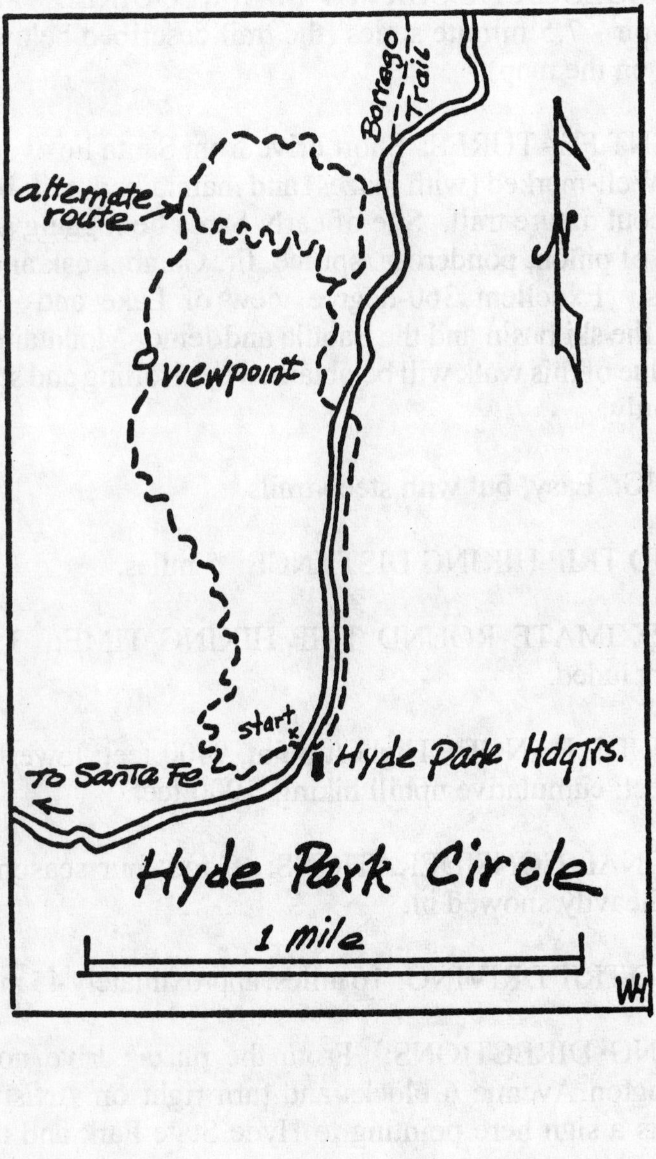

Borrego Trail

N

altemate
route →

viewpoint

start
×

to Santa Fe

Hyde Park Hdqrs.

Hyde Park Circle

1 mile

WH

HYDE PARK CIRCLE TRAIL

by
John H. Muchmore

U.S. GEOLOGICAL SURVEY MAP REQUIRED: McClure Reservoir - 7.5 minute series (the trail described below is not shown on the map).

SALIENT FEATURES: Short drive from Santa Fe over paved road. Well-marked (with blazes) and maintained trail; includes Girl Scout nature trail. Site of early Santa Fe logging activity. Stands of piñon, ponderosa, spruce, fir, Gambel oak and wildflowers. Excellent 360-degree view of Lake and Tesuque Peaks, the ski basin and the Sandia and Jemez Mountains. The real value of this walk will be obtained by strolling and stopping frequently.

RATING: Easy, but with steep trails.

ROUND TRIP HIKING DISTANCE: 5 miles.

APPROXIMATE ROUND TRIP HIKING TIME: 3 hours, stops included.

ALTITUDE RANGE: Highest point, 9400 feet; lowest point, 8400 feet; cumulative uphill hiking, 1000 feet.

SEASONAL CONSIDERATIONS: Good four season walk, unless heavily snowed in.

ROUND TRIP DRIVING: 16 miles; approximately 45 minutes.

DRIVING DIRECTIONS: From the plaza, drive north on Washington Avenue 6 blocks and turn right on Artist Road. There is a sign here pointing to Hyde State Park and the Ski

Basin. Measure your mileage from the turn. Drive 7.4 miles to Hyde Memorial State Park Headquarters on your right. There are parking spaces in a large lot below the headquarters on the right-hand side of the road and in a smaller lot above the headquarters on the left side. Pay your entrance and use fees at the self-service payment box. The trailhead is directly across the road from the stone store and is marked by a "Hiking Trail" sign.

HIKING INSTRUCTIONS: Begin your walk by crossing Little Tesuque Creek on the stone bridge opposite the general store, then turning left (south). The trail, well marked with tree blazes, climbs steeply through a series of switchbacks, then gradually levels off as it serpentines along an ascending ridge. Check your watch as you cross the bridge and plan to stop at half hour intervals to enjoy the surrounding vistas and view the distant mountains. At your first stop, you will be about 500 feet above the campground. Looking ahead to the northeast, you will see the Santa Fe Ski Basin with the watershed rising to Tesuque and Lake Peaks. Behind you to the southeast, Thompson Peak is showing above the Black Canyon notch. At your next stop, northwest and southwest views should have your attention. Southwesterly are the Sandia and Ortiz Mountains. Westerly and northwesterly are the Jemez Peaks with the Buckman flats and the Caja del Rio in the middle foreground.

Your trail now rollercoasts along the ridge and another five minutes brings you to a 360-degree view point. There are two picnic tables here that invite you to stop for lunch or a snack. Although downed timber gives evidence of some harsh winter weather, this trail's southern ascent makes it inviting even during years of heavy snows. Turn-of-the-century logging is evident along the ridge. A word of caution: during summer thunderstorm activity, portions of this ridge have taken direct lightning strikes. You will see several large trees that have been hit by lightning.

Before moving on, consider the options. If you continue on the trail, you will reach the ski basin road in half an hour. It takes another half hour of hiking in close proximity to that road to get to your car. To avoid the traffic noise on the last part of the circle you might opt to turn around now and return the way you came.

If you continue along the ridge, you will see a branch of the trail just beyond the first picnic table. This right-branching trail will bring you down a series of switchbacks to the recreational vehicle hookup section of the Hyde Park Campground and will cut off about 30 minutes of your walking circuit. However, we suggest that you continue straight ahead past the second picnic table. The main trail continues a gradual traversing descent along the northeast or right side of the main ridge.

Within five minutes, your trail swings sharply to the east (your right) and drops steeply through a series of descending switch-backs to the trail's end at the northern boundary of the Hyde Park Campground. As you leave the trail, the paved Ski Basin road will be directly in front of you and can be followed down to your car. However, let us avoid the paved road. There are a series of short trails running down the canyon approximately 50 to 100 feet above the west side of the road. Keeping the paved road on your left, follow any of these intersecting trails until you pass the recreational vehicle section. You will soon cross the alternate descending trail from the ridge above you. This trail almost immediately converges with the Girl Scout nature trail with its metal and wooden identification signs pointing out various types of trees, shrubs and wildflowers. The nature trail continues for about ten minutes and soon returns you to the paved road. At this point, cross the paved road, then Little Tesuque Creek and then take any of the dirt roads or trails that follow the creek back down to the Park Headquarters, the store and your car.

The entire circuit can be covered in three leisurely hours. With a picnic and a clear warm day the circuit could be extended to all day. Snow cover may require three strenuous hours for the circuit. Experienced hikers will walk this trail in under two hours. Novices should not attempt it in deep snow.

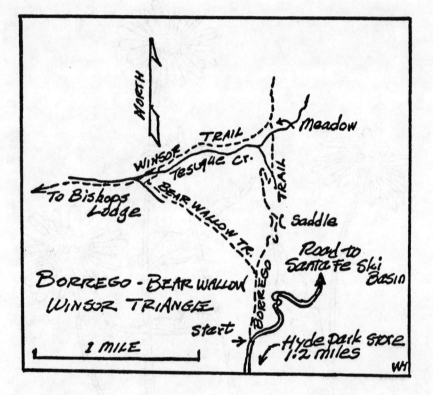

BORREGO - BEAR WALLOW WINSOR TRIANGLE

NORTH

WINSOR TRAIL

Meadow

Tesuque Cr.

To Bishops Lodge

BEAR WALLOW TR.

TRAIL

Saddle

Road to Santa Fe Ski Basin

BORREGO

Start

Hyde Park Store 1.2 miles

1 MILE

WH

BORREGO-BEAR WALLOW-WINSOR TRIANGLE

by
Bill Chudd

U.S. GEOLOGICAL SURVEY MAPS REQUIRED: Aspen Basin, and, for the first five or six hundred yards only, McClure Reservoir - 7.5 minute series.

SALIENT FEATURES: An easily accessible short hike along good trails, partly stream-side, and through pleasant woods rife with seasonal wildflowers. You will make two stream crossings. If spring runoff is unusually high, the crossings can present some problems. On summer weekends you'll encounter many hikers and bike riders. If you are a seeker of solitude go somewhere else! Trail signs are sometimes destroyed or switched. In case of doubt ignore suspicious signs.

RATING: Easy.

ROUND TRIP HIKING DISTANCE: 4 miles.

APPROXIMATE ROUND TRIP HIKING TIME: 2 hours 15 minutes, with stops.

ALTITUDE RANGE: Highest point, 8880 feet; lowest point, 8240 feet; cumulative uphill hiking, 760 feet.

SEASONAL CONSIDERATIONS: Usually snowed-in in midwinter. Can be hot in midsummer, but is fairly well shaded.

ROUND TRIP DRIVING: 17.5 miles; approximately 40 minutes.

DRIVING DIRECTIONS: From the plaza, drive north on Washington Avenue 6 blocks and turn right onto Artist Road.

There is a sign here pointing to Hyde State Park and the Ski Basin. Measure your mileage from the turn. Drive a little over 8.5 miles to the small paved parking area on the left side of the road. To alert you to your approach, you will notice an RV parking area at the left of the road 0.2 miles before the Borrego Trail parking area.

HIKING INSTRUCTIONS: The trail starts down from the far left corner of the parking lot. There is a sign identifying this as the Borrego Trail 150 and giving the distance to Trail 182 as ½ miles and the distance to Trail 254 as 1 ½ miles. After 4 or 5 twists, the trail becomes wide and easy to follow. You have entered a lovely forest of firs, aspens and, shortly, a few ponderosa pines. Later you may see some shrubby Gambel oaks trying valiantly to become full-fledged trees.

This is the Borrego Trail along which shepherds brought their flocks to market in Santa Fe from towns to the north, before modern roads and other developments made life easier and less interesting. In about half a mile the trail passes between two wooden signposts. If these remain intact, the left hand one will point out the Bear Wallow Trail, with Big Tesuque Creek 1 mile away. The right hand sign will show the Borrego Trail 150, with Big Tesuque Creek and the Winsor Trail 254, 1¼ miles ahead. Take the left fork, the Bear Wallow Trail 182, which heads west of north. (You will return on the right fork.) After about 15 minutes you will get glimpses through the trees ahead of a transverse ridge, indicating your approach to Big Tesuque Creek. Begin listening for the always pleasant sound of its flow. Continue down the switchbacks to the stream bank, one mile from the Borrego Trail.

There is usually a somewhat flimsy log crossing a bit down-stream from the trail. Cross the creek at the trail or over the log bridge. The Winsor Trail 254, marked by a sign, parallels the stream. Your route will be upstream, a right turn after crossing the creek. If the season is right, look around for raspberries in this vicinity. Other berries you are apt to encounter in the course of this hike are strawberries (many plants but few berries), edible (but not choice) thimbleberries, non-poisonous (but hardly edible unless cooked or prepared) Oregon grape, kinnikinnick and poisonous baneberry.

Make the right turn and continue on the Winsor trail. It's all upstream and uphill, but you knew you'd have to pay for all that lovely downhill trail behind you. Note the ridge on your right, across the creek. Eventually, you're going to have to get over that. After one mile, you will reach the junction of the Winsor and the Borrego trails. It is marked by a post with two signs. Turn right, southeast, through a small meadow, onto the Borrego Trail. You will shortly cross the Big Tesuque Creek. A huge fallen ponderosa over the creek will make your crossing easier. Soon thereafter attack the ridge you saw earlier by a winding switchback trail. After topping the ridge, the trail descends for a while, levels off, then returns to the junction with Bear Wallow Trail which comes in from the right. You have now completed a triangle of the Bear Wallow, Winsor and Borrego Trails, each leg about one mile.

Continue up the Borrego Trail one-half mile to your car. Next time, take this circuit in the reverse direction. It will seem like a different walk.

I never saw a discontented tree.
–John Muir

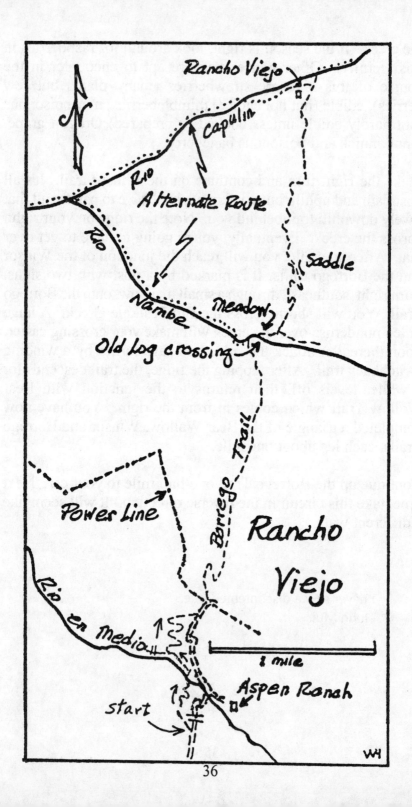

Rancho Viejo

Capulin

Rio

Alternate Route

Rio

Saddle

Nambe

Meadow

Old Log crossing

Power Line

Borrego Trail

Rancho

Viejo

Rio en Media

½ mile

Aspen Ranch

start

WH

RANCHO VIEJO

by
Betsy Fuller

U.S. GEOLOGICAL SURVEY MAP REQUIRED: Aspen Basin - 7.5 minute series.

SALIENT FEATURES: Lovely meadows and fast-running clear streams; wildflowers in season and good stands of ponderosa, spruce, fir and aspen. Not recommended for low-slung cars. During winter, the road from the Ski Basin down to the "T" junction of 102 and 412 is closed to vehicular traffic and reserved for skiers.

RATING: Strenuous.

ROUND TRIP HIKING DISTANCE: 11.5 miles.

APPROXIMATE ROUND TRIP HIKING TIME: 6½ hours.

ALTITUDE RANGE: Highest point, 9200 feet; lowest point, 8187 feet; cumulative uphill hiking, 2300 feet.

SEASONAL CONSIDERATIONS: Not a winter hike.

ROUND TRIP DRIVING: 34 miles; approximately 2 hours.

DRIVING DIRECTIONS: From the plaza, drive north on Washington Avenue 6 blocks and turn right onto Artist Road. There is a sign here pointing to Hyde State Park and the Ski Basin. Measure your mileage from the turn. At about 12 miles (0.5 miles beyond the Big Tesuque picnic area) turn left onto the Pacheco Canyon Road (Forest Road 102, a dirt road) and continue downhill for 3 miles until the road comes to a "T" junction with Forest Road 412. Take your mileage here again.

37

Turn right onto Forest Road 412 and continue on up over the ridge (on a sometimes very bumpy road), passing several secondary roads and an old corral up the hill to your right. About 1.4 miles beyond the junction of 412 and 102, you will come to a flat parking area on the right side of the road. Park here.

HIKING INSTRUCTIONS: Walk about 100 yards farther along the road to the trailhead on the left side. It is signed "Trail 163, Trail 150." The trail starts uphill and winds through a mixed forest of pines and occasional aspens. Then it descends via switchbacks to the Rio en Medio, a small, easily-crossed stream (possibly more impressive during spring runoff). Cross the stream and go left and up the opposite bank until you come to a fork marked with a sign. Take the right fork: Borrego Trail 150.

Follow this trail as it zigzags up the hill until it joins the old Lucky Star Mine road. The sign here reads: "Borrego Trail 150, Rancho Viejo." Turn left here (noting this junction for your return). Follow the road uphill until you come to a saddle where the road turns sharply to the right. Leave the road here and look for a trail that starts leftwards and downhill to the north. There is a sign here: "Borrego Trail 150, Rio Nambé, Rancho Viejo, Aspen Ranch", with appropriate arrows.

Trail 150 is part of the historic Borrego Trail which as recently as the mid-20th century was used to herd sheep from the high mountains east of Chimayo and Truchas to Santa Fe. As you walk down the small drainage, you'll be going through a dark forest of spruce and fir. In the summer, you may see the spectacular flowering green gentian, which sometimes grows as tall as 5 feet. If there is any water in the small drainage, watch for the one-sided pyrola in the wet dirt.

After about a mile and a half of steady descent you'll come to a tiny stream where the trail forks. The left fork is Trail 160 (which you'll return on if you choose the alternate way back mentioned in the final paragraph of this description). For now, continue onwards towards Rancho Viejo as indicated by sign.

You'll soon arrive at the Rio Nambé which flows west to the Nambé Indian Pueblo about 6 miles downstream. Cross the river to the north bank. You will have to cross the river by wading (and having wet feet the rest of the trip) or by scouting up and down the river for stepping stones or a fallen log.

Just right and upstream from the crossing, you will find yourself in a lovely open meadow. This is a good spot for your first rest stop and snack, especially since the next mile and a half will involve climbing from an elevation of about 8200 to 8800 feet.

After your rest, continue on upstream for about a quarter of a mile. At this point you will see the trail divide, one branch going on up the river and the other (still your Trail 150) going to the left (north) up the slope away from the river. You will be climbing through ponderosa pines. The trail is lined with mountain mahogany which you can identify by its curlicue seeds. As you top the ridge and start down the trail on the north-facing slope into the Rio Capulin (chokecherry) valley, you'll be going through an evergreen forest with an occasional scrub oak grove.

It's approximately 2.5 miles from the Rio Nambé crossing where you had your snack to the Rio Capulin. Walk downstream for a few hundred yards on Trail 158 through a beautiful meadow and you will find the burned-out remains of a log cabin that was once used by the sheepherders of the old Spanish ranch known as Rancho Viejo. Have a good rest in this lovely sloping meadow because retracing your steps back to your car will be more strenuous than the outbound trip, especially the long, final ascent out of the Rio Nambé valley.

Return the way you came. If you come to a gate as you are walking down the old Lucky Star Mine road, then you have missed the place where your trail takes off to zigzag down to the Rio en Medio. Walk back up the road about 75 yards and you will see the trail you came up on. Also, if you come to the gate on the Rio en Medio Trail, turn back for about 50 yards and you will see where the trail heads down the bank to the stream crossing.

Someday, you may want to extend this walk by following Trail 158 downstream from the burned-out cabin along the Rio Capulin to the junction of this stream with the Rio Nambé and then back up the Nambé on Trail 160 to rejoin the Borrego Trail at the point where you crossed the tiny stream several hours before. This added loop would increase your hike by about 3 miles.

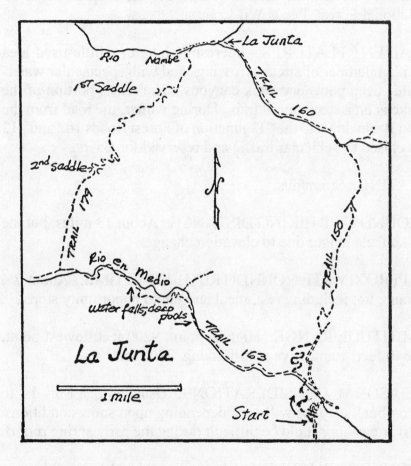

La Junta

Rio Nambe

La Junta

TRAIL 160

1st Saddle

2nd saddle

TRAIL 179

Rio en Medio

Water falls, deep pools

TRAIL 158

TRAIL 163

La Junta

1 mile

Start

LA JUNTA CIRCUIT

by
Art Judd, E. J. Evangelos and John Jasper

U.S. GEOLOGICAL SURVEY MAP REQUIRED: Aspen Basin - 7.5 minute series. Other helpful maps: Santa Fe National Forest, Pecos Wilderness.

SALIENT FEATURES: Interesting hike in a little-used area with a number of stream crossings and with spectacular waterfalls, deep pools and rock canyons. The return portion of the hike is on a steep uphill trail. During winter, the road from the Ski Basin down to the "T" junction of Forest Roads 102 and 412 is closed to vehicular traffic and reserved for skiers.

RATING: Strenuous.

ROUND TRIP HIKING DISTANCE: About 13 miles, but the hike feels longer due to elevation changes.

APPROXIMATE ROUND TRIP HIKING TIME: About 7½ hours, not including rest, meal and photo opportunity stops.

ALTITUDE RANGE: Highest point, 9200 feet; lowest point, 7640 feet; cumulative uphill hiking, 2800 feet.

SEASONAL CONSIDERATIONS: Usually open May 1st to October 1st. This will vary depending upon snow conditions. River crossing could be difficult during the early spring runoff.

ROUND TRIP DRIVING: Approximately 34 miles; 2 hours.

DRIVING DIRECTIONS: From the plaza, drive north on Washington Avenue 6 blocks and turn right onto Artist Road. There is a sign here pointing to Hyde State Park and the Ski

Basin. Measure your mileage from the turn. At about 12 miles (0.5 miles beyond the Big Tesuque picnic area) turn left onto the Pacheco Canyon Road (Forest Road 102, a dirt road) and continue downhill for 3 miles until the road comes to a "T" junction with Forest Road 412. Take your mileage here again. Turn right onto Forest Road 412 and continue on up over the ridge (on a sometimes very bumpy road), passing several secondary roads and an old corral up the hill to your right. About 1.4 miles beyond the junction of 412 and 102, you will come to a flat parking area on the right side of the road. Park here.

HIKING INSTRUCTIONS: Walk about 100 yards farther along the road to the trailhead on the left side of the road, where a sign marks the entrance to Trails 163 and 150. The trail starts uphill and winds through a mixed forest of pines and occasional aspens. Then it descends via switchbacks to the Rio en Medio, a small, easily-crossed stream (possibly more impressive during spring runoff).

Cross the stream and go left and up the opposite bank until you come to a fork marked with a sign. Take the right fork: Borrego Trail 150. This is a loop hike. You will return to this point later when you hike upstream along the Rio en Medio on Trail 163.

Follow Trail 150 as it zigzags up the hill until it joins the old Lucky Star Mine road. Turn left here. Follow the road uphill until you come to a saddle where the road turns sharply to the right. Leave the road here and look for a trail that starts downhill to the north. There is a sign here: "Borrego Trail 150, Rio Nambé, Rancho Viejo, Aspen Ranch", with appropriate arrows.

The trail makes a steep descent for about 1.7 miles to the Rio Nambé. The Rio Nambé begins to make itself heard as you near the last quarter mile or so. Just before you get to the river, notice the huge moss-covered boulder on the left of the trail. In the spring, garlands of wildflowers bedeck this rock.

At the Rio Nambé, take Trail160 downstream for a few hundred yards and either ford the river or cross on dead-fall. Continue on down the river for about half an hour (a little over a mile) to the junction of the Rio Nambé with the Rio Capulin ("La Junta" means the meeting point). You'll come to a fork in the trail when you get close to this junction. Take either one; they both lead to La Junta. The Rio Capulin comes in from the right. Cross it and continue on downstream for several hundred yards to the junction of your trail (160) with Trail 179. A sign marking this junction is tacked onto a large ponderosa pine, so watch for it. Trail 179 crosses the river here. Usually adequate dead-fall bridges the river at this point. Cross with care, especially in early spring and on frosty mornings, as the tree trunks are often coated with ice and can be very slippery.

After crossing the river turn right. Trail 179 climbs up a deeply scoured arroyo. After about 45 minutes on this trail, you'll top out at a saddle -- a good place for a rest and a snack. The trail now turns downhill, passes through another valley and then ascends to the top of another saddle. At one place on this portion of the hike, the trail divides -- take the left trail which weaves up an arroyo on the left side of the streambed, then switches back and forth ascending to the second saddle. The power line crosses the trail at this saddle and you will now begin the one-mile descent to the Rio en Medio, a total of three miles from La Junta. Just before reaching the Rio en Medio, a trail sign states "Aspen Ranch 3 miles." A sharp left turn here onto Trail 163 will take you up the Rio en Medio, the first stream you crossed at the beginning of the hike. At the junction, Trail 163 may be narrow and heavy with vegetation.

This is probably the most beautiful and strenuous leg of this lovely hike: three miles of waterfalls, deep pools, rock canyons, wildflowers, mushrooms and trout. The trail crosses the Rio en Medio numerous times and goes steeply up to gain the elevation lost in the descent to La Junta. It's about 3.5 miles up the Rio en Medio, the first half steep, the rest a gentle rise through a wider stream valley. At the sign "Borrego Trail 150, Trail 163" turn right, cross the stream and return to your car.

To return to Santa Fe, either go back up the Pacheco Canyon Road the way you came or continue down Forest Road 412 past Vigil Meadows on the left to Rancho Encantado and the village of Tesuque and back to Santa Fe. FR 412 has a gate near the bottom which the Forest Service tells us is open between snow seasons. Chances are it's open if FR 102 was, but call the Española Ranger station to be sure: 505-438-7801.

This grand show is eternal. It is always sunrise some-where; the dew is never all dried at once; a shower is forever falling; vapor is ever rising. Eternal sunrise, eternal sunset, eternal dawn and gloaming, on sea and continents and islands, each in its turn, as the round earth rolls.
–John Muir

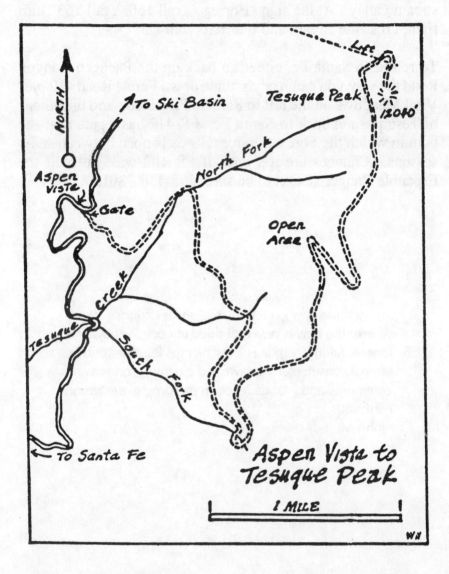

North

To Ski Basin

Tesuque Peak

Lift

12,040'

Aspen Vista

Gate

North Fork

Open Area

Creek

Tesuque

South Fork

To Santa Fe

Aspen Vista to Tesuque Peak

1 MILE

WN

ASPEN VISTA TO TESUQUE PEAK

by
Walt Kunz

U.S. GEOLOGICAL SURVEY MAP REQUIRED: Aspen Basin - 7.5 minute series. The 1977 topo map shows the road on which you will be walking. A "Visitor's Guide to the Pecos Wilderness" also shows the road and is available from the Forest Service.

SALIENT FEATURES: Good stands of aspen, spruce and fir, clear streams, large open areas with excellent views. Trail is a dirt road. Especially beautiful in the fall when the aspens are golden. This is a popular and often crowded area at the height of the aspen viewing in late September and early October.

RATING: Easy - strenuous.

ROUND TRIP HIKING DISTANCE: 12 miles for the entire hike.

APPROXIMATE ROUND TRIP HIKING TIME: 6 hours for the entire hike. Fastest round trip time by runners is about one and a quarter hours.

ALTITUDE RANGE: Highest point, 12,040 feet; lowest point, 10,000 feet; cumulative uphill hiking for the entire hike, 2040 feet.

SEASONAL CONSIDERATIONS: Usually snowed in at higher altitudes in winter and spring and popular with cross country skiers in the winter. Even in July you may encounter snow. Bring adequate clothing.

ROUND TRIP DRIVING: 27 miles; approximately one hour.

DRIVING DIRECTIONS: From the plaza, drive north on Washington Avenue 6 blocks and turn right onto Artist Road. There is a sign here pointing to Hyde State Park and the Ski Basin. Measure your mileage from the turn. Drive 12.6 miles, then turn right into a large parking lot marked by a large sign for Aspen Vista.

HIKING INSTRUCTIONS: There is a gated access road on the east side of the parking area which is the start of the trail to Tesuque Peak. The "not for public use" sign refers to vehicles only; hiking (as well as cross country skiing) is permitted. This is the service road for the microwave relay station at the peak.

The first 2.5 miles are through aspen forest (spectacular in the fall); the last 3.5 miles are through fir and spruce alternating with large treeless areas. About 0.5 miles in you can catch a glimpse of your destination, the bare peak with microwave towers straight ahead. At 0.8 miles you cross the north fork of Big Tesuque Creek, at 1.6 miles, two more forks of the creek, and at 2.3 miles, the last fork. Water-loving flowers abound along the banks of the creeks. Late in the summer the lower stretches of the road are lined with masses of yellow senecio and purple asters.

Just past the last creek crossing, the road makes a switchback to the north (left) and enters a fir and spruce forest. At 3.8 miles the road traverses a large open area which affords good views of the Rio Grande valley north of Santa Fe. A bit farther along you get a panoramic view of Santa Fe. On your left you will see a large outcropping of rock which makes a good rest area and a turnaround point if you don't want to hike the entire distance.

At 5 miles, after a few more switchbacks, the road turns northeast and enters the forest again. (This section has had 3 feet of snow across the road in mid-July.) At 5.5 miles the road enters another large open area. Below, to the northwest, you can see the top of a chair lift at the Santa Fe Ski Basin. The long fence straight ahead is a snow fence along one of the ski trails served by the ski lifts under which you will pass farther up the road. Above, to the northeast, are the microwave towers on Tesuque Peak, about half a mile away by road.

At the top, the terrain drops steeply eastward into the Santa Fe River valley, a closed area which provides a main part of Santa Fe's water supply. To the north is Lake Peak, about a mile away. Return by the same route.

An alternate return route, with another car having been shuttled to and left at the Santa Fe Ski Basin, is to take one of the ski trails (if you know the trails) down to the ski basin parking lot. This maneuver would increase considerably the steepness of the descent but would shorten the hike by approximately 4 miles.

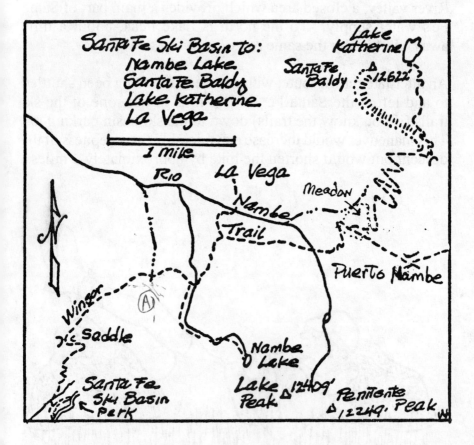

Santa Fe Ski Basin to:
Nambe Lake
Santa Fe Baldy
Lake Katherine
La Vega

Lake
Katherine

Santa Fe
Baldy △ 12622'

1 mile

Rio   La Vega

Nambe   Meadow

Trail

Puerto Nambe

Winsor

Ⓐ

Saddle

Nambe
◯ Lake

Santa Fe
Ski Basin
Park

Lake △ 12409'   Penitente
Peak   △ 12249' Peak

Ⓐ Raven's Ridge

50

NAMBÉ LAKE

by
Carolyn Keskulla

U.S. GEOLOGICAL SURVEY MAP REQUIRED: Aspen Basin - 7.5 minute series. This trail is not shown on the topo map but does appear on the Pecos Wilderness map available at U.S. Forest Service headquarters. See sketch map on page 50.

SALIENT FEATURES: You will have the special treat of seeing Nambé Lake, which nestles under the cliff face of Lake Peak. Good hiking shoes are a necessity: the trail is very steep and in some places rocky as it climbs alongside Nambé Creek.

RATING: Moderate in distance, but there are some steep, rocky climbs.

ROUND TRIP HIKING DISTANCE: 7 miles.

APPROXIMATE ROUND TRIP HIKING TIME: About 5 hours, allowing time for lunch and a stroll around the lake.

ALTITUDE RANGE: Highest point, 11,400 feet; lowest point, 10,250 feet; cumulative uphill hiking, 2100 feet.

SEASONAL CONSIDERATIONS: Generally accessible from mid-June to first heavy snow; may be snowed-in at other times.

ROUND TRIP DRIVING: 30 miles; 1 hour 20 minutes.

DRIVING DIRECTIONS: From the plaza, drive north on Washington Avenue 6 blocks and turn right onto Artist Road. There is a sign here pointing to Hyde State Park and the Ski Basin. Measure your mileage from the turn. Continue 14 miles to the Ski Basin. At the Ski Basin, keep to the left and park in

51

the lower parking lot. Look for a sign that says, "WINSOR TRAIL."

HIKING INSTRUCTIONS: After crossing the small wooden bridge, turn right and start uphill on the well-used Winsor Trail 254. After a half mile or more of steep climbing you will be at the wilderness boundary fence, 600 feet higher than the trailhead. Watch for the lovely wildflowers among the aspen and spruce. In June you may see shooting star and fairy slipper orchid. After passing through the fence you start gently downhill coming, in about a quarter of a mile, to a little noticed trail on the left, marked with the sign "Trail 403 Rio Nambé 1 3/4" This is a very steep trail to the Rio Nambé nicknamed the "elevator shaft." DON'T TAKE THIS TRAIL: it goes to the Nambé river, not the lake.

Continue past this junction another 1 1/4 miles or so. You will come to a clearing on your right. Ahead of you, the Winsor Trail drops down to cross the Nambé Lake Creek. A sign to the right of the main trail says "Nambé Lake." Look for a trail going up to the right (south) which will bring you alongside a lovely, cascading alpine stream. There is no officially maintained trail to Nambé Lake, which is hidden behind the high ridge to the southeast. Instead, there are several paths, all of which will eventually lead you to the lake. By using your own instinct and following the stream and the paths, you will reach the lake, the source of the Rio Nambé.

The trail consists of several steep ascents separated by level stretches. After the first such ascent keep to the left bank. The basic rule: keep the stream within earshot as you climb steeply. The lake will eventually appear surrounded by spruce forest and talus slopes.

The shallow lake nestles under the cliff face of Lake Peak. Flowers grow in profusion in July along the stream and around the lake. Parry's primrose, mertensia and marsh marigold are spectacular in early July. Later there will be fireweed, yampa, monkshood and many others. You may also see marmots and pika scampering around the slopes.

Return by the same route.

LA VEGA

by
Norbert Sperlich

U.S. GEOLOGICAL SURVEY MAP REQUIRED: Aspen Basin - 7.5 minute series. How to locate La Vega on the topo map? Find the Ski Area first, called "Santa Fe Recreation Area" on the map. Now find Aspen Peak (northwest of the Ski Area) and Santa Fe Baldy (northeast of the Ski Area). Place a ruler over the tops of Aspen Peak and Santa Fe Baldy. Starting at Santa Fe Baldy, follow the ruler down for 4 inches. You will come to a level area, indicated by the absence of contour lines. This is La Vega, Spanish for "meadow" or "pasture land." See sketch map on page 50.

SALIENT FEATURES: This hike through aspen, fir and spruce takes you to an open meadow at the foot of Santa Fe Baldy. La Vega offers a beautiful setting away from the sometimes crowded Winsor Trail. Many wildflowers in season. Spectacular in late September and early October, when the aspens are golden.

RATING: Moderate.

ROUND TRIP HIKING DISTANCE: Approximately 7 miles.

APPROXIMATE ROUND TRIP HIKING TIME: 3 to 4 hours.

ALTITUDE RANGE: Highest point, 10,840 feet; lowest point, 10,000 feet; cumulative uphill hiking, approximately 1500 feet.

SEASONAL CONSIDERATIONS: Do not attempt this hike in snow.

ROUND TRIP DRIVING: 30 miles; about 1 hour 20 minutes.

DRIVING DIRECTIONS: From the plaza, drive north on Washington Avenue 6 blocks and turn right onto Artist Road. There is a sign here pointing to Hyde State Park and the Ski Basin. Measure your mileage from the turn. Continue 14 miles to the Ski Basin. At the Ski Basin, keep to the left and park in the lower parking lot. Look for a sign that says, "WINSOR TRAIL."

HIKING INSTRUCTIONS: From the trailhead, you will cross a small stream and go up on the Winsor Trail (to the right, Trail 254). The trail zigzags up through a forest of aspen, fir and spruce trees and crosses several small meadows. After half an hour or so of steep climbing you come to a meadow and the entrance gate to the Pecos Wilderness. You have reached the highest point of the hike (10,850 feet). Time to catch your breath and to feed the gray jays that are usually waiting here for handouts from hikers.

The trail now descends gradually through stands of conifers and aspens. After about an hour of hiking time (from the Ski Basin) you will reach a clearing to the right of the trail. Just before the clearing, a smaller trail goes off to the right to Nambé Lake (see page 51 for the Nambé Lake hike). You will continue straight ahead on the Winsor Trail which, right after the clearing, crosses Nambé Creek. Check the time at this point. In about five minutes you will reach the turnoff to La Vega, a small trail that goes down to the left. Look for a sign on the right side of the trail. The sign says: UPPER NAMBE TRAIL 101 - RIO NAMBE - LA VEGA.

Here, you leave the well-traveled Winsor Trail and take the trail to La Vega. This trail is not on the topo map!

For a while, the trail stays on top of a ridge, then it drops down into the valley to the right of the ridge. Keep your eyes on the trail. It is overgrown in some places and obstructed by fallen aspen trees in others. At the valley bottom, the trail enters a conifer forest and then comes to a stream (a tributary of the Nambé River). At this point, you have hiked for about 20 minutes on the La Vega Shortcut Trail. You have now reached the lowest point of the hike (approximately 10,000 feet). Cross the stream on a bridge of slippery logs.

The trail now turns left and goes up on the other side of the creek. About 30 yards away from the stream, your trail merges with Trail 160 (Rio Nambé Trail). The junction is marked by a signpost with two signs. One of them points in the direction from which you came; the other sign, indicating the Rio Nambé Trail, says "Trail 160." You take the left branch of the latter trail.

For a while, the trail descends slowly, with the stream on your left within earshot. After a few minutes, you will be going uphill again and the trail moves to the right, away from the stream. Some 10 minutes after passing the last sign (near the creek), the trail will take you up to a low ridge. Ahead of you is a clearing and a signpost. The sign, about chest high (likely to be destroyed by vandals) will tell you: LA VEGA ← RIO NAMBÉ TRAIL ← BORREGO TRAIL 4 ← ASPEN RANCH 7.

The trail is not clearly visible beyond this point. Walk 10 yards or so past the signpost and you will look down on La Vega, a large meadow (altitude about 10,100 feet) interspersed with spruce and fir trees and patches of gooseberry bushes. Opposite you, to the north, the meadow is framed by two ridges that lead up to Santa Fe Baldy. (The top of Santa Fe Baldy is not visible from this point.) A little stream comes down the valley between the two ridges and meanders through the meadow, turning to the west to join Nambé Creek further down. If you are lucky, you might see deer bounding across the meadow. More likely, you will encounter a herd of grazing cattle.

56

Before you move on to explore La Vega or to relax at the bank of the stream, memorize the location of the LA VEGA signpost. You will have to return to this post in order to find the trail. When exploring the meadow, watch out for swampy areas.

Start your return at the sign post and go back the way you came. After a few minutes of hiking you will hear the creek below you on the right. Once the creek comes into your view, watch for the turnoff to the right and the sign on the left side of the trail. Turn to the right and go down to the stream. Cross the stream and retrace your steps back to the Winsor Trail. When you reach the Winsor Trail, turn right and go back to the Ski Basin.

SANTA FE BALDY

by
Arnold and Carolyn Keskulla

U.S. GEOLOGICAL SURVEY MAP REQUIRED: Aspen Basin - 7.5 minute series. See sketch map on page 50.

SALIENT FEATURES: You will experience the satisfaction of achieving the summit of a beautiful mountain with unsurpassed views and lovely wildflowers. There are steep grades and high altitudes. Pick a clear day to make your climb and be well equipped with full canteen, poncho, lunch and energy. This is a strenuous hike and you should be in good shape. Start as early as you can in order to be off the peak before the usual summer afternoon thunderstorms begin.

RATING: Strenuous.

ROUND TRIP HIKING DISTANCE: 13 to 14 miles.

APPROXIMATE ROUND TRIP HIKING TIME: 8 hours.

ALTITUDE RANGE: Highest point, 12,622 feet; lowest point, 10,250 feet; cumulative uphill hiking, 3600 feet.

SEASONAL CONSIDERATIONS: Generally accessible from mid-June to early October. The best time to climb Santa Fe Baldy is in late June or early July because the thunderstorm season may not have begun and the forget-me-nots and other alpine flowers are in profusion.

ROUND TRIP DRIVING: 30 miles; approximately 1 hour 20 minutes.

DRIVING DIRECTIONS: From the plaza, drive north on Washington Avenue 6 blocks and turn right onto Artist Road. There is a sign here pointing to Hyde State Park and the Ski Basin. Measure your mileage from the turn. Continue 14 miles to the Ski Basin. At the Ski Basin, keep to the left and park in the lower parking lot. Look for a sign that says, "WINSOR TRAIL."

HIKING INSTRUCTIONS: After crossing the small wooden bridge turn right and start uphill on the well-used Winsor Trail 254. In a half mile or more of steep climbing you will be at the wilderness boundary fence, 600 feet higher than the trailhead. Watch for the lovely wildflowers among the aspen and spruce. In June you may see shooting star and fairy slipper orchid. From the fence you start gently downhill, passing in about a quarter of a mile a little-noticed trail on the left. This is a very steep trail to the Rio Nambé nicknamed the "elevator shaft." Continue past it for about one mile. Here a trail goes south up to lovely Nambé Lake beneath Lake Peak (see page 51 for the Nambé Lake hike).

However, you go straight ahead across the Rio Nambé and continue along the Winsor Trail. After crossing two streams (which feed into the Rio Nambé), start up the switchbacks which will lead you to a trail junction at 11,000 feet, 4.5 miles from the Ski Basin. The level grassy meadow here is generally, though inaccurately, referred to as Puerto Nambé. Before continuing, take a look at the way you came: on the way back people occasionally wander mistakenly down the meadow and into the Nambé River drainage.

The junction is marked by sign posts. The left branch of the trail is the beginning of the Skyline Trail. This trail goes to Lake Katherine and beyond. The right branch (the Winsor Trail) goes to Spirit Lake and down into the Pecos Valley.

Take the left fork, Trail 251 (not shown on the USGS map) which leaves the Winsor Trail and goes northeasterly up long switchbacks to the top of a saddle. From the saddle leave the trail and strike for the summit up the ridge to your left (north) by line of sight. There is a rough trail near the edge of the ridge.

This is a steep ascent, so you may have to make your own switchbacks and rest occasionally. There may be a few snow patches. Along with your lunch, enjoy the superb views from the top and don't miss looking down on Lake Katherine by walking a short distance to the northeast. The unforgettable blue forget-me-nots, fairy primroses, sky pilots and other beautiful alpine flowers will be abundant early in the season. Later, bistorts, gentians, composites and others will appear. You have climbed to the summit of a 12,622 foot peak, a memorable experience!

Remember to turn back at any sign of a thunderstorm. Before you leave the top, check your bearings by sight or compass so that you can reach Puerto Nambé and the trail back to the ski basin. Don't try to take a shortcut down; rather, return by the same route you ascended. Many hikers have gotten themselves lost by trying to take a shortcut back to the Winsor Trail.

> When we try to pick out anything by itself, we find it
> hitched to everything else in the universe.
> –John Muir

LAKE KATHERINE

by
Kenneth D. Adam

U.S. GEOLOGICAL SURVEY MAPS REQUIRED: Aspen Basin and Cowles - 7.5 minute series. The current maps do not show the trail from Puerto Nambé to Lake Katherine, but the Pecos Wilderness Map from the Forest Service and Drakes's "Mountains of Santa Fe" both do. See sketch map, page 50.

SALIENT FEATURES: A high altitude hike over well-marked trails through aspen, fir and spruce forest and high alpine meadows, ending in a beautiful alpine lake in a spectacular setting. Fine views of nearby peaks and distant valleys.

RATING: Strenuous.

ROUND TRIP HIKING DISTANCE: 14.5 miles.

APPROXIMATE ROUND TRIP HIKING TIME: 7-8 hours, plus stops.

ALTITUDE RANGE: Highest point, 11,742 feet; lowest point, 10,250 feet; cumulative uphill hiking, 3300 feet.

SEASONAL CONSIDERATIONS: Practical from about early June, depending on snow, until the first major snowfall.

ROUND TRIP DRIVING: 30 miles; approximately 1 hour 20 minutes.

DRIVING DIRECTIONS: From the plaza, drive north on Washington Avenue 6 blocks and turn right onto Artist Road. There is a sign here pointing to Hyde State Park and the Ski Basin. Measure your mileage from the turn. Continue 14 miles

61

to the Ski Basin. At the Ski Basin, keep to the left and park in the lower parking lot. Look for a sign that says, "WINSOR TRAIL."

HIKING INSTRUCTIONS: From the trailhead, immediately cross a small stream (the upper part of the Rio en Medio), turn right and start to climb. The trail starts with the steepest climb of the day through mixed aspen and conifer forest (very spectacular in the fall). In about 20 to 30 minutes, after two or three switchbacks and a couple of small meadows (wild iris in season), you will arrive at the entrance gate of the Pecos Wilderness in a meadow at the top of the first climb. This pass is between the watersheds of the Rio en Medio and Rio Nambé. The elevation here is 10,850 feet.

The trail now traverses the north slope of the divide. About 10 to 15 minutes after passing through the Wilderness Gate you come to a fork in the trail. Trail 403, to Rio Nambé, goes to the left. You continue straight ahead on the Winsor Trail, gradually losing altitude for a little over a mile until you reach a sparkling stream, the Nambé Creek. You will have been walking about one hour at this point. Just before the creek a fork leads upstream to Nambé Lake but you continue forward, crossing Nambé Creek on a log bridge.

The trail continues to traverse, without much altitude change, to the northeast. Keep to the main trail (Winsor Trail 254, now climbing slightly through aspen groves and small meadows. You will cross three minor streams and pass by two places where trails lead off to the left from the main trail. Stay on the main trail. The three-quarters of a mile uphill stretch from the last stream to Puerto Nambé will seem more like a mile. After twenty or twenty five minutes you will finally reach the "Y" trail junction in a beautiful high meadow. There are fine views of Santa Fe Baldy to the north and Lake Peak and Penitente Peak to the south and southeast. While you stop to rest at the junction, several gray jays will probably pester you for a handout. With just a little patience on your part, they will eat from your hand. Before continuing, take a look at the way you came: on the way back people occasionally wander mistakenly down the meadow and into the Nambé River drainage

You now leave the Winsor Creek Trail and take the Skyline Trail, the left trail at the "Y." The Winsor Trail, which you leave at this point, is the trail to the right (it takes you across Puerto Nambé to Spirit Lake). From here on, the trail is not shown on the USGS topo map (but is on Drake's). It crosses the meadow and starts up a series of long, long switchbacks which finally bring you to a saddle at the divide between the Rio Nambé and Pecos watersheds. You will have been walking about three hours at this point. This is a wonderful rest/snack spot with dramatic scenery in all directions: the upper Pecos basin to the east, the Rio Grande valley and Jemez Mountains to the west, Santa Fe Baldy right next to you on the northwest and Lake Peak and Penitente Peak to the south and southeast.

You are at the edge of a steep dropoff to the east and looking down you can see your trail zigging and zagging down in a series of seven switchbacks. After dropping down these switchbacks, the trail starts a climbing traverse to the northwest across the upper edge of a large talus slope, then through open forest. Level stretches of trail are interrupted with short climbs up switchbacks. Be on the look-out for abrupt changes in trail direction that mark switchbacks. You finally leave the forest and cross an open talus-covered area. The trail is not very definite here so keep a close eye on it. At the end of the talus area is a sign reading "Lake Basin closed to camping and fires." You cannot see the lake yet. A short walk through open forest brings you to the eastern shoreline of Lake Katherine, elevation 11,742 feet.

You are in a high alpine bowl, with Santa Fe Baldy directly above you to the southwest. The peak is so close that you may be tempted to climb it on your way home. This can be done by climbing the steep grassy slope above the west shore of the lake and following the ridge to the summit. It involves an extra 900 feet of climbing at high altitude, however, and is emphatically not recommended unless every member of your party is in excellent shape and you know your way back from the summit.

The recommended return is by retracing your route in reverse. When leaving Lake Katherine, the trail can be difficult to find again. Hike to the southeastern shore of the lake and toward the southern wall surrounding the lake. Then head east and look for the "no camping" sign you saw on the way in.

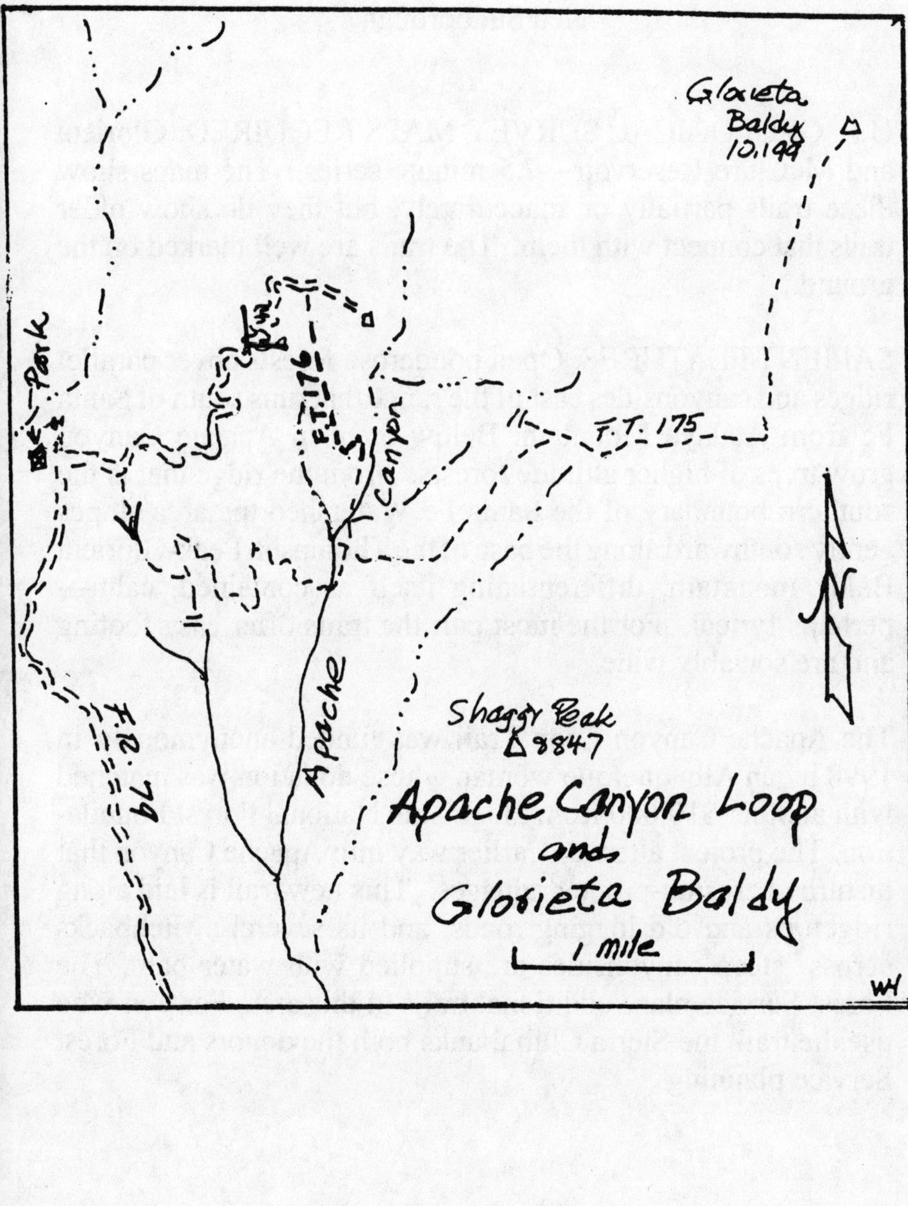

Glorieta
Baldy
10,199

F.T. 175

Elk Park

F.T. 175

Canyon

Apache

Shaggy Peak
8847

Apache Canyon Loop
and
Glorieta Baldy

1 mile

F.R. 79

N

WH

APACHE CANYON LOOP
and
APACHE CANYON TO GLORIETA BALDY

by
Ned Sudborough

U.S. GEOLOGICAL SURVEY MAPS REQUIRED: Glorieta and McClure Reservoir—7.5 minute series. The maps show these trails partially or inaccurately, but they do show older trails that connect with them. The trails are well marked on the ground.

SALIENT FEATURES: Open ponderosa forests cover parallel ridges and canyonsides east of the range that runs south of Santa Fe from Atalaya Mountain. Below them in Apache Canyon grow trees of higher altitude forests. From the ridge that is the southern boundary of the Santa Fe Watershed the area slopes gently southward along the base of the Thompson Peak-Glorieta Baldy mountain, differentiating itself as contained, calm---perhaps lyrical. For the most part the trails offer easy footing and are sociably wide.

The Apache Canyon Loop Trail was funded anonymously in 1998 by an Albuquerque woman whose donation was matched with another $10,000 from the private National Forest Foundation. The project alters an earlier way into Apache Canyon that disturbed erosion-prone drainages. This new trail is laid along ridgetops and old logging roads, and its several switchbacks across steep canyonsides are supplied with water bars. The Forest Service plans additional trails in this area. For you who use the trail, the Sierra Club thanks both the donors and Forest Service planning.

RATING: Easy-moderate/strenuous. The trail is pleasant step by step: returning from anywhere on the way into Apache Canyon provides a rewarding, easy hike. The Apache Canyon Loop trail is a moderate hike. The hike to Glorieta Baldy is strenuous.

ROUND TRIP HIKING DISTANCE: The Loop Trail is approximately 6 miles long. The round-trip hike to Glorieta Baldy is approximates 13 miles long.

ROUND TRIP HIKING TIME: Expect approximately 4 hours for the loop, 8 hours for Glorieta Baldy.

ALTITUDE RANGE: The Loop Trail's highest point is 8400 feet; its lowest point is 7760 feet (Apache Canyon bottom) with cumulative uphill of 800 feet. The figures for Glorieta Baldy are 10,199 feet and 7760 feet with cumulative uphill of 2820 feet.

SEASONAL CONSIDERATIONS: The Loop Trail can be hiked in all seasons. Glorieta Baldy is not usually climbed until after snows have melted. The approach on Forest Road 79 may be a problem in soaking wet weather of any season.

ROUND TRIP DRIVING: From the Santa Fe Plaza, 27 miles; allow 1 ½ hours.

DRIVING DIRECTIONS: From downtown Santa Fe, drive south on Old Santa Fe Trail, setting odometer at Paseo de Peralta, by the New Mexico State Capitol Building. Continue south on Old Santa Fe Trail but at 0.4, bearing left where it separates from Old Pecos Trail. (A left-turn lane is available beyond a "Do Not Enter" sign: turn left after the "Old Santa Fe Trail" street sign). Out of town, from 3.5, are surprising curves. For a mile afer 4.0 there are occasional glimpses eastward of Sierra Pelada, with cliffs bulging just below the horizon. At 4.5

67

pass El Gancho Way on the right. The road curves to cross a bridge over Arroyo Hondo (Big Ravine). At 6.4, a third of a mile beyond an I-25 locator sign, the road curves through a small drainage. (Old Santa Fe Historical Trail, which sometimes coincided with the route you've been traveling, here leaves the paved road for good. The trail continues beside the road in the drainage on the right and crosses out of sight through the slight saddle in the ridge ahead.)

The road climbs to reach around the southern end of the hills, and its crest provides the first views of the Apache Canyon area at 8.0. The great mountain on the eastern horizon is named Glorieta Baldy on the south and Thompson Peak (10,554 feet) on the north. Conspicuous in the foreground is Shaggy Peak (8845 feet), whose cliffs show the area's Precambrian granites gneissly. At 8.3 bear left and follow the county signs: "Cañada Village Road" and "67A." The road passes downhill through the village of Cañada de los Alamos (Cottonwood Canyon), once part of a 1785 land grant. Some of the interesting buildings are made of logs as well as of adobe. At the lower end of the village the pavement ends. The road passes between corrals, crosses the Cañada de los Alamos and turns uphill.

Curve left at several subsequent choices, as you climb to the ridge, and notably at 9.9, avoid the road signed "Herencia de Prada." At a cattleguard on the ridge, at 10.6, you pass a national forest boundary sign, and the road becomes Forest Road 79. From the highest stretch of the road, less than two miles ahead, little Aspen Peak can be seen on the left, with Lake Peak stepping away to the right, followed by Penitente Peak and Santa Fe Baldy behind them all. Near, leftward, is Sierra Pelada, seen earlier from Santa Fe. The road quickly drops to the trail junction: a sign announces "Baldy Trailhead." Altitude at the trailhead is 8150 feet. Park only on the left, where indicated.

HIKING INSTRUCTIONS: The hike starts across from the parking area on the road marked "Baldy Trailhead." Down the road a quarter mile is a locked gate. At the ridgetop just beyond it, find a sign for Forest Trail 175 on the right. FT 175 is a route to Glorieta Baldy and is the first part of the Apache Canyon Loop Trail. Follow this trail out on the ridge a quarter mile, and then down to an unused logging road that has become a trail. Turn left. Hikers planning to return this way should note the site for later recognition. The road will curve through several small drainages that beg a question: "Is there water this time, or not?"

In warm weather, a sniff into the vanilla/butterscotch-scented bark of the large trees will confirm that they are ponderosa pines. After winding down the road for a mile, you will see a Forest Service sign on the right advising that you continue forward on the road. The trail behind it reaches private property in Apache Canyon.

In sight up the road is another Forest Service sign: it directs you to the descent into Apache Canyon. The trail crosses a second unused logging road. The proximity of the roads suggests the intensity of the logging of this forest in the mid-1970s. (The present Santa Fe National Forest Plan allows logging here for forest health and disallows logging with commercial intent. From Apache Canyon nearly to the top of Glorieta Baldy, the slopes are classed as close to "wilderness" as administrative decision allows: hence no logging there.)

As you switchback steeply downward, the tree types change to Douglas fir, white fir, aspen, southwestern white pine and blue spruce as you near the canyon bottom. These are Mixed-conifer (Canadian) Zone trees that around Santa Fe usually succeed ponderosa pines above 8200 feet, but here grow below them, favored by cool mountain air drafting down the canyon.

69

Cottonwood, box elder, willow and the lacy Rocky Mountain juniper also grow in the canyon.

Near you at the bottom is the Apache Canyon stream; it flows throughout the year, though sometimes in some places it flows underground. It runs in a place of different character six miles south of here, marked by the I-25 sign "Cañoncito at Apache Canyon." The Santa Fe National Historical Trail is there, too. But here you can admire the trees and listen to the water and to the quiet of the canyon.

Take the trail leftward. But negotiate with any cows for quiet passage. Dilly-dally, eat lunch in the shade, as less than a half mile of trail is in the canyon. Beyond the grove of Douglas firs the trail crosses the brook. Ahead is a mound of logging refuse rising from the streambed, and just to the left of the path are the minimal remains of a sawmill, dated circa 1900. In the flat on the right, the forest is reclaiming the logging camp site. As these come into sight, note a trail sign on the right that announces FT 176 to complete the Loop Trail. The sign also directs a right turn to the canyon wall for the climb eastward out of the canyon to reach Glorieta Baldy on FT 175. *Continued description of the Glorieta Baldy trail begins with the second paragraph following.*

To complete the shorter Loop Trail, continue forward across the brook to the left side of the canyon, where FT 176 starts westward out of the canyon. The trail climbs 300 feet up the steep canyon wall back to the open ponderosa pine forest. In its next mile the path rises gently on a ridge alongside Apache Canyon and reaches the road on which the hike began. Elevation at this junction is 8300 feet. Turn left to return to the parking area 2.5 miles up the road. The ridges that you cross are the same ridges that you crossed on the trail into Apache Canyon, but now the crossings are as much as 200 feet higher in elevation.

To Glorieta Baldy. The trail switchbacks steeply out of Apache Canyon to the lower branch of a network of ridges rising toward Glorieta Baldy. At about two miles out of Apache Canyon, open space beyond the trees ahead signals a right turn onto the crest of the next to last ridge leading to the mountain-top. A set of shallow dips mark the beginnings of Grasshopper Canyon, that runs southward along the eastern base of Shaggy Peak. The trail is easy to follow as it climbs, and Shaggy Peak, near on the right, quickly drops below.

Three miles or more out of Apache Canyon, at 9300 feet, the trail passes between two well-separated signless posts. They make a gate onto the ridge by which the trail will reach the top. The ridge rises along the mountain's primary north-south axis. Enter the meadow just beyond the posts, turn left and, following signs, cross toward the trees, where the trail will reappear. This is the first of five pocket meadows between here and Glorieta Baldy, and in their greenery may be found purple asters bleaching to white, yellow composites, tiny blue harebells, red-green Indian paintbrush, scarlet bugler, scarlet gilia and flat-up white yarrow.

After the second meadow are the first views eastward; they open onto the lower Pecos Valley. The village of Pecos is there, and Interstate 25, slashing toward Las Vegas under the cliffs of Glorieta Mesa. The distant, steep roadcut leads to the top of Rowe Mesa.

From the third meadow the Glorieta lookout tower—your destination—can be seen braced above the trees. Just beyond this meadow, on the left, is a small abandoned mine opening. No gold there. On the right the ridge slopes into Ruiz Canyon, whose far side rises to a lower ridge that carries the hiking trail from the Glorieta Baptist Conference Center. The tower can be seen again on entering the fifth meadow. The trail breaks from the shading trees just below the top, passes through a junction

71

with the trail from Glorieta, and delivers you to the last turn of the tower's service road. You are at the base of the tower and the top of the mountain.

The walls of the lookout tower face north, south, east and west: you approached it from the south. From this height the view southeast shows 10 or more miles of I-25, paved through the valley over traces of the Santa Fe Trail, traces that run over Spanish horse tracks on top of Indian footpaths.

The Pecos Valley lies within a mountain rim, a green horseshoe, edged due east of here by Bear Peak (10,423 feet), a rise on the smooth high ridge that has another prominence to the northeast named Elk Mountain (11,661 feet). Most of the Pecos Wilderness lies north and west of Elk Mountain. Twenty-five bird miles northward is another edge, the jagged Truchas Peaks (13,102 feet); to their left, just ten miles away, are the profiles of Lake Peak and adjacent Penitente Peak. The bold cliffs low in the foreground are the north walls of Dalton Canyon, 3 1/4 miles away. All these hills and mountains immediately north of I-25 form the southern terminus of the Rocky Mountain Front, a range that begins in Wyoming.

To the southeast, the plains may be visible. To the southwest lies an area of mountain blocks and desert valleys, with the smooth, rounded profile of Sandia Mountain (10,678 feet) on the horizon and the pointy, smaller San Pedro and Ortiz mountains before it.

On returning, note the trail junction just down from the top: continue straight ahead to return to your car the way you came. (The junction is with a trail described on page 74 under the title "Glorieta Baldy.") On hiking down FT 175 in warm weather, you can anticipate the cool, shallow water of Apache Canyon for head, hands and feet.

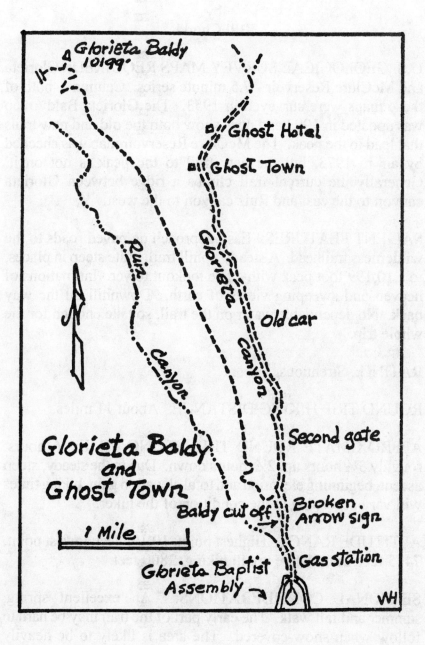

Glorieta Baldy
10199'

Ghost Hotel

Ghost Town

Ruiz Canyon

Glorieta Canyon

Old car

Second gate

Glorieta Baldy
and
Ghost Town

1 Mile

Baldy cut off →

Broken
Arrow sign

Glorieta Baptist
Assembly →

Gas station

WH

GLORIETA BALDY

by
Bill Chudd

U.S. GEOLOGICAL SURVEY MAPS REQUIRED: Glorieta and McClure Reservoir - 7.5 minute series. Caution -- both of these maps were surveyed in 1953. The Glorieta Baldy map was updated in 1993 and does show both the old and new trails that lead to the peak. The McClure Reservoir map was checked by air in 1973, but the new trail to the peak is not on it. Generally the current trail climbs a ridge between Glorieta canyon to the east and Ruiz canyon to the west.

SALIENT FEATURES: Easy approach on paved roads to the wilderness trailhead. A steady uphill trail, quite steep in places, to a 10,199 foot peak with a fire lookout tower. Intimations of heaven and sweeping views of earth. Downhill all the way back. No dependable water on the trail, so take enough for the whole trip.

RATING: Strenuous.

ROUND TRIP HIKING DISTANCE: About 11 miles.

APPROXIMATE ROUND TRIP HIKING TIME: 6 hours; roughly 3½ hours up, 2½ hours down. Due to the steady, steep ascent, beginning elevation and total elevation gain, hiking times will vary according to the condition of the hiker.

ALTITUDE RANGE: Highest point, 10,199 feet; lowest point, 7475 feet; cumulative uphill hiking, 2800 feet.

SEASONAL CONSIDERATIONS: An excellent spring, summer and fall walk. The early part of the trail may be hard to follow when snow-covered. The area is likely to be heavily snowed-in in midwinter. In summer start early enough to be off the peak shortly after noon to avoid the afternoon lightning storms. Carry a flashlight in all seasons; the Director of the Maintenance Department at the Conference Center says that 20-30 people get lost on this trail every summer.

ROUND TRIP DRIVING: 40 miles; about an hour.

DRIVING DIRECTIONS: From Santa Fe, take I-25 toward Las Vegas, New Mexico, to exit 299 at Glorieta. Following the direction signs for the Glorieta Conference Center, turn left at the top of the ramp and again at the "T". This road parallels the interstate and takes you to the Conference Center guard station. Stop at the gatehouse and, if there is a security officer there, advise him or her of your hike plan.

On leaving the gatehouse, immediately turn right onto Oak Street. Follow Oak Street through the conference grounds. At 0.6 mile from the gate, Oak Street turns right. Do not go straight onto Willow Street, but continue on Oak Street to the right. There is a small street sign at this street fork. At 0.9 mile, you will see a bicycle rental shop (the old firehouse) on the right. Park here.

HIKING INSTRUCTIONS: Walk back and turn right onto Holly Street. About 200 yards along this road (dirt now) you will find a fence with a trail register at the right of the road. Register your hike and pass through the fence to continue along the road. About 200 yards past the fence you will see a prominent sign marking Broken Arrow, the trail to Glorieta Baldy on your left and to Ghost Town straight ahead. Leave the road, turning onto the trail to your left.

Follow this trail uphill through scrub oak and to the left where it levels off among large boulders and seems to end. Do not go downhill but proceed directly to your right, maintaining your altitude. This section of trail is mostly unmarked from either direction. By neither climbing nor descending you will shortly see and pass through a wood gate, after which the trail is much clearer. You will shortly cross another rock outcropping which is also mostly unmarked. Watch the ground for the worn spots and you will be able to follow the trail.

The trail makes a number of small switchbacks and keeps climbing, with nice views toward the west, south and east. In the west, behind a ridge, you will see the top of Shaggy Peak. Shortly, you will reach the top of a ridge, a good place to get your bearings. Eastward, to your right, you will be looking down into Glorieta Canyon or across to La Cueva Ridge. Westward, to your left, you are looking into Ruiz Canyon. The broad trail follows the top of the ridge, climbing gently. You will see occasional blazes on trees. Along the trail are gilia so bright they look like orange cable markers.

About 2 miles into the hike you will see a trail merging in from the right with a sign, "Trail Closed." Continue straight ahead. After this junction the trail widens and becomes progressively steeper. The ridge, too, widens until you are simply climbing up a hillside. After you have been hiking for about 3 miles the trail becomes sharply steeper and narrower. You should have your first clear view of the fire tower ahead. You descend now for 1/4 mile to cross a small, and usually dry, drainage. This eventually runs into Glorieta Canyon. After crossing the ravine, the trail turns left and goes steeply upward on the right side of the drainage.

The ponderosa pines have given way to firs and, at about 9500 feet, patches of aspen appear. These will announce themselves with shouting golden hues in late September and October. From time to time you will get dramatic views back toward Glorieta and an occasional view of the lookout tower ahead through the tree tops.

76

In the last mile the slope becomes increasingly steep and the trail begins to switch back and forth across a runoff channel which is often used as the trail. **Please stay on the switchbacks**. Your trip will be only slightly longer, but much easier, and you will not contribute to the serious erosion problem in the runoff channel. Because of the heavy use of the runoff channel as the trail it is easy to get confused about the switchbacks. Simply keep going up and you will again pick up a switchback leading uphill to the top.

This trail meets the trail up from Apache Canyon (see page 66 for "Apache Canyon to Glorieta Baldy" description). At this intersection, which is just below the fire tower, turn right, and follow the trail as it curves up to the fire tower.

Look around. Wasn't it worth it? I've sat here on a day with broken clouds rolling below, revealing glimpses of hilltops, mesas and distant plains, as though looking down from heaven. On another unheavenly, still day with a temperature inversion, I looked to the southwest to see Albuquerque smog snaking around the north slopes of Sandia Mountain and sending a gray-brown plume out over the plains to the east. It's an ever-changing, always remarkable view.

From the steps of the fire tower you can see north to all the mountains bounding the Pecos Valley and Pecos Wilderness. You can see Starvation Peak to the southeast and the Ortiz Mountains in front of Sandia Mountain to the south. Only to the west and the Jemez is the view obstructed.

Descend by the same trail. When you reach the lower, flatter part of the ridge where yucca and other dry plants grow, it is easy to be misled by the many trails that lead off from campfire rings and campsites. The main trail is broad and gently descends, however, and is not easily lost here. Enjoy the scent of sunbaked pine needles as you move along. After descending off the ridgeline, pay careful attention to the trail as it moves back toward the northeast and crosses the rock outcroppings.

When you get back to the Conference Center, you may wish to explore this curious city in the wilderness. From your parking area, you may choose to continue to the left on Oak Street, which completes a circuit of the Conference Center grounds and returns you to the entrance gate.

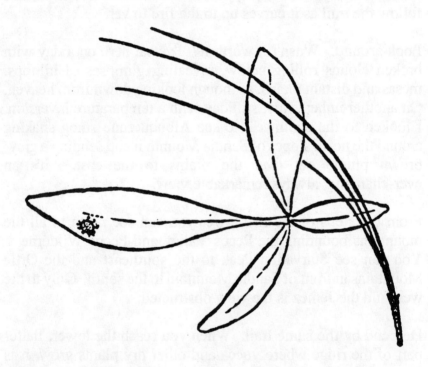

GLORIETA GHOST TOWN

by
Bill Chudd

U.S. GEOLOGICAL SURVEY MAPS REQUIRED: Glorieta and McClure Reservoir - 7.5 minute series. This hike appears on these maps as the lower part of an old trail to Glorieta Peak. That trail has long been abandoned and no longer exists. See sketch map on page 73.

SALIENT FEATURES: An easy-to-reach trail along a forest stream in Glorieta Canyon to a "ghost town." I have been told there was a lumber mill at the ghost town 60 or 70 years ago and you will see a large pile of lumber mill leftovers. There were also some mining activities in this area. The only remaining ruins are those of a two-story log hotel (collapsed) and one other wooden building. A secluded walk through mixed conifer and deciduous woods. Some aspens and oaks pick up the sunlight in the autumn and provide touches of gold and reddish brown. Small meadows along the way contain a good mix of wild-flowers in season. The geologic strata start with sandstone, followed by fossil-bearing limestone, and finally granite-like cliffs. The trail may be heavily used some days, empty others.

NOTE: The Forest Service warns that most of this trail is on private land. The Forest Service does not maintain it nor provide signs. Each year many people wander off the path described here, get lost and have to be rescued. **Don't improvise.**

RATING: Easy.

ROUND TRIP HIKING DISTANCE: Just short of 6.5 miles.

APPROXIMATE ROUND TRIP HIKING TIME: 3½ hours.

ALTITUDE RANGE: Highest point, 8420 feet; lowest point, 7475 feet; cumulative uphill hiking, 950 feet.

SEASONAL CONSIDERATIONS: This can be an all-year walk, although accessibility in winter will depend on the amount of snowfall. The lower section can be an easy and beautiful cross country ski route. The stream flow varies widely with the seasons. It may present difficult crossings at the height of the spring runoff or may be completely dry after prolonged drought.

ROUND TRIP DRIVING: 40 miles; one hour.

DRIVING DIRECTIONS: From Santa Fe, take I-25 toward Las Vegas, New Mexico, to exit 299 at Glorieta. Following the direction signs for the Glorieta Conference Center, turn left at the top of the ramp and again at the "T". This road parallels the interstate and takes you to the Conference Center guard station. Stop at the gatehouse and, if there is a security officer there, advise him or her of your hike plan.

On leaving the gatehouse, immediately turn right onto Oak Street. Follow Oak Street through the conference grounds. At 0.6 mile from the gate, Oak Street turns right. Do not go straight onto Willow Street, but continue on Oak Street to the right. There is a small street sign at this street fork. At 0.9 mile, you will see a bicycle rental shop (the old firehouse) on the right. Park here.

HIKING INSTRUCTIONS: Continue on Oak Street about 100 feet to the first intersection, with Holly Street. Turn right onto Holly. About 200 yards after leaving the paved road for a dirt road you will come to a trail register and a fence. After registering your hike, continue along the road. Soon you will reach a sign marking Broken Arrow and the turnoff to Glorieta Baldy. Stay straight ahead to Ghost Town. The trail is well used and very obvious. Some five minutes later, you will reach a fork in the road. Take the right branch. It goes past a campground on the left and soon crosses the little stream that stays close to the trail all the way to Ghost Town. You will cross the stream from time to time and even walk in it for some of the trip. The water is usually quite shallow.

Many local wildflowers can be seen beside the trail. At the lower sections of the trail are large cottonwood trees which give way to aspens at the higher levels. There are some junipers and ponderosa pines throughout the hike. About a half mile in, you will come to a fence with an open field beyond. This field has a heavy growth of mullein and also some yellow or yellow-brown prairie coneflowers, not too common in our area. In addition there are wild roses and strawberries all along the trail, with some New Mexico columbine just to the east of the last stream crossing before Ghost Hotel. You may also hear the sweet song of a meadow lark.

Beyond the field, just before the road bears right, you may be reassured by a sign pointing back toward the trailhead and ahead to Ghost Town (at this time--1998--the sign is leaning against a tree). You will now be walking along what remains of the road to the old "Ghost Hotel." There are occasional side trails, but the main trail remains obvious. Some twenty minutes past the sign post, you will find an ancient car parked in the stream bed. The road climbs gradually. While the ascent totals about 900 feet, there are only two moderately steep parts. The good news is that it's downhill all the way back.

About three miles in you will see the remains of an old wooden bridge on your left, then the first of the two ruins, an old wooden building, will also be on your left. Here the trail narrows to a thin path between the ruin and the stream, then broadens again to the width of a primitive road. You may see "Posted" signs on several trees, telling you it is "Private Land - Keep Out."

In less than a half mile you will reach another meadow. The ridge to your right across the stream features towering cliffs. Ahead and to your left, at the northwest end of the field, is your destination, "Ghost Hotel." Alas, the once imposing structure has collapsed in recent years. A trail does continue along the stream for a ways. At one time it connected with the road to Glorieta Baldy, but has since completely disappeared.

You may want to explore a bit of the surrounding area. Beyond the hotel ruin, toward the northwest, you can follow a barely visible path for about 200 feet to the entrance of an old mine gallery carved into the hillside rock on the right side of a small canyon. Due to the buildup of earth at the entrance the gallery remains flooded. After your exploration, sit a while. Enjoy a snack. Watch the ravens soaring above and the ground squirrels foraging at your feet. Looking at the cliffs to the east, across the stream, imagine, as I did, a colorful sunrise over these hills at the time the Ghost Hotel was in its heyday.

Upon your return to the parking area, continue driving further on Oak Street, which completes a circuit of the Conference Center grounds and returns you to the entrance gate.

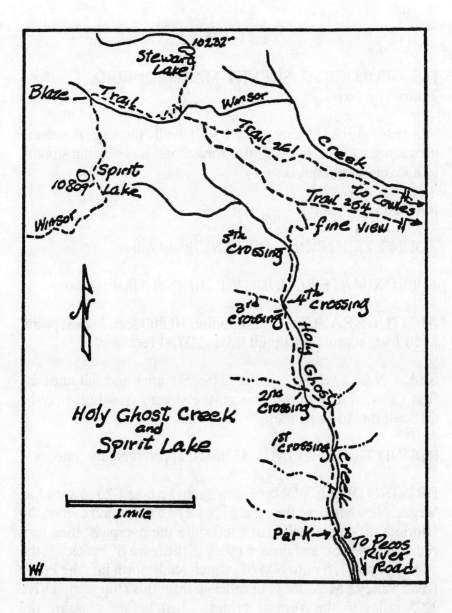

Holy Ghost Creek
and
Spirit Lake

1 mile

WH

HOLY GHOST CREEK AND SPIRIT LAKE
(The Espiritu Santo Walk)

by
Carl Overhage

U.S. GEOLOGICAL SURVEY MAP REQUIRED: Cowles - 7.5 minute series.

SALIENT FEATURES: An uphill walk through flowering meadows, aspen groves, spruce forest, past a cascading stream, to a lovely mountain lake.

RATING: Strenuous.

ROUND TRIP HIKING DISTANCE: 14 miles.

APPROXIMATE ROUND TRIP HIKING TIME: 9 hours.

ALTITUDE RANGE: Highest point, 10,800 feet; lowest point, 8150 feet; cumulative uphill hiking, 2750 feet.

SEASONAL CONSIDERATIONS: Summer and fall until the first snow. Early in the season, the stream crossings may be difficult due to snow melt.

ROUND TRIP DRIVING: 81 miles; approximately 3 hours.

DRIVING DIRECTIONS: From Santa Fe take I-25 toward Las Vegas, New Mexico, for approximately 15 miles and exit on the Glorieta off-ramp 299. Turn left onto the overpass, then turn right onto NM 50 and drive 6 miles to the town of Pecos. At the stop sign turn left onto NM 63, which leads north into the Pecos River valley. Measure your mileage from this stop sign. Drive 13.5 miles to the Terrero bridge. Just before crossing the bridge, swing left on Forest Road 122 leading to Holy Ghost

Campground. There is a direction sign at this intersection. Follow the paved road 2.4 miles to a parking area located about 100 yards before the campground entrance. Watch for speed bumps along this 2.4 mile road. A sign opposite the parking area points to the trailhead. Parking in the area before the campground entrance costs $2 per day. There is additional parking in the campground, but it is only for campground users and costs $8 per day.

HIKING INSTRUCTIONS: There are two ways to begin the initial approximately twenty minutes of the hike. The first option is to head uphill on the trail opposite the parking area, where there is a trailhead sign. The advantage of this route is that it bypasses the entire campground. The trail goes uphill, passes the campground, then descends to cross the Holy Ghost stream on a foot bridge.

The second option is to walk through the campground. This is a bit quicker. Follow the paved road through the individual camping sites and past the group campground area. Continue past the ground camping area on a dirt path. In a few minutes, you will come to the foot bridge that crosses the Holy Ghost stream.

Once you cross the footbridge, you will follow Holy Ghost Creek upstream. After about twenty minutes and after passing through some large meadows you will cross Holy Ghost Creek from west to east. Another twenty minutes takes you to the second crossing and back to the west bank. In the meantime, you will have seen many wildflowers, including iris, and you will have been greatly tempted to linger among them.

Next, you have a short steep climb up on a ridge. You come to some aspen groves with beautiful fern; then you descend to the creek where you cross for the third time. You will cross the creek again very soon. After this fourth crossing there is a steep uphill. At this point you will be back on the west bank. You pass a small meadow, and soon afterwards cross the creek for the fifth time.

After the fifth crossing you turn away from the stream and begin the climb up the ridge between Holy Ghost Creek and Winsor Creek. During the next half hour, by a series of switchbacks, you will gain 650 feet in elevation. On the way up, you pass a small promontory, from which there is a fine view down into the Holy Ghost valley. You reach the top of a ridge and, at the northwest end of a large meadow, the intersection with Trail 254 coming up from Cowles. You are now three hours away from the starting point, and this is a good place to rest for a brief snack.

From the meadow, follow Holy Ghost Trail 283. The walk continues in a northwesterly direction through a beautiful forest. In about thirty minutes you come to the intersection with another (shorter) trail (261) from Cowles coming up on your right. Fifteen minutes later, you come to a point where you cross the main branch of Winsor Creek, which descends from Lake Katherine. After crossing the creek on a large log to its north bank, the trail splits in two. The Winsor Trail to Spirit Lake bears left, toward west. (The trail to the right goes north to Stewart Lake, less than half an hour away, and only one hundred feet above this junction. If you feel tired at this time, you may decide to go to Stewart Lake, instead of walking more than one hour and climbing seven hundred feet to Spirit Lake.)

After leaving the Winsor Creek crossing, the trail to Spirit Lake climbs fairly steeply, following Winsor Creek upstream. In several places, you get beautiful views of the stream as it cascades down its steep course. The trail becomes gradually easier as it passes some lush green meadows a short distance to the left. Twenty minutes after leaving the Winsor Creek crossing, you should begin to look for a trail junction, where the trail to Lake Katherine takes off to the right. Follow the sign straight ahead to Spirit Lake.

Five minutes later you will come to a somewhat confusing spot, where the trail crosses Winsor Creek from its north bank to the south bank. As you come closer to the creek, keep looking at the opposite bank for a blaze on a large spruce and for a low cairn. This marks the place where the Winsor Trail crosses to the south bank. Disregard the abandoned former Lake Katherine trail, which continues up the north side of Winsor Creek. Once across the creek, the trail is easy to follow as it climbs up the low ridge separating the Winsor and Holy Ghost drainages. You will reach the lake about half an hour after the last Winsor Creek crossing and about five hours from the beginning of the walk. At the time of this revision (June 6, 1998) there was spotty snow on the last 45 minutes of the trail to Spirit Lake.

The return trip will present no special problems. At the junctions with the trails from Cowles, remember to keep right. Shortly after the third crossing of Holy Ghost Creek on the return walk, as you walk parallel to the stream on its right (west) bank, you will come to a trail fork which you may not have noticed in the morning on the way up. Take the right branch, which goes up steeply for a short distance. On the home stretch through the streamside meadows, you may now feel that you have time for a more leisurely look at the many wildflowers.

(John Muchmore's helpful observations during joint walks over this route are gratefully acknowledged.)

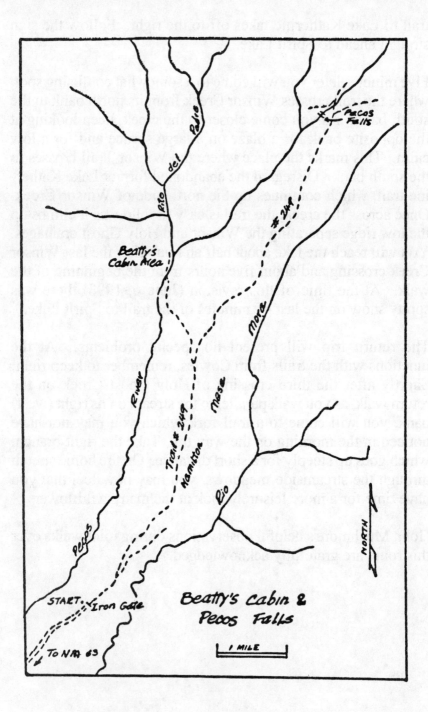

Beatty's Cabin &
Pecos Falls

1 MILE

BEATTY'S CABIN
and
PECOS FALLS

by
Philip L. Shultz

U.S. GEOLOGICAL SURVEY MAPS REQUIRED: Pecos Falls and Elk mountain - 7.5 minute series. Note that "Beatty's Cabin" is called "Beatty's" on the Pecos Wilderness map and "Beatty's Flats" on the USFS map.

SALIENT FEATURES: This hike goes through some of the most beautiful high meadows of the Pecos Wilderness, with outstanding views of the Truchas Peaks, Pecos Baldy and Lake Peak from the east side. In early summer the irises are spectacular.

RATING: Beatty's Cabin, strenuous; Pecos Falls, very strenuous.

ROUND TRIP HIKING DISTANCE: Beatty's Cabin, 10 miles; Pecos Falls, 17 miles.

APPROXIMATE ROUND TRIP HIKING TIME: Beatty's Cabin, 5 hours; Pecos Falls, 8 hours, stops not included.

ALTITUDE RANGE: Beatty's Cabin: Highest point, 10,200 feet; lowest point, 9400 feet; cumulative uphill hiking, 1640 feet. Pecos Falls: Highest point, 10,600 feet; lowest point, 9400 feet; cumulative uphill hiking, 1300 feet.

SEASONAL CONSIDERATIONS: This is not a winter hike. Four-wheel drive is required whenever the road is likely to be muddy. Trail can be muddy during monsoon season (July, August).

ROUND TRIP DRIVING: 94 miles; approximately 3½ hours.

DRIVING DIRECTIONS: From Santa Fe take I-25 toward Las Vegas, New Mexico, for approximately 15 miles and exit on the Glorieta off-ramp 299. Turn left onto the overpass, then turn right onto NM 50 and drive 6 miles to the town of Pecos. At the stop sign turn left onto NM 63, which leads north into the Pecos River valley. Measure your mileage from this stop sign. From the Pecos stop sign, drive 18.5 miles, passing several camp and picnic grounds and the little settlement of Terrero. At the top of a grade turn right onto Forest Road 223. A sign here will direct you to Iron Gate Campground. The distance between this junction and the campground is 4 miles; the road is steep and rough in places. Four-wheel drive is essential when the road is wet and muddy. (Remember the road may be dry in the morning but wet in the afternoon when you return after a summer shower.) Near the entrance of the campground you will find a parking area for hikers. This is a fee area: pay your fee before starting your hike. The parking fee is $2 per day. Camping costs $4 per night.

HIKING INSTRUCTIONS: The trail starts at the far end of the campground. Trail 249 gently zigzags northeast from the gate at the Iron Gate Campground. It rises about 300 feet in a little under half a mile, through spruce, fir and aspen to a usually well-marked junction with Trail 250 (which goes essentially straight and makes up the right fork of the junction). Remain on Trail 249, bearing slightly left and still climbing. This is a popular trail for hikers and equestrians, so the trail marker signs may be torn down or defaced. In another quarter of a mile or so the trail comes out of the aspen, still climbing gently through the first meadow. In June the irises are gorgeous for the next 2 miles. Also, look for mariposa lilies. Kestrels are common and I have seen elk in these meadows on several occasions. The trail tops out at about 10,200 feet, a beautiful point for a rest stop, with fine views of the Truchas Peaks to the north. Three and a half miles from the start is the next marked trail junction, and the point of decision of whether to do the very long walk to Pecos Falls.

If you decide on the shorter trip to Beatty's Cabin, bear left (downhill to the northwest), entering the woods promptly for the winding descent to the Pecos River. Cross the good bridge and find a spot on the lovely grassy slope for a rest. The actual cabin is long gone. It was upstream near the confluence with the Rito del Padre. However, for those who like to see cabins, there is a new one located southwest of the bridge up on the side of the ridge. Return by the same route for a lovely, not too strenuous hike.

If you decide on the longer trip to Pecos Falls, instead of taking the left-hand trail to Beatty's Cabin, bear right on your original Trail 249. The trail generally follows the 10,200 foot contour through meadows and islands of aspen for about 4 miles to the falls, which are quite beautiful during the spring runoff. Return by retracing your walk along Trail 249 all the way back to Iron Gate Campground.

This wonderful high country is at its best in early summer when the irises are at their height and in late September when the aspen leaves are golden. Enjoy it!

Walking is man's best medicine.
–Hippocrates

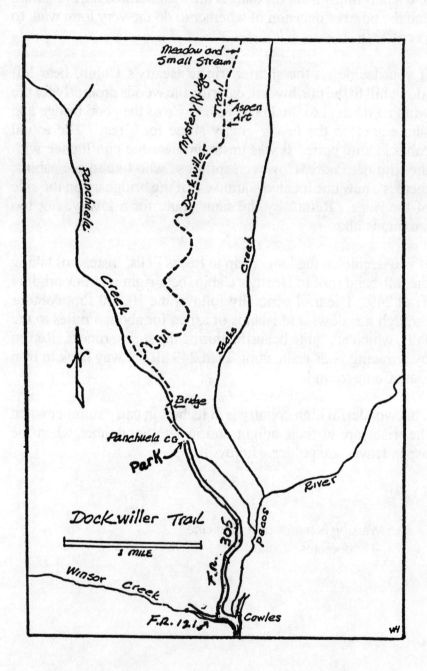

Meadow and
Small Stream

Mystery Ridge

Aspen
Art

Panchuela

Dockwiller Trail

Creek

Jacks Creek

Gin

Bridge

Panchuela CG

Park

Dockwiller Trail

1 MILE

River

Pecos

F.R. 305

Winsor Creek

F.R. 121A

Cowles

WH

DOCKWILLER TRAIL

by
Ann Bancroft

U.S. GEOLOGICAL SURVEY MAP REQUIRED: Cowles - 7.5 minute series.

SALIENT FEATURES: Three-season hike (not winter). Rife with wildflowers. Wonderful in fall when aspens are turning. This is a little-used trail and, although the views are not expansive, the wildflowers, aspens, and high, grassy meadows are beautiful and the opportunity for solitude will invite you to linger.

RATING: Moderate.

ROUND TRIP HIKING DISTANCE: 8 miles.

APPROXIMATE ROUND TRIP HIKING TIME: 5 hours.

ALTITUDE RANGE: Highest point, 10,040 feet; lowest point, 8350 feet; cumulative uphill hiking, 1700 feet.

SEASONAL CONSIDERATIONS: Unhikeable in winter. Cool in summer because of dense aspen groves.

ROUND TRIP DRIVING: 91 miles; approximately 3 hours.

DRIVING DIRECTIONS: From Santa Fe take I-25 toward Las Vegas, New Mexico, for approximately 15 miles and exit on the Glorieta off-ramp 299. Turn left onto the overpass, then turn right onto NM 50 and drive 6 miles to the town of Pecos. At the stop sign turn left onto NM 63, which leads north into the Pecos River valley. Measure your mileage from this stop sign. From the Pecos stop sign, drive 20 miles to the road fork where the

93

little settlement of Cowles used to be. Turn left, across the bridge onto Forest Road 121 and after just a few hundred yards turn sharply right uphill on Forest Road 305 toward Los Pinos Ranch and Panchuela Campground (it's now just a parking lot). The road dead-ends at Panchuela "Campground" in about 1.5 miles. Park here. There is a $2 per day parking fee.

HIKING INSTRUCTIONS: Follow the wide trail at the north end of the parking area (just past the fee station). It leads a short distance upstream to a bridge which spans Panchuela Creek. Cross the bridge and continue hiking upstream along a well-defined, now narrow trail. Twenty or so minutes of walking will bring you to a fork sign: straight to follow Panchuela Creek (this is Trail 288 which takes you up to Cave Creek and then on to Horsethief Meadow), right for Dockwiller Trail 259. Take the right fork uphill, following the Dockwiller.

This steeply ascending, switchbacked trail is named after a man who lived in the Cowles area and ran a sawmill. It is also sometimes referred to as the Mystery Ridge Trail. What the mystery is I haven't been able to discover. The trail takes you uphill out of the Panchuela Creek drainage. In about 40 minutes (about half way up the switchbacks) you may spot the snow cornice between Santa Fe Baldy and Lake Peak toward the west. These peaks are visible by looking up a canyon at a point where the trail direction changes from west to east.

After more severe switchbacks, at approximately 9200 feet, you will begin skirting the Jack's Creek drainage on the eastern flank of Mystery Ridge. Continue along the trail through aspen forests, interrupted by occasional grassy areas in the trail, which may become less well-defined. Off and on, aspen art may be spotted: if you're lucky you may find the words "Dios nos libre, Amen" etched around a cross, or names, possibly of sheepherders, dating as far back as 1919, not to mention the numerous carvings of more recent visitors.

After approximately 2½ hours, having taken a leisurely-paced hike with breaks, the turn-around point of this hike comes at a large, sloping, aspen-encircled meadow with a small stream running through it at approximately 10,000 feet. The trail continues on, but for this hike it's time to turn back, retracing your steps to Panchuela Campground.

This hike leads to many other beautiful areas in the Pecos Wilderness. Someday you may want to go on to Beatty's Cabin or Horsethief Meadow or, if you have someone to do a drive-around, return to Jack's Creek Campground via the Round Mountain trail.

Watching the circling seasons, listening to the songs
of the waters and winds and birds, would be endless
pleasure. And what glorious cloud-lands I would
see, storms and calms, a new heaven and a new
earth every day.
–John Muir

Stewart Lake

1 mile

STEWART LAKE

by
Betsy Fuller and Ann Young

U.S. GEOLOGICAL SURVEY MAP REQUIRED: Cowles - 7.5 minute series. The map called "Pecos Wilderness" put out by the National Forest Service is also helpful.

SALIENT FEATURES: A lovely mountain tarn reached through a deep aspen/conifer forest rife with wildflowers. Return along a ridge with distant views of the Pecos Wilderness.

RATING: Moderately strenuous.

ROUND TRIP HIKING DISTANCE: 10.5 miles.

APPROXIMATE ROUND TRIP HIKING TIME: About 6½ hours, including time for breaks and snacks.

ALTITUDE RANGE: Highest point, 10,332 feet; lowest point, 8400 feet; cumulative uphill hiking, 2500 feet.

SEASONAL CONSIDERATIONS: Beautiful in spring as soon as the snow disappears; good through fall until the first heavy snows.

ROUND TRIP DRIVING: 90 miles; 2 hours 45 minutes.

DRIVING DIRECTIONS: From Santa Fe take I-25 toward Las Vegas, New Mexico, for approximately 15 miles and exit on the Glorieta off-ramp 299. Turn left onto the overpass, then turn right onto NM 50 and drive 6 miles to the town of Pecos. At the stop sign turn left onto NM 63, which leads north into the Pecos River valley. Measure your mileage from this stop sign. From the stop sign, drive 20 miles to the junction where the little settlement of Cowles used to be. Turn left over the bridge onto Forest Road 121 and continue straight ahead for a little over a mile to the end of the road at Winsor Creek Campground.

HIKING INSTRUCTIONS: From the parking area, start hiking up the trail that parallels the creek. You'll walk through grassy meadows, aspen glades and wildflower patches. In 20 minutes or so you'll cross the stream to the left (south) bank and continue on the well-defined trail still paralleling the creek just below you.

About one hundred yards after crossing the stream, you'll pass the trail to your left (the Winsor Trail 254) that you will return on. It is not marked in any way so you might not notice it. Not to worry: it will be clear coming back. For now, just continue straight ahead (it's now Trail 261).

The aspens give way to deep conifer forests. You may notice a large, low rock sticking out partway into the trail with a USGS marker imbedded in it indicating that the elevation is 9405 feet. This is a good place for a break since you will have been hiking for about an hour by now. Beyond this point the trail climbs higher and higher above the stream and finally you'll lose the sound of it below you. After about 15 more minutes of climbing beyond the rock, the trail levels out a little. Another 15 minutes will bring you to a trail joining from the left. This is the Winsor Trail 254. Note this junction well because on the return trip you will take this higher trail.

For now, though, continue on the trail ahead of you (which is now the Winsor Trail). In about 10 minutes of level walking you will cross a stream over a big log. This is the main fork of the Winsor Creek that you were paralleling down below. A sign here indicates the Skyline Trail. For this hike continue straight ahead. Another 15 minutes will bring you to Stewart Lake.

You'll have to climb up a little rise to get to it. There are many well-worn paths here, so take any one.

This little gem of a lake is spring fed and from its banks you can look up to the west and see the flanks of Santa Fe Baldy. Fishermen have worn a path around the lake. After a snack and a rest you may want to walk around it. It won't take more than 15 or 20 minutes with time for admiring the wildflowers included.

To return, take the same path from the lake that you arrived on until you come to the trail junction mentioned previously. You can return the way you came, but a much more interesting way (although longer by about a mile and a half) is to take the righthand trail (Winsor Trail) that goes along the forested ridge above the trail you came in on. (This trail does not show on the Cowles topo map, but if you have the map put out by the Forest Service called "Pecos Wilderness," you'll see it marked.)

In about 20 to 25 minutes from the junction you'll arrive at a meadow with a sign indicating that this is the Pecos Wilderness area. This sign may be vandalized, so if it isn't there or has been replaced by another sign don't worry. At this point -- the very beginning of the meadow -- your trail goes 90 degrees off to the left.

It's quite faint here. Stay to the left of the meadow for a minute or two until the trail becomes more well defined. (If you find yourself crossing the meadow and dropping down into Holy Ghost Canyon to the right, you've missed your trail. Go back again to the top of the meadow and try again.) The trail is level or very slightly rising and in places where the grass is high becomes a little indistinct, but you should have no trouble finding it. It goes through aspen and then conifer forests and sometimes seems to be following an open swath through the trees. Was this once an ancient sheep-herding trail? You may see an occasional blaze on an old aspen. About 35 minutes after you've left the meadow, an open view will begin to be visible in front of you. This is a nice spot for another break.

Continue on the trail for another 20 minutes or so as the trail begins to descend. Now you come to a place where you have to keep your eyes open because the trail takes a poorly marked sharp turn to the left. (This is about an hour from the trail junction and about 20 minutes from the place where the distant views become visible.) The landmarks to look for are a few large branches to block passage straight ahead and, to your left, a large fallen ponderosa. Go past this ponderosa and the tall standing stump from which it broke and you'll quickly find the well-defined trail going down the other side of the ridge you've been walking on. The trail turns back on itself toward the left. There may also be a small rock cairn here marking this important turn. (If you suddenly find yourself casting about for the trail you have probably gone a few yards too far. Back up a little and look for the landmarks mentioned above.)

From here on there are no problems. Look off to your right once in a while and you'll catch glimpses of Pecos Baldy, Round Mountain, Hamilton Mesa and Grass Mountain. The trail goes down, down, down, seemingly without end. After about 45 minutes, you'll hear the stream below you and then come to the trail on which you walked up to the lake. Turn right onto this trail. Another 20 minutes downstream will bring you to your car.

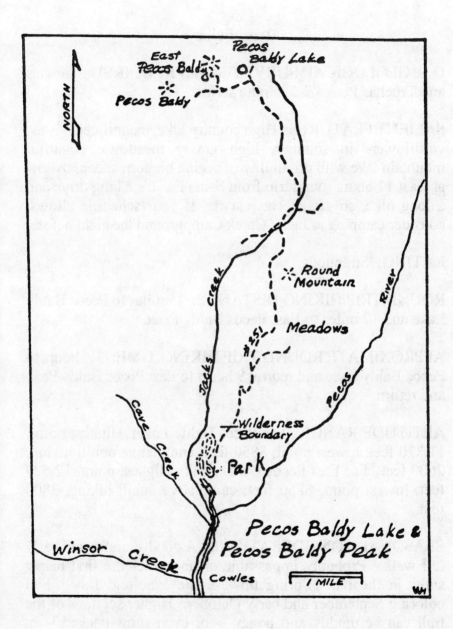

PECOS BALDY LAKE and PECOS BALDY PEAK

by
Betsy Fuller

U.S. GEOLOGICAL SURVEY MAPS REQUIRED: Cowles and Truchas Peak - 7.5 minute series.

SALIENT FEATURES: High country hike, magnificent vistas, wildflowers in summer, high grassy meadows, beautiful mountain lake with possibility of seeing bighorn sheep. Allow at least 11 hours round trip from Santa Fe. It's a long drive and a long hike, so get an early start. If your schedule allows, consider camping at Jack's Creek Campground the night before.

RATING: Strenuous.

ROUND TRIP HIKING DISTANCE: 15 miles to Pecos Baldy Lake and 17 miles to East Pecos Baldy Peak.

APPROXIMATE ROUND TRIP HIKING TIME: 7½ hours to Pecos Baldy Lake and return; 9 hours to East Pecos Baldy Peak and return.

ALTITUDE RANGE: For Pecos Baldy Lake: Highest point, 11,320 feet; lowest point, 8850 feet; cumulative uphill hiking, 2600 feet. For East Pecos Baldy Peak: Highest point, 12,529 feet; lowest point, 8850 feet; cumulative uphill hiking, 3800 feet.

SEASONAL CONSIDERATIONS: A good summer and early fall walk. Probably impassable on foot after the first heavy snow in the fall. Spring flowers late June and July. Fall coloring September and early October. Higher sections of the trail can be muddy and boggy -- or even snow-packed -- in spring and early summer.

102

ROUND TRIP DRIVING: 102 miles; 3½ hours.

DRIVING DIRECTIONS: From Santa Fe take I-25 toward Las Vegas, New Mexico, for approximately 15 miles and exit on the Glorieta off-ramp 299. Turn left onto the overpass, then turn right onto NM 50 and drive 6 miles to the town of Pecos. At the stop sign turn left onto NM 63, which leads north into the Pecos River valley. Measure your mileage from this stop sign. From the Pecos stop sign drive 20 miles to the road fork where the little settlement of Cowles used to be. Do not take the road to the left which crosses the river, but keep straight ahead for another three miles following the Forest Service signs to Jack's Creek Campground. Keep to the right at every junction following the road to "Wilderness Parking" until you arrive at a large loop where there are picnic tables, a corral and parking areas. Pay your fee at the self-service payment box. Parking costs $2 per day, camping $10 per night.

HIKING INSTRUCTIONS: The trailhead is to the north of the parking area where there is a Forest Service sign. The trail starts with a long climb (about a mile) through a conifer forest up the side of a hill. During this climb you will enter the Pecos Wilderness. Soon after the initial long climb, the trail goes into a series of long switchbacks still rising, until finally, after about another mile, the trail levels off a little. Just after another short climb, you will reach an open sloping grassy area. At this point, there is a signpost marking a "Y" trail junction. You will have walked about 2.5 miles and climbed about 1050 feet. Your altitude here is 10,026 feet.

Take the left (north) fork of the trail and continue through the meadow toward the aspen trees. After passing through the aspens, the trail swings slightly to the right. Watch for beautiful distant views of the Pecos Valley to the east and the mountains to the west as you look all around you. The trail climbs up through an open meadow in a northerly direction. Soon you will get your first view of the barren Pecos Baldy Peaks looming above the forests to the northwest. At the northern end of this meadow the trail enters a conifer forest and drops down to Jack's Creek, which is shallow most of the year and can easily be crossed on stepping stones. At this point you will have walked another 2 miles in about 45 minutes to an hour.

Crossing Jack's Creek, follow the trail to the right paralleling the stream. In 5 minutes, the trail swings away from the stream. Fifteen minutes after crossing Jack's Creek, the trail splits. Go straight ahead to Pecos Baldy, not right to Beatty's Cabin. Continue climbing through deep and dark conifer forests. Your altitude here is now over 10,500 feet and the trail is steep in some places, so take it easy as you continue your ascent.

Finally, about 2 miles (and over an hour's walking) after you crossed Jack's Creek, you will leave the forest behind you and will see the summit of East Pecos Baldy Peak ahead of you. One last steep climb brings you out at yet another junction from which point you will see Pecos Baldy Lake just a few hundred feet away. As you approach the lake, note the ridgeline of East Pecos Baldy Peak sloping downward to your left and ending at a high open saddle. This is the open saddle you cross on the way up to the peak.

If you're tired (and you will be!) go down to the lake for a snack and a rest. As you're recovering from the steep walk, search the sides of the mountain for bighorn sheep which are often found here in the summer months. Sometimes the sheep are overly friendly, nuzzling into your knapsack if it's left unattended. It will make a great picture, though.

You may want to end the outward bound trip here. If you've still got enough energy and time left, you might want to consider two options: climb East Pecos Baldy Peak or climb the ridge north of the lake.

Option #1: To climb East Pecos Baldy (2 miles round trip, 1100 feet up), go back up a couple of hundred feet to the place where you first saw the lake and where there is a marker prohibiting camping in the lake basin. Take the trail to the southwest (to your right as you walk away from the lake) and follow it for about one-half mile through a forested hillside south of the lake until it comes out onto an open saddle. Don't take the trail to the left that goes downhill through the woods, but continue across the open saddle in the same general direction that you were following when you arrived. You will have no trouble finding the rocky path that now zigzags up the steep side of the mountain. The climb from the saddle to the top of East Pecos Baldy is another 680 feet and a hard pull at this elevation (12,529 feet when you reach the top), so take your time and enjoy the ever enlarging views as you climb to the top. Don't attempt this part of the hike if it's stormy. There's no protection on top and lightning and strong winds are not good companions when you're on the top of a bare rocky peak in the high mountains. There is frequently a snow cornice along the peak, with a considerable overhang. <u>Do not walk out on any snow field along the edge of the peak.</u>

Option #2: To go up to the saddle on the ridge north of the lake (1 mile round trip, 400 feet up). Keeping the lake on your left, walk to the north side of the lake and then up to the saddle. There are several trails leading in the same direction. Your reward will be terrific views of the mountains to the north. And yes, those are fossils in the gray shale outcrops. Go back to the lake the same way you came up.

Your return trip is over the same route as the one you came up on, the only difference (an important one!) being that you'll be going downhill most of the time.

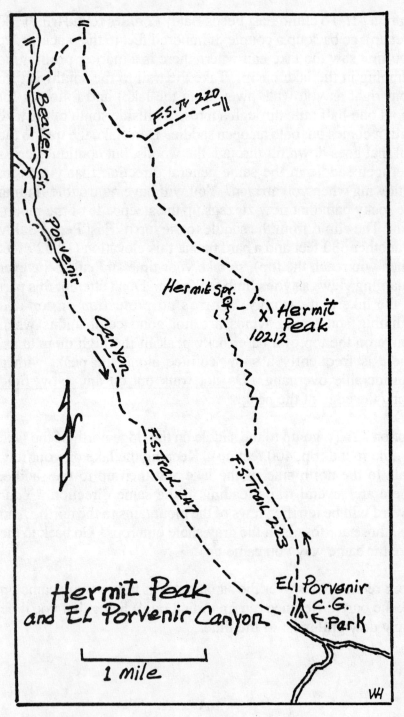

F.S. Tr. 220

Beaver Cr.

Porvenir

Canyon

Hermit Spr.

x Hermit
Peak

10212

F.S. Trail 247

F.S. Trail 223

El Porvenir
C.G.

← Park

Hermit Peak
and El Porvenir Canyon

1 mile

WH

HERMIT PEAK
and
EL PORVENIR CANYON
(as an optional extension)

by
Norbert Sperlich

U.S. GEOLOGICAL SURVEY MAPS REQUIRED: El Porvenir, and, for the extended hike, Rociada - 7.5 minute series. On top of Hermit Peak, a section of Trail 223 (from Hermit Spring to the east rim) has been rerouted; this new route does not appear on the topo map.

SALIENT FEATURES: Hermit Peak is a rugged granite peak and major landmark in the southeastern corner of the Pecos Wilderness. It is named for a hermit who lived in a cave near the summit in the 1860s. The approach to the trailhead is on paved roads. The trail is quite steep. From the summit are great views toward the eastern plains.

The extension of this hike takes you into beautiful El Porvenir Canyon with its meadows, wildflowers, waterfalls and rugged cliffs. You will be challenged by 27 stream crossings. An extra pair of sneakers and socks, a walking stick and mosquito repellent might be helpful for this adventure. Don't attempt the canyon during spring runoff! It is a long hike and a long drive, so start early. To get an early start, you might want to spend the night at El Porvenir Campground.

RATING: Hermit Peak, moderate in distance, but strenuous if you are not used to steep climbs. Hermit Peak and El Porvenir Canyon, strenuous.

ROUND TRIP HIKING DISTANCE: Hermit Peak, 8 miles. Hermit Peak and El Porvenir Canyon, about 14 miles.

107

APPROXIMATE ROUND TRIP HIKING TIME: Hermit Peak, 5 hours. Hermit Peak and El Porvenir Canyon, about 7 hours, stops not included.

ALTITUDE RANGE: Highest point, 10,212 feet; lowest point, 7550 feet; cumulative uphill hiking, approximately 2700 feet for Hermit Peak, about 2800 feet for Hermit Peak and El Porvenir Canyon.

SEASONAL CONSIDERATIONS: Not a winter hike. For the El Porvenir Canyon portion of the hike, avoid the spring runoff.

ROUND TRIP DRIVING: 170 miles; approximately 3½ hours.

DRIVING DIRECTIONS: Take I-25 toward Las Vegas, New Mexico. Take the first exit (Exit 343) into Las Vegas and turn left onto road 329. There is a sign, "United World College," at the turnoff. Turn left again at a stop light where road 329 crosses Hot Spring Road. You are now on road 65, which will take you to the trailhead. After passing United World College (on the right) in Montezuma, the road starts to climb and becomes narrow, with many blind curves. When you approach the village of Gallinas, the rocky face of Hermit Peak appears in the background. Look for green mileage markers on the right side of the road. After mile 13, you will come to a fork. Take the right branch to El Porvenir. After about 2.7 miles, you will reach the parking lot at the entrance to El Porvenir Campground. Park here. A sign, "Hermit Peak Trail Head," points to a wooden bridge.

HIKING INSTRUCTIONS: Cross the wooden bridge next to the parking lot. After a few minutes, you will be back on the road that leads to the campground. Look for a trailhead marked, "Hermit Peak, Trail 223," just before the road comes to the campers' self-service pay station. The trail starts to climb right away. After a few minutes, it goes through a fence. Shortly after, the Dispensas Trail branches off to the right. Keep on going straight, following the sign, "Hermit Peak 4." The trail crosses two drainages. Next, two old roads merge with the trail, coming in from the right. Some 40 yards past the place where your trail joins the second road, this road turns left, crossing a low spot where two drainages come in from the right. Here, your trail leaves the road and goes off to the right at a 90 degree angle and up a ridge between the two drainages that come in from the right. This junction is usually marked.

From now on, the trail is wide and obvious and there are no more forks until you reach the summit plateau. You can forget about the trail for a while and enjoy your surroundings. As you go up and up, ponderosa pines give way to Douglas firs and aspen. The slope gets steeper and the trail starts to zigzag up a canyon formed by the cliffs of Hermit Peak. An intermittent stream runs through this canyon and you might notice a sign, "Trail Spring," which points to the stream. After about 2 hours of hiking, you will come to the top of the cliffs. Enjoy the view.

The trail now moves away from the rim. In a minute or two, you might notice an old trail going up to the right. Ignore it. Soon, you will reach a clearing. Here is Hermit Spring, enclosed in rock walls and protected with a metal cover. Hermit Peak (actually the east rim) is only one-half mile away and you have a choice of two trails to get there. The new, official route, passing to the left of the spring, is indicated by a trail sign. The old trail, no longer marked, turns right in front of the spring. It is lined with wooden crosses. Only the new trail has a marked junction where you can go in the direction of Lone Pine Mesa and eventually into El Porvenir Canyon. So, if you plan to do the extended hike, use the new trail, as described here.

After about 10 more minutes of hiking, you will come to a fork in the trail. Trail 223, the trail you have been on, turns sharply to the left and goes to Lone Pine Mesa. You go straight ahead on Trail 223A, toward the peak, as indicated on the signpost. Soon the rim of the summit plateau will appear on your left. In 5 minutes, you will be at the edge of Hermit Peak, looking across the plains to the east.

There are several old trails on the summit plateau. Make sure you return the way you came, with the mountain's edge close to your right. After about 5 minutes, you will come to the marked trail fork again. The left fork will take you back the same way you came up. If you are planning to take the long way back by way of El Porvenir Canyon, you should now take the right branch, toward Lone Pine Mesa. You have 10 more miles ahead of you! Do you have enough time?

The trail to El Porvenir Canyon will take you through a conifer and aspen forest, heading in a northwesterly direction. Soon it starts to drop down, staying on a ridge all the time. After some ups and downs, the trail levels out. About two miles from Hermit Peak, you will come to a trail junction marked by signposts and a cairn. Your trail (223) goes left toward Lone Pine Mesa. Trail 220 (Rito Chavez Trail) goes straight ahead (Trail 220 does not appear on the 1965 topo map). The trail is little-used and faint in places. It goes down, then up again, following a ridge which becomes narrow and rocky. About 1.2 miles or 25 minutes after the last trail junction, you will come to another fork marked by signposts and cairns. Take the trail that goes down to the left, towards Beaver Creek Canyon. On your way down, you will get glimpses of the canyon, and after about 25 minutes of steep downhill hiking you will reach Beaver Creek and a "T" junction marked by a cairn and a signpost. A marker, "Lone Pine Mesa, Hermit Peak," points in the direction you have come from. This is a great place for a stop. Right across from the trail, Beaver Creek forms a waterfall and a pool.

To continue the hike, take the left branch of the "T" junction, following Beaver Creek downstream. From now on, you will hike along lively streams, first Beaver Creek, then Porvenir Creek. This is the wild and wonderful part of the hike, 5 miles of hiking through meadows and woods, alongside rushing water and towering cliffs. If you brought extra sneakers for the stream crossings, now is the time to put them on.

After crossing Beaver Creek 4 times, you will reach a marked trail junction where the trail you are on (Trail 247) meets Trail 219 (Hollinger Creek Trail), the latter coming in from the right. Keep on going downstream on Trail 247.

You are now in Porvenir Canyon. Soon the canyon narrows, with the granite cliffs of Hermit Peak on one side and El Cielo Mountain on the other. And yes, there are stream crossings galore. Stick to the trail and do not try to skip a crossing by staying on "this side." It does not work. The last two miles of the hike are on private land; stay on the trail to avoid trespassing. When the canyon widens again, you are coming to the end of the hike. You will pass campsites and the remains of a log cabin, and reach a sign directing you to the Parking Area. Go through a gate and soon you will arrive at the parking lot where you left your car. By now, you will be bouncing along in exhilaration, looking for more stream crossings, or you may be staggering on wobbly legs. It is up to you!

> Walking is the best possible exercise. Habituate
> yourself to walk very far.
> –Thomas Jefferson

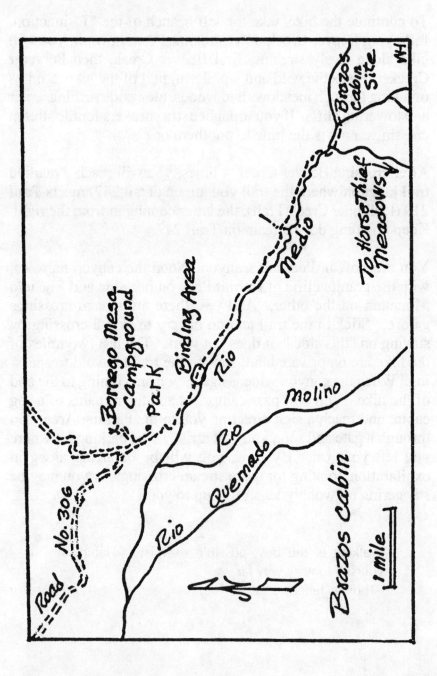

BRAZOS CABIN

by
John O. Baxter

U.S. GEOLOGICAL SURVEY MAPS REQUIRED: Sierra Mosca and Truchas Peak - 7.5 minute series. (The trail shown on these maps is different from the current trail described here.)

SALIENT FEATURES: This trail into the Pecos Wilderness is used less than trails starting at the Santa Fe Ski Basin. A beautiful mountain country hike, mostly in the trees, with good bird and flower sightings likely. The destination of this hike is a high meadow with views of Pecos Baldy.

The Forest Service access road 306 was in good condition in 1998. After prolonged rains, you should check with the Forest Service about road conditions.

RATING: Strenuous.

ROUND TRIP HIKING DISTANCE: 11 miles.

APPROXIMATE ROUND TRIP HIKING TIME: 7 hours.

ALTITUDE RANGE: Highest point, 9200 feet; lowest point, 8250 feet; cumulative uphill hiking, 1550 feet. There is a sharp drop (8850 to 8250 feet) in the first half mile, then a gradual climb to Brazos Cabin at 9200 feet.

SEASONAL CONSIDERATIONS: May be snowed-in in winter.

ROUND TRIP DRIVING: 78 miles; approximately 2½ hours.

DRIVING DIRECTIONS: Take US 84/285 northbound to Pojoaque (about 16 miles from Santa Fe). Continue across the bridge in the Española lane and turn right onto NM 503 at the Nambé turnoff (traffic signal). Note the mileage at the turnoff. At the Cundiyo-Chimayo junction (about 7.5 miles), go straight ahead toward Cundiyo. Drive carefully through Cundiyo (about 10 miles; narrow road, free-roaming dogs). About two miles past Cundiyo, you will pass a turnoff to Santa Cruz Lake on your left, County road 98A. About 100 yards past this turnoff, look for Forest Road 306, a dirt road which goes off to the right. There is a very small sign with "306" and an arrow. If you drive past the top of the ridge you've gone too far (we did the first time). This turnoff is 13.5 miles from the Nambé turnoff, where you took your odometer reading.

Reset your odometer to zero. Turn right onto FR 306. At about 7.5 miles, you will pass a turnoff on your right marked Trail 150, Borrego Trail. This is not your trail. At 9 miles, close to the Borrego Mesa Campground, the road forks. FR 306 curves to the left, but you turn right onto FR 435, which takes you to the entrance of the campground. Now take the road in front of the entrance that goes off to the right. It is about 300 yards to the trailhead of Trail 155. The last part of this road was very rutted in September 1998. You might want to park closer to the entrance of the campground, especially if rain is expected, and just walk the extra 300 yards.

HIKING INSTRUCTIONS: At the trailhead, to the right of the road, you will find an information board. A wooden sign directs you to Rio Medio Trail 155, which reaches the junction with the Rio Capulin Trail after 5 miles and Trail Riders Wall after 10 miles. You will follow this trail to Brazos Cabin for about 5.5 miles. The trail sets off in an easterly direction, rising slightly for 100 yards before plunging sharply down into Rio Medio Canyon. Much of this trail was rerouted in 1992. If you find yourself on a washed-out, rutted trail, you have probably strayed from the new, narrow trail onto the old one, which forks off to the right. This is most likely to happen on the stretch between the trailhead and the place where the trail reaches the river for the first time. Retrace your steps and get back on the new trail. Or, trudge on: the new and old trails rejoin a short ways further down.

On the southern horizon the green silhouette of Sierra Mosca looms over the valley to the south. Winding through towering ponderosas and patches of oak, the trail makes a descent of 600 feet in the first half mile, leading to the clear waters of the Rio Medio (not to be confused with Rio en Medio). Don't forget that this same steep slope must be negotiated in reverse at the end of the hike when the scenery may seem less remarkable. This part of the trail has many false paths and shortcuts, but the main course is clear. It takes about ½ hour to reach Rio Medio.

Continuing eastward, the track follows the north bank of the river upstream. Birders should find several mountain species in this area such as Steller's jays, hairy woodpeckers and western wood peewees. Broadtailed hummingbirds are often seen feeding at the scarlet penstemon blossoms which border the trail. Unfortunately, the canyon is also the home of some of New Mexico's most belligerent insects, including clouds of voracious gnats in June and equally hungry deer flies later on. THAT'S why they call it Sierra Mosca (Fly Mountain)!

After staying close to the Rio Medio for about a mile, the trail leaves the bottom of the canyon turning abruptly leftwards to climb up on the north bank for the next 2.5 miles or so, making several swings away from the river to cross a series of arroyos and occasional streams which come down from the north. If a snack now seems in order, reward yourself with the tiny raspberries which grow in profusion nearby as the trail returns to the Medio. At this point a large boulder protrudes over the rushing stream, which older hikers will instantly recognize as the perch of the White Rock nymph, one of the classic advertising symbols of an earlier era. Chances of seeing the maiden herself are less certain. (Note: 1998 reviewers missed this and the raspberries. We suspect the trail was rerouted to join the Medio further upstream).

After making an easy crossing on a huge (2 feet in diameter) ponderosa, followed by a few minutes through treefall, the trail passes through a log fence into a horse corral and comes to a marked fork. Here, Trail 158 goes off to the right toward Horse Thief Meadow. Stay on the left fork, Trail 155, the Rio Medio Trail. It takes you out of the corral, through a most picturesque section of the canyon, and in a few short minutes you cross a small stream and proceed directly to the beautiful meadow where Brazos Cabin once stood. Of the cabin, only some foundation stones remain. In this part of the valley, which opens rather suddenly, there are many pleasant locations to enjoy your lunch and the beauty of the Sangre de Cristos before retracing your footsteps to the trailhead.

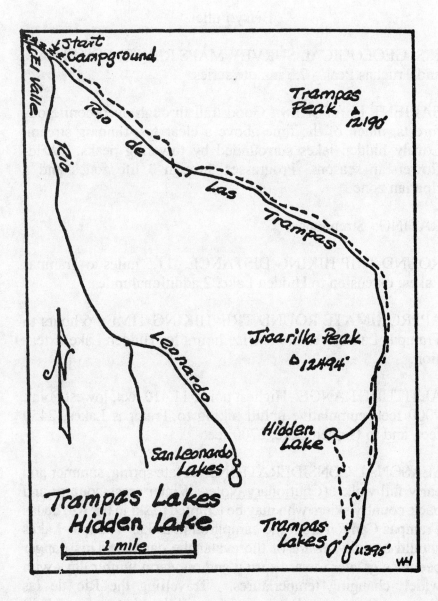

Start
Campground

El Valle

Rio de Las Trampas

Rio

Trampas Peak ▲ 12,190'

Jicarilla Peak △ 12,494'

Leonardo

San Leonardo Lakes

Hidden Lake

Trampas Lakes 11,395'

N

Trampas Lakes
Hidden Lake

1 mile

WH

TRAMPAS LAKES - HIDDEN LAKE

by
Betsy Fuller

U.S. GEOLOGICAL SURVEY MAPS REQUIRED: El Valle and Truchas Peak - 7.5 minute series.

SALIENT FEATURES: Good trail through deep coniferous forests, much of the time above a clear fast-running stream. Lovely hidden lakes surrounded by towering peaks. Wildflowers in season. Progresses through 3 life zones and a riparian zone.

RATING: Strenuous.

ROUND TRIP HIKING DISTANCE: 11.5 miles to Trampas Lakes; extension to Hidden Lake, 2 additional miles.

APPROXIMATE ROUND TRIP HIKING TIME: 6 hours to Trampas Lakes. Additional 1½ hours for Hidden Lake extension.

ALTITUDE RANGE: Highest point, 11,410 feet; lowest point, 9000 feet; cumulative uphill hiking to Trampas Lakes, 2450 feet, and to Hidden Lake, 2700 feet.

SEASONAL CONSIDERATIONS: A late spring, summer and early fall walk. (<u>Cautionary Note</u>: Winter cross-country and back-country skiers who may be tempted to ski in the Rio de las Trampas Canyon from the campground to Las Trampas Lakes should be fully aware of the avalanche danger. This danger becomes greater toward spring and on warm winter days with widely-changing temperatures. Travelling the Rio de las Trampas Canyon trail during such conditions is to be avoided.)

ROUND TRIP DRIVING: About 108 miles; 3 hours.

DRIVING DIRECTIONS: Take US 84/285 northbound to Pojoaque (about 16 miles from Santa Fe). Continue across the bridge in the Española lane and turn right onto NM 503 at the Nambé turnoff (traffic signal). About 7.5 miles from the turn-off onto NM 503, take a left turn (north) onto County Road 98 to Chimayo. Go through the village of Chimayo until you come to the junction with NM 76. Turn right (east) on NM 76 toward Truchas (Spanish: trout). About 7.7 miles from this junction and just as you get into the settled part of the village of Truchas, 76 takes a sharp turn to the left (north). The turn here is between two buildings and hardly looks like a main thorough-fare but there is a sign here showing that the road goes to Peñasco and Taos.

Take a new odometer reading and continue on 76 through the villages of Ojo Sarco (Spanish: clear spring) and Las Trampas (Spanish: traps). Soon after you pass through the village of Las Trampas, be sure to notice the old log flume on the right, still carrying water from the higher elevations over the ravine to the irrigation ditches of the village below. About 8.7 miles past Truchas and about a mile beyond Trampas, you come to Forest Service Road 207 (sometimes unmarked) going off to the right (east). Take this road and drive past the settlement of El Valle. From El Valle to the very end of FS 207 is about 8.1 miles. The road ends at a primitive campground. Park here.

HIKING INSTRUCTIONS: Now you can get a close look at the Rio de las Trampas whose course you have been following in the car. It comes rushing out of a deep little canyon, probably the reason the road comes to an end here.

Look for a sign reading Trampas Lake Trail 31 near an outhouse sited on a bank to the left of the road and your parked car. Start walking up the trail, a steady upward path. You are at about

119

8960 feet here and you have about 2400 feet to climb to the lakes, and over 5 miles. You will soon pass through a gate (be sure to close it behind you). Close to an hour in, the trail will cross to the south side of the stream and then again to the north side. This is where a snow avalanche came down the side of the mountain a few years ago taking all the trees with it (see Cautionary Note under SEASONAL CONSIDERATIONS, above). The area is now regenerating into an aspen forest usually filled with a profusion of wildflowers. Shortly after this open spot, rimmed on the north with striking cliffs, you will encounter a large blowdown which extends the better part of a mile or more. Fortunately the forest service has sawed off a sufficient number of the trees blocking the trail so that there is an easy passage through the devastation.

Until you get very near the lakes, you will be walking along the left side of the river, most of the time quite far above it, but within earshot of it and with occasional glimpses of it rushing below you. There are many long switchbacks that help ease your way up, and, finally, a river crossing which, except during the spring snow melt, should be no problem. Fallen tree trunks and stepping stones can be useful in crossing.

At the right time of year, usually early to mid-July, you find unbelievably beautiful gardens of marsh marigolds, brook cress, false hellebore, wild candytuft, thimbleberry, cranesbill, osha, cow parsnip, Parry's primrose and many, many other flowers. Look back down the valley once in a while and you may catch a glimpse of the flat land around Española far below you in the Rio Grande valley.

Finally you will top out at a level, usually marshy, area. A sign indicates Trampas Lakes to the left and Hidden Lake ahead. Veer left and you will see a faint path along the shallow streamlet. Although you cannot see the lakes from here, there should be a sign identifying Lower and Upper Trampas Lakes.

A walk of a few hundred yards further ahead will bring you to Upper Trampas to the right and Lower Trampas to the left. They are separated from each other by a low ridge and both provide majestic sites for lunch and photographs. Interestingly though both sit in bowls under the cliffs, Lower Trampas Lake is much deeper and darker green than Upper Trampas Lake.

From these lakes you can either return directly to your car down the trail over which you have just come or you can take the trail to Hidden Lake at the junction you passed.

EXTENSION: This extension will consume about 1½ hours including time for a snack at the lake and will add about 2 miles to the total distance. You will be walking along a good trail that is almost parallel with the trail you came on, but above it. Gradually the trail to Hidden Lake will bear off to the left, and, after a couple of mild switchbacks, you will descend to the lake itself. You will have dropped about 280 feet from the Trampas Lakes to Hidden Lake and you will now have to climb back up in order to start the return trek home.

The return trip to your car is over the same trail on which you walked to get to the lakes. Tighten your boot laces because it's downhill all the way!

We see that everything in Nature called destruction
must be creation—a change from beauty to beauty.
–John Muir

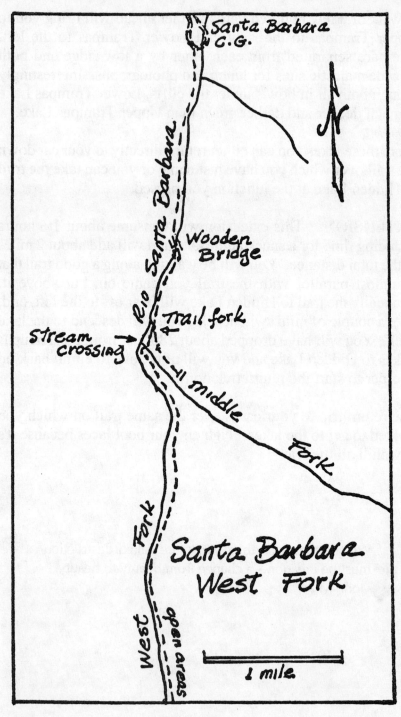

Santa Barbara
C.G.

N

Rio Santa Barbara

Wooden
Bridge

Trail fork

stream
crossing

Middle

Fork

Fork

Santa Barbara
West Fork

West
Fork

open areas

1 mile

SANTA BARBARA WEST FORK

by
Linda and John Buchser

U.S. GEOLOGICAL SURVEY MAP REQUIRED: Jicarita Peak - 7.5 minute series.

SALIENT FEATURES: This trip takes you to the north end of the Pecos Wilderness. Following the West Fork of Santa Barbara Creek, you will hike through lush meadows and aspen forest to alpine tundra, depending on the distance you travel.

RATING: Strenuous.

ROUND TRIP HIKING DISTANCE: 12 miles.

APPROXIMATE ROUND TRIP HIKING TIME: 7 hours.

ALTITUDE RANGE: Highest point, 9880 feet; lowest point, 8868 feet; cumulative uphill hiking, 1100 feet.

SEASONAL CONSIDERATIONS: Road closed several miles before Santa Barbara campground during snow season.

ROUND TRIP DRIVING: 143 miles; 2½-3 hours.

DRIVING DIRECTIONS: From Santa Fe take US 84/285 north to Española. In Española, stay on the main road as US 84/285 goes off to the left. Continuing straight ahead, you will be on NM 68 headed toward Taos. Go through Velarde and along the Rio Grande just past Embudo, where you turn right (east) onto NM 75. Continue through Dixon and Peñasco. When you come toward the end of Peñasco, NM 75 turns sharply left (toward Vadito). Don't take this left turn. Keep on going straight ahead toward Rodarte. After about 1.5 miles, just past

123

a sign to the Sipapu Ski Area, the road you are on will turn right. Just before you come to this turn, look for a road that goes off to the left. This is your road, Forest Service Road 116. There is a brown Forest Service sign directing you to Santa Barbara campground. Follow this road (first part paved, the rest dirt) for six miles to Santa Barbara campground. Park in the area before the cattle guard entrance to the campground. No fee if you park here. $5 per night if you park inside.

HIKING INSTRUCTIONS: Hike around (not through) the campground on the trail which starts to the right of the parking area entrance. After 10-15 minutes you'll be past the campground. At about one mile, the trail is rerouted to avoid a washed-out area and ascends through an aspen stand. Looking down from this higher portion, one can see a beaver lodge and a dam on a side area of the creek. Later, the trail runs along the main flow of Rio Santa Barbara.

In a normally wet year there is a continuous show of wildflowers from April through September, and a great variety, since the changes in habitat and elevation provide a wide range of growing conditions. At about 1.6 miles, there is a wooden bridge crossing the Rio Santa Barbara. This first section of trail, and the return, is an easy day hike for those with small children or small energies. Now the trail increases its rate of ascent. At about 2.3 miles you will come to a trail fork marked by a sign. The left fork, which you do not take, is Middle Fork Trail 24. Go straight ahead on West Fork Trail 25. In another 0.2 miles there is a stream crossing which often has a number of peeled logs jammed across as a makeshift bridge.

If it is the rainy season, you may find these logs dry enough to cross on the way in, but under water on the way out. In this case, the creek may be forded just upstream of the logs, but use caution in the swift water and expect to get wet up to your hips.

During the spring runoff, the stream may be too deep to ford at all.

The stream you have just crossed is actually a combination of the East and Middle Forks and you are now between them and the West Fork, which is out of sight at this point. The trail moves higher on the mountainside, and though the West Fork is now often visible, access to it is down inconveniently steep and loose slopes.

At about mile 4.7, you come out of the trees and pass through open areas. On the stream below are more beaver dams. These intermittent meadows continue to the end of the valley. Cattle grazing is permitted here only in the fall of every third year, so meadow wildflowers can be magnificent when there has been sufficient rain. Chimayosos Mountain comes into view spectacularly to the south.

Approximately 5 miles in, you will pass on the right a sign for the Dominguez Trail, which connects the West Fork drainage with the Trampas River drainage. This rerouting of an old sheepherding trail was the product of several year's worth of national Sierra Club trail maintenance service trips.

You reach the end of the meadows at about mile 6, with a sign indicating another 6 miles to the divide. The trail goes on up to the Santa Barbara Divide, but this is the turnaround point for this hike.

Return by the same route.

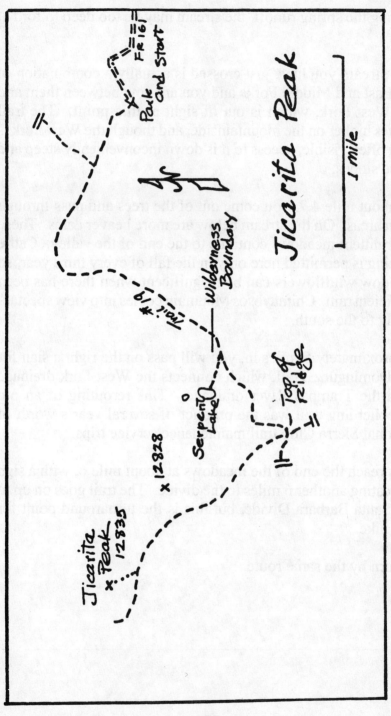

Jicarita Peak

Park and Start

FR 161

Wilderness Boundary

Trail #19

Top of Ridge

Serpent Lake

x 12828

Jicarita Peak
x 12835

1 mile

JICARITA PEAK

by
Norma McCallan

U.S. GEOLOGICAL SURVEY MAP REQUIRED: Jicarita Peak - 7.5 minute series shows this area, but it neither shows Forest Road 161 nor is an accurate portrayal of the current trail. Use the USFS Pecos Wilderness map.

SALIENT FEATURES: This hike to the tenth highest peak in New Mexico affords marvelous vistas of the surrounding countryside, incredible displays of alpine wildflowers and a sense of being on the very top of the world. The peak itself is easily climbed and can be done as a day hike. Because the peak and its approach are well above timberline, caution is urged in the event of approaching storms. Frequent thunderstorms play around the Santa Barbara Divide in the summer and that exposed terrain is not the place to be when lightning is striking.

RATING: Strenuous.

ROUND TRIP HIKING DISTANCE: Approximately 11 miles.

APPROXIMATE ROUND TRIP HIKING TIME: About 8 hours, stops included.

ALTITUDE RANGE: Highest point, 12,835 feet; lowest point, 10,400; cumulative uphill hiking, 2435 feet.

SEASONAL CONSIDERATIONS: June to October would be best; earlier or later one may run into snow. Even June or October could be risky. The dirt road to the trailhead is not plowed in the winter.

ROUND TRIP DRIVING: 151 miles; 4 hours.

127

DRIVING DIRECTIONS: Take US 84/285 northbound to Pojoaque (about 16 miles from Santa Fe). Continue across the bridge in the Española lane and turn right onto NM 503 at the Nambé turnoff (traffic signal). About 7.5 miles from the turnoff onto NM 503, take a left turn (north) onto NM 520 to Chimayo (you'll see a blue sign indicating Restaurante de Chimayo). Go through the settlement of Chimayo until you come to the junction with NM 76. Turn right (east) onto NM 76 toward Truchas. About 7.7 miles from the turn and just as you get into the settled part of the village of Truchas, NM 76 takes a sharp turn to the left (north). The turn here is between two buildings and hardly looks like a main thoroughfare, but there is a prominent sign here showing that the road goes to Chamisal and Peñasco. Continue on NM 76 through the villages of Ojo Sarco, Las Trampas and Chamisal. Turn right onto NM 75 just before the village of Peñasco and continue through Peñasco. At the end of Peñasco, turn left, still on 75, through Vadito. Ten minutes from Peñasco you come to a "T" intersection. Turn right onto NM 518. This road goes past a number of Forest Service campgrounds and through the small village of Tres Ritos. At 1.7 miles past the sign to the private Angostura Camp and at 0.9 miles past the sign for Mora County, turn right onto Forest Service Road 161. It is marked with a large brown sign on the highway. Stay on this rough but passable road until it dead ends at a road block (dirt piled up) after 4.6 miles and park.

HIKING INSTRUCTIONS: At the road block there is a small sign "HEAD TRAIL" pointing toward the extension of the road you have been driving on. Proceed on the road for about 5 minutes until the road ends. There is a sign indicating that the trail to the right is Angostura Trail 493. The trail to the left goes to Serpent Lake and Santa Barbara Campground. Follow the left hand trail. In about 10 minutes you will see a trail coming in from the right. Ignore it, and remember to ignore it on the way back. Very shortly you will cross a fast-flowing ditch;

there should be enough stones and logs to make a relatively easy crossing.

The trail continues through the forest, going upward at a comfortable incline. About 1.5 miles in you will pass a series of meadows, which make a good spot for a rest stop since this part of the trail is mostly heavy forest. Slightly more than 2.5 miles in, you will come to a boundary sign for the Pecos Wilderness. Soon thereafter, as you turn a corner, you will see the stark outline of the Santa Barbara Divide through the trees. Less than a half mile further you will come to the intersection of the Serpent Lake Trail, heading off to the right, while the main trail has a sign showing that it is 11 miles further to Santa Barbara Campground and 10 miles back to Agua Piedra Campground. Serpent Lake is only about a quarter mile down the side trail.

Continue up the main trail. It soon leaves the forest and starts to switchback up through the scree and isolated clumps of stunted spruce and bristlecone pine. As you go higher, these pygmy forests give way to dense patches of willow, and magnificent bouquets of alpine flowers dot the scree. By September, most flowers have died off, but the willows are turning gold and so are the aspen in the surrounding forests. Just before you get to the top of the Divide you will pass a small spring, which takes the form of a shallow pond, on the right.

Once on top you will find an old sign pointing back down the trail with the barely legible legend that Serpent Lake is 2 miles and Agua Piedra Campground is also that way. About 50 feet further stands a post where a sign used to be, showing the Santa Barbara Campground to be 9 miles away. Do not continue any further on this Angostura Trail, which meanders over the ridge and switchbacks down to the Middle Fork of the Santa Barbara River, even though it will have the more prominent cairns and better worn path. Instead, while standing by this post, look to your right, and you should see one large cairn, and perhaps patches of trail heading northwest. Walk there. Once at this first cairn, look in the same direction you have just walked and you should see a second cairn and then a third. Follow these cairns as the trail contours along the ridge near the top of the Divide and detours around the south side of a large unnamed 12,828 foot peak. In some stretches, alternate trails and cairns exist -- don't worry, they all seem to end up in the same place.

Not until you are well around this peak will Jicarita Peak itself be visible -- its flat top and trapezoidal shape suddenly dominate the horizon in front of you. Stay on this small trail until you reach the closest corner of Jicarita. The trail itself contours around the south and west sides of Jicarita and meets the trail coming up from Indian Creek at the northwest corner of Jicarita. Get off the trail and walk up the southeast corner of Jicarita. If you watch closely you will find patches of trail going up through the scree and grass of the slope. Soon you will be on the flat, wide top, with vistas in all directions and several rock shelters if you want to eat your lunch out of the ever-present wind. The southern horizon is particularly awesome, with the jagged Truchas Peaks and the gentler slopes of Trampas and Chimayosos Peaks dominating the skyline. Always observe caution when up on the Divide and watch for storm clouds; summer thunderstorms can roll in fast and you do not want to be above timberline when the lightning starts striking.

Return the way you came. As you near the post without its sign on the ridge, you may find it harder to follow the cairns and the patches of trail. Veer slightly down (southeast) instead of staying at contour, or you will end up in a large pile of scree.

Note: If you want to make this into a backpack trip, Serpent Lake is an ideal campsite halfway up the trail. It is situated in a lovely grassy meadow. You can set your tent up in the dwarfed trees just north of the lake, then proceed on up to

Jicarita Peak. Weather permitting, you can return to the divide the next day and walk in the other direction, to the southwest, following sketchy trails along the top of the Santa Barbara Divide and drinking in the magnificent 360-degree views. I do not know why the lake got its name, other than that several little grassy hummocks in the lake look rather like a small serpent swimming along, when viewed from the trail above.

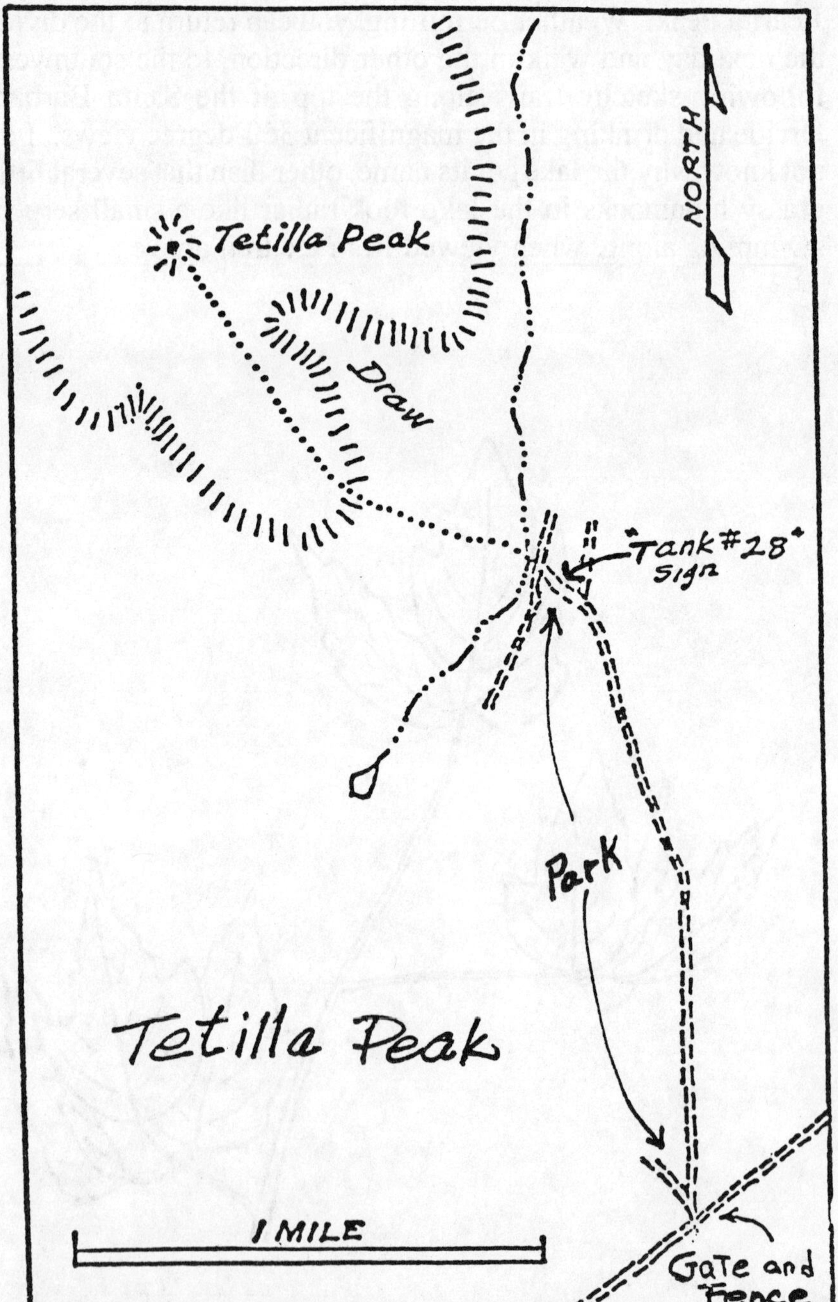

NORTH

Tetilla Peak

Draw

"Tank #28"
Sign

Park

Tetilla Peak

1 MILE

Gate and
Fence

KH

TETILLA PEAK

by
Ingrid Vollnhofer

U.S. GEOLOGICAL SURVEY MAP REQUIRED: Tetilla Peak - 7.5 minute series.

SALIENT FEATURES: Tetilla Peak is a prominent volcano on the Caja del Rio Plateau, a volcanic field formed some 2.6 million years ago. An open area with a lot of cholla cactus and juniper. Wonderful panorama from Tetilla Peak of Mount Taylor and the Jemez, Taos, Sangre de Cristo, Ortiz and Sandia Mountains. There is a lot of cactus on the way, so hiking boots are recommended. The last six miles of driving are on a rough, rutted road, which will be muddy and probably impassable during or after wet weather. A vehicle with high clearance will make this drive less scary. Bring plenty of water.

RATING: Easy but steep.

ROUND TRIP HIKING DISTANCE: 2.5 miles. Add 2.8 miles if the last stretch of road is too rough for your car.

APPROXIMATE ROUND TRIP HIKING TIME: 2-3 hours, including breathing, vista, water and snack breaks.

ALTITUDE RANGE: Highest point, 7206 feet; lowest point, 6260 feet; cumulative uphill hiking, 946 feet.

SEASONAL CONSIDERATIONS: Pretty hot in summer.

ROUND TRIP DRIVING: 40 miles; approximately 2 hours.

DRIVING DIRECTIONS: From downtown Santa Fe go west on Alameda. Alameda follows the river, then climbs up onto a plateau and becomes County Road 70. About 4.6 miles from the plaza you will come to an intersection with a stop sign and a sign indicating that CR 70 is to the right. Turn right here. Shortly you will reach a T-junction with the bypass road (599). Take a left. In 4.9 miles you will come to an intersection with traffic lights. Turn right onto CR 56. Continue past the sewage treatment plant and past a large red scoria boulder on your right. About 1.3 miles past this boulder look for a road coming in from the right. In January 1999 this road was marked by two signs: "Soccer" and "Santa Fe Horse Park." Turn right here. This graded dirt road crosses a cattle guard, then climbs the hill to the left. At the top, when the road turns sharply to the right, drive straight ahead onto a rough, primitive road. Go straight on this road, ignoring roads that branch off to the sides. After 4.5 endless miles you will come to a fence line and a metal gate. If the gate is open drive through it and turn right.

Stop and check the road that follows the fence toward Tetilla Peak. How deep are the ruts, how high the tumbleweed piles? If the road looks bad, park your car here and start walking toward Tetilla Peak. If you can, drive another 1.4 miles on this road to a fork. Turn left at a battered "Tank 28" sign and park.

HIKING INSTRUCTIONS: There is no trail. This walk is a free-for-all. Head for Tetilla Peak in front of you. There is no other peak around. Avoid the draw which you see ahead of you. Keep to the left of it and stay high. While climbing, look back and note some distant high landmark in the direction of your car to guide you on the way down. It is easier to go off course than this open landscape would lead you to believe. At the very last stretch, the walk is quite steep, almost a scramble. Don't forget, the view at the top is magnificent.

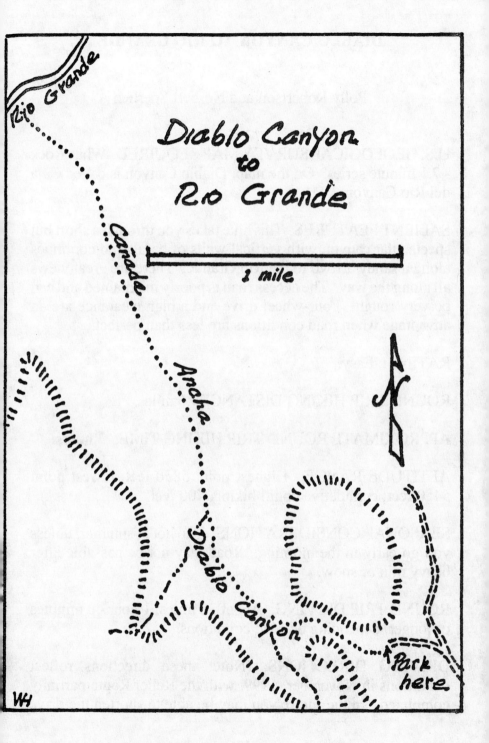

Diablo Canyon
to
Rio Grande

Rio Grande

Cañada

Ancha

Diablo Canyon

1 mile

N

Park here

WH

DIABLO CANYON TO RIO GRANDE

by
Polly Robertson and Norbert Sperlich

U.S. GEOLOGICAL SURVEY MAP REQUIRED: White Rock - 7.5 minute series. On the map, Diablo Canyon is called Caja del Rio Canyon.

SALIENT FEATURES: This hike takes you through a short but spectacular canyon with vertical walls of basalt and continues along a sandy arroyo to the Rio Grande. There are great views all along the way. The access road is poorly maintained and can be very rough. Four-wheel drive and a high clearance are an advantage when road conditions are less than perfect.

RATING: Easy.

ROUND TRIP HIKING DISTANCE: 6 miles.

APPROXIMATE ROUND TRIP HIKING TIME: 3 hours.

ALTITUDE RANGE: Highest point 5850 feet; lowest point 5450 feet; cumulative uphill hiking, 400 feet.

SEASONAL CONSIDERATIONS: Too hot in summer, unless you go early in the morning. Road may not be passable after heavy rain or snow.

ROUND TRIP DRIVING: About 38 miles; 1 hour 40 minutes or longer, depending on road conditions.

DRIVING DIRECTIONS: (Note: these directions reflect conditions in November, 1999, with the Relief Route partially completed. In the future you may be able to shorten the drive somewhat by going north on Calle Nopal, across the Relief Route, and onto Camino la Tierra. As of November, 1999, access from Calle Nopal to the Relief Route was closed.)

Take Washington Avenue north from the plaza. Turn left in front of the pink-stuccoed Scottish Rite Temple onto Paseo de Peralta. At the intersection with Guadalupe Street, turn right onto Guadalupe, which joins US 84/285. On 84/285 go into the right lane. Very soon, you will come to the exit for the Santa Fe Relief Route (599) on your right. Take that exit. Some 4.2 miles after leaving 84/285, turn right at the traffic light onto Camino la Tierra.

At the next 4-way stop intersection continue straight ahead. Further on, when the road forks, with the right branch going toward Las Campanas, stay on the left branch (La Tierra). Occasionally, the road splits and there will be trees and bushes separating the two lanes. Stay in the right lane and go straight ahead at intersections. Four miles past the intersection with the Relief Route the pavement ends. Slow down! You will encounter washboard surface, cattle guards, and ruts or deep sand where the road is crossed by drainages.

After four miles on the dirt road you will pass a windmill (Dead Dog Well) and a corral on your left. Take a mileage reading here. At this point a wide arroyo (Cañada Ancha) comes in from the left. This arroyo follows the edge of the Caja del Rio volcanic field. The latter is now visible on your left, forming a basalt-capped escarpment. The road stays to the right of the escarpment, going downhill over sandy terrain. Soon, the vertical cliffs of Diablo Canyon will appear ahead of you to the left. The canyon separates a small mesa that is edged by basalt cliffs from the lava mesa to the west. At 4.3 miles from the windmill look for a secondary road that branches off to the left and toward Diablo Canyon. Take this road to an open area close to the mouth of the canyon. Park your car here.

HIKING INSTRUCTIONS: Head toward the arroyo that goes into the canyon. You will have to cross a fence. At the entrance of the canyon, vertical cliffs rise up some 300 feet. As you go deeper into the canyon, you will notice that the basalt columns rest on sand and gravel -- a very unstable foundation, indeed. About ten minutes into the hike, you will come to a place where water is seeping out of the ground. To the right of this spot, where basalt columns form an overhang, cliff swallows like to build their nests. In the summertime, you can see swallows feeding their young. The unique descending scale call of the canyon wren can often be heard here. Soon, the canyon widens and, on your right and toward the top of the mesa, basalt cliffs give way to layers of ashes and cinders that have been eroded into jagged shapes.

As you walk out of the canyon, the arroyo widens and heads north for a while, toward Buckman Mesa. The arroyo soon swerves left (northwest) and descends slowly toward the Rio Grande. If you look skyward once in a while, you may see hawks or ravens circling above. Ahead of you, on the other side of the (still hidden) Rio Grande, you will see dark basalt cliffs topped by orange tuff. The basalt comes from the Caja del Rio volcanoes; the tuff was produced by eruptions of the Jemez caldera. After hiking a little over an hour, you will come to the river. From this point look upstream toward Buckman Mesa and its small peak. Does it look like a hound dog or a crocodile in profile? Had you been here around the turn of the century, you would have encountered a bridge crossing the river, a railroad line and a settlement built by lumberman Henry Buckman. It's all gone now. The Buckman area is important for Santa Fe, however, because here are wells that produce part of the water supply.

Return to your car the way you came. When driving back to Santa Fe, get in the right lane of the Relief Route as you approach Highway 84/285, and take the exit ramp on your right.

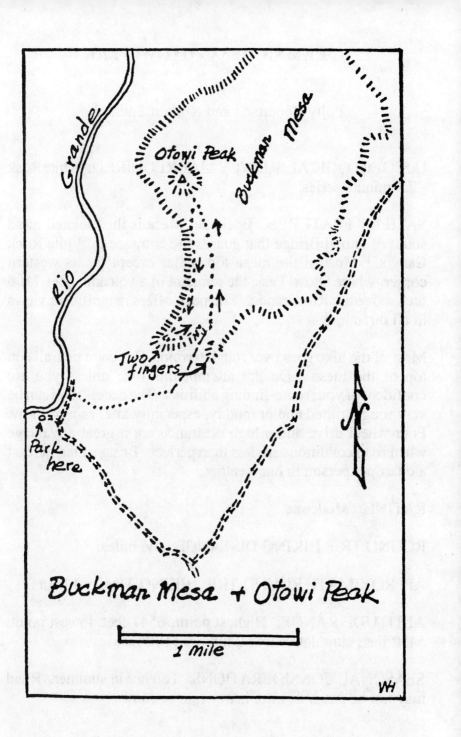

Grande

Rio

Otowi Peak

Buckman Mesa

Two
fingers

Park
here

N

Buckman Mesa + Otowi Peak

1 mile

WH

BUCKMAN MESA - OTOWI PEAK

by
Polly Robertson and Norbert Sperlich

U.S. GEOLOGICAL SURVEY MAP REQUIRED: White Rock - 7.5 minute series.

SALIENT FEATURES: Buckman Mesa is the isolated mesa south of Otowi Bridge that guards the entrance to White Rock Canyon. Most of the mesa top is flat except for its western corner, where Otowi Peak, the remnant of a volcano, rises 1100 feet above the Rio Grande. The peak offers magnificent views in all directions.

Most of the hike goes over rough terrain. There are no trails on top of the mesa. Do not attempt this hike unless you are confident of your route-finding abilities. The access road can be very rough, rutted and/or muddy, especially after rain or snow. Four-wheel drive and a high clearance are a great advantage when road conditions are less than perfect. Bring water, at least a quart per person in hot weather.

RATING: Moderate.

ROUND TRIP HIKING DISTANCE: 5½ miles.

APPROXIMATE ROUND TRIP HIKING TIME: 4 hours.

ALTITUDE RANGE: Highest point, 6547 feet; lowest point, 5450 feet; cumulative uphill hiking, 1100 feet.

SEASONAL CONSIDERATIONS: Too hot in summer. Road may not be passable after heavy rain or snow.

ROUND TRIP DRIVING: 44 miles; about 2 hours.

DRIVING DIRECTIONS: Follow the driving directions for the Diablo Canyon Hike (page 136) up to the point 4.3 miles past the windmill, where a secondary road branches off to the left and toward Diablo Canyon. Since your destination is the Rio Grande, stay on the main road and go past the turnoff. You have about three more miles to go.

Further down the road, ignore roads that go off to the right or left. Drive slowly and look for ruts. The last few road miles can be bad! A grove of tamarisks ahead will tell you that the river is near. Shortly after the Rio Grande comes in sight, the road turns left and up to an open spot. Park your car here.

HIKING INSTRUCTIONS: Before starting the hike, you may want to spend a few minutes at the bank of the river. Its muddy waters are always a welcome sight in this dry country. Upstream, to your right, Buckman Mesa rises steeply. No trail going up is to be seen from here. This hike will take you to the southern end of the mesa. There, Buckman Mesa ends in two long "fingers," and a rough trail climbs up to the mesa top between the two fingers.

First, go back on the road that you just drove on. While still in the tamarisk grove, look for a secondary road that goes off to the left (north). Follow this road for about 5 minutes to a fence (with a gate) and some 30 yards beyond the fence to a wide arroyo. Follow the arroyo upstream. Soon it narrows into a canyon with vertical walls of compacted sand. After hiking in the arroyo for about 8 minutes, you may have to cross a fence (sometimes the fence is rolled back.). A few minutes later you will come to a place where the arroyo turns to the right. On your left is a vertical wall of sand. Some 30 yards further, you will see a much eroded trail going up on the left. It is usually marked by cairns. If you miss the trail, you will see a small

141

drainage coming in from the left at ground level, creating a break in the canyon wall and affording you a glimpse of the southern tip of Buckman Mesa. You have gone too far! Go back about 30 yards and look for the trail.

The first part of the trail is rough and getting worse every year, due to erosion. Look for "ducks" (small rocks placed on top of larger rocks) and footprints if you lose sight of the trail. The general direction is up, keeping the drainage on your right. After about half an hour of climbing, you are close to the top of the mesa. Just before you reach the mesa top, the trail moves into the drainage and then to the right side of it. Look around when you reach the top. You will have to find this place on your way back.

Otowi Peak is not yet in sight and the trail fizzles out. Keep going straight ahead. In a minute or so you will see the peak. Go for it! Occasionally you will have to make a detour to the right to avoid a steep gully.

Vegetation on the mesa consists of piñon and juniper bushes, sage, grasses and flowers. September, when the snakeweed is blooming yellow, is my favorite time for this hike. November is great for watching the sandhill cranes fly south.

After hiking for about 20 minutes on the flat mesa top, you come to the cinder-strewn slope of Otowi Peak. Going up, take the path of least resistance and avoid the steep, rocky parts if possible. If, some 30 to 40 yards below the top, you come upon a faint, fairly level trail, you might want to follow it to the left (west). It leads to the blowhole, an opening dating back to the time when the volcano was spewing steam or hot gases. This entrance to the underworld is hidden from view behind rocks until you are very close to it. It is very dangerous and drops down steeply after a few yards, so keep out of the hole. Most likely, you will reach the top without having seen the blowhole.

Time to enjoy the views. To the west and southwest, the Rio Grande flows through White Rock Canyon, and the Jemez Mountains appear in the distance. Black Mesa can be seen to the northeast and the Sangre de Cristos stretch across the horizon toward the east and northeast. Closer by, to the south, you will see the Caja del Rio volcanic field with its dark hills. Special note: Otowi Peak is just south of the San Ildefonso Indian Reservation boundary line, beyond which a permit is needed. Respect the land and do not wander any further north than the peak itself.

Before leaving the peak, take time to study your topo map and look at the terrain to the south. (Interesting note: the rocks on the peak are magnetic and compass readings will be inaccurate.) The trail that will take you down from the mesa top starts where the two "fingers" of the mesa meet. To get to this point, you will take a different route on the way back. Instead of heading straight for the trail, you will follow the western edge of the mesa all the way to the tip of the west "finger" and then you will continue along the east side of the finger to your trail. This route offers dramatic views into White Rock Canyon.

Leave the peak in a southerly direction and, after bypassing the first gully at the foot of the peak, head for the edge of the mesa on your right. Stay close to the edge, swerving left only to avoid steep drainages. Take time to look back once in a while. Awesome views of Otowi Peak and the canyon below!

Just before you reach the tip of the finger, you will come to a place where the mesa's edge on your right forms an overhang. Watch it! Some 40 minutes after leaving the peak, you should come to the tip of the finger. Turn left now, still following the edge of the mesa. You are heading toward the place where the two fingers join. Stay on top of the mesa, close to the edge. Soon the terrain descends a bit and you will come to a drainage. Cross the drainage and remain on top of the mesa. Two or three minutes later, you will come to a second drainage. This drainage is your landmark. Look for a trail or cairns on the other side of the drainage and start heading down. (If you did not notice the second drainage and kept hiking along the edge of the mesa, you will soon end up at the tip of the second finger. Admire the great views, then go back along the edge and look for the drainage and/or cairns.) Go down the way you came up and back to your car.

When driving back to Santa Fe, get in the right lane of the Relief Route as you approach Highway 84/285 and take the exit ramp on your right.

Glory be to God for dappled things...
All things counter, original, spare, strange;
   Whatever is fickle, freckled (who knows how?)
    With swift, slow; sweet, sour; adazzle, dim;
He fathers-forth whose beauty is past change;
      Praise him.
–Gerard Manley Hopkins

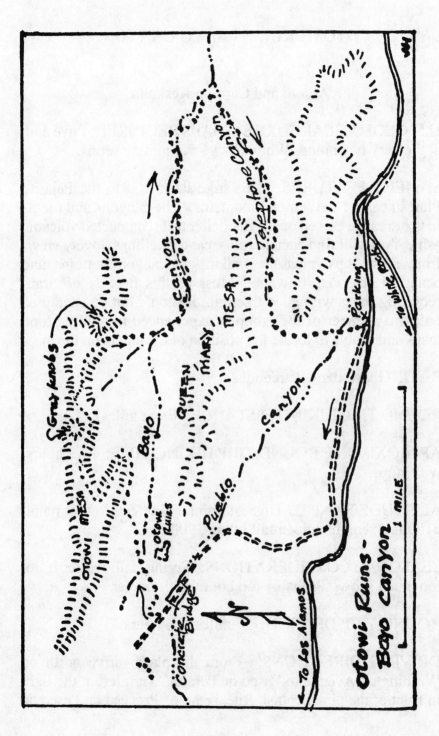

Otowi Ruins –
Bayo Canyon

1 MILE

OTOWI RUINS - BAYO CANYON

by
Arnold and Carolyn Keskulla

U.S. GEOLOGICAL SURVEY MAPS REQUIRED: Puye and, at the very beginning, White Rock - 7.5 minute series.

SALIENT FEATURES: This hike takes you to the Pajarito Plateau east of the Jemez Mountains. The canyons and mesas in this area are carved out of Bandelier tuff (compacted volcanic ash). You willl find ancient ruins, cave dwellings, lovely views from mesa tops, pleasant walking in canyon bottoms and beautiful seasonal flowers. Most of this hike is off trail, requiring shoes with good traction. It should not be attempted unless a member of the group is experienced in reading topo maps and is able to locate the position of the hikers on the map.

RATING: Moderate/strenuous.

ROUND TRIP HIKING DISTANCE: Eight miles.

APPROXIMATE ROUND TRIP HIKING TIME: Five hours, with stops.

ALTITUDE RANGE: Highest point, 6800 feet; lowest point, 6100 feet; cumulative uphill hiking, 900 feet.

SEASONAL CONSIDERATIONS: Spring, fall, winter if not too much snow. Probably too hot in midsummer.

ROUND TRIP DRIVING: 57 miles; 1½ hours.

DRIVING DIRECTIONS: From the plaza, drive north on Washington Avenue to Paseo de Peralta. Turn left at the light in front of the pink Scottish Rite Temple. Proceed on Paseo de

Peralta to the third stoplight. Turn right onto Guadalupe, which merges into US 84/285. Drive north on 84/285 about 15 miles to Pojoaque. Take the Los Alamos exit ramp to the right and swing left under the overpass. After the traffic light proceed west on NM 502, which crosses the Rio Grande and climbs to a well-marked "Y" intersection about 28 miles from Santa Fe. Take the left fork toward Los Alamos for 0.3 miles. Turn right into a paved road leading off toward two gates and a maintenance yard. Park before the left gate, leaving enough room for large trucks to get by. The hikers' entrance is to the right of this gate.

HIKING INSTRUCTIONS: Go through the hikers' gate and follow the gravel road northwesterly through ponderosa pines with a view of Chicoma Peak ahead. The road heads uphill for a while, then drops down into Pueblo Canyon. Notice a funny smell? The little stream on your right originates at the Los Alamos sewage treatment plant. About 1.75 miles (40 minutes) into the hike, the road crosses the stream. Look to your right. About 40 yards past the little concrete bridge, you will see an old jeep trail going off to the right into the trees. This turnoff may be marked by a small cairn. Turn right here. Immediately after the turnoff, the trail passes between two small boulders and snakes up a low ridge that separates Pueblo Canyon from Bayo Canyon. In about 5 minutes you will come to the top of the ridge and a "T" junction with another trail. Turn right (east). The trail stays on the ridge top and leads in another 5 minutes to the fenced-in ruin of Otowi Pueblo (inhabited from the 1300s to the 1500s).

The ruin has been excavated and backfilled. What you can see now are mounds of rubble covered with weeds. However, go to the highest part of the site to appreciate the beautiful setting. To the east, the pueblo dwellers could see the Truchas Peaks; to the west, Pajarito and Caballo Mountain. To the north, the cliff face of Otowi Mesa towers over Bayo Canyon. Note the numerous cave cliff dwellings at the base of the cliffs; they are your next destination.

Leave the ruins by the gate you entered, follow the fence on your right (north) to the edge of the ridge. There, turn left (west) and follow the edge for 15 yards. You will see two boulders on your right. A steep trail goes down between these boulders, taking you into Bayo Canyon. Go downstream (east) on the sandy bottom. After about 300 feet, and before a sharp bend in the arroyo, go up the bank on the left and angle northeast. There is no obvious trail here. Go north up the hillside toward the cliffs. If a mere dozen caves will do, cut to the right halfway up the hill and bear for a point near the corner of the cliffs. There is a faint trail that you might find, marked here and there with small cairns.

At the base of the cliffs are many soot-blackened caves with viga holes, Moki stairways, and accumulations of dung from burros and sheep. In front of this cliff there are also some lovely flowers in the late summer, such as Rocky Mountain bee plant and an unusual white gilia with blue anthers *(ipomopsis polyanthis)*. When you come to the pointed end of the mesa, go around it and follow the cliff face on the other side (in a northwesterly direction). After hiking about 100 yards (5 minutes), you will come to a place that is usually marked by small cairns. Here you can get on top of the cliffs that form the vertical edge of the mesa. (Mark this place if you want to return this way instead of completing the hike as described.) Follow the edge of the mesa.

You will see to the northwest that this mesa joins another which stretches out to the east and which has two large gray domes. Stay at the level you are on, heading northwest until you can follow the level around to the gray-domed mesa. Proceed eastward toward the first gray dome. Wind and water have sculpted it into rounded forms. After climbing and descending the first dome, continue eastward. The mesa becomes very narrow, then widens again. Stay on the right (south rim) side. A little more than halfway between the first and second dome, there is a break in the cliff face, probably marked with cairns. This is where you go down -- in a little while.

First, continue on to the second gray dome to enjoy the sweeping views: to the east and northeast, the Sangre de Cristos span the horizon. More to the north are the Taos and Latir mountains. The Jemez Mountains appear to the west. The nearby mesa south of you is the "Queen Mary" Mesa, presumably named after the ocean liner. Further to the south are the dark hills of the Caja del Rio volcanic fields, and in the distance the Sandia Mountains.

Time to go back. As you head west, with the mesa edge on your left, look for the break in the cliffs (about 100 yards after you leave the smooth gray rock). It is much easier to see approaching this way. Down you go. After a short rock scramble, you will be on the sloping shoulder of the mesa.

Angle steeply down (south) over the loose rocks to a small sandy-bottomed canyon that soon joins Bayo Canyon. From this junction continue down Bayo Canyon (east) for about 1.5 miles (approximately 45 minutes to an hour) to the first major arroyo coming in from the right. At the junction, look for cairns.

On your way to this junction you will see several lesser arroyos coming in from the right and good views to your right of the north side of the "Queen Mary" mesa. Your objective is a canyon that will lead you westward on the south side of this mesa. You will know you are at the right junction when you can look up the canyon and see the narrow bow of the "Queen Mary" bearing directly toward you.

149

Go up this winding side canyon for about half an hour, until you come to a trail that climbs out of the arroyo to the left. This trail follows a telephone line. Stay on this trail until it reaches the ridge top. To your left (south) you will see the Los Alamos road. Leave the trail and head toward that road, in the direction of a white water tower, visible above the road. In a few minutes you will reach the bottom of Pueblo Canyon and the little stream. If recent rains have swollen the stream to make a wet crossing likely, you may, with a little searching, find a log on which to cross. Now the maintenance yard should be clearly visible. Keep it to your left while you go up to the road where you started your hike and back to your car.

How glorious a greeting the sun gives the mountains! To behold this alone is worth the pains of any excursion a thousand times over. The highest peaks burned like islands in a sea of liquid shade. Then the lower peaks and spires caught the glow, and long lances of light, streaming through many a notch and pass, fell thick on the frozen meadows.
–John Muir

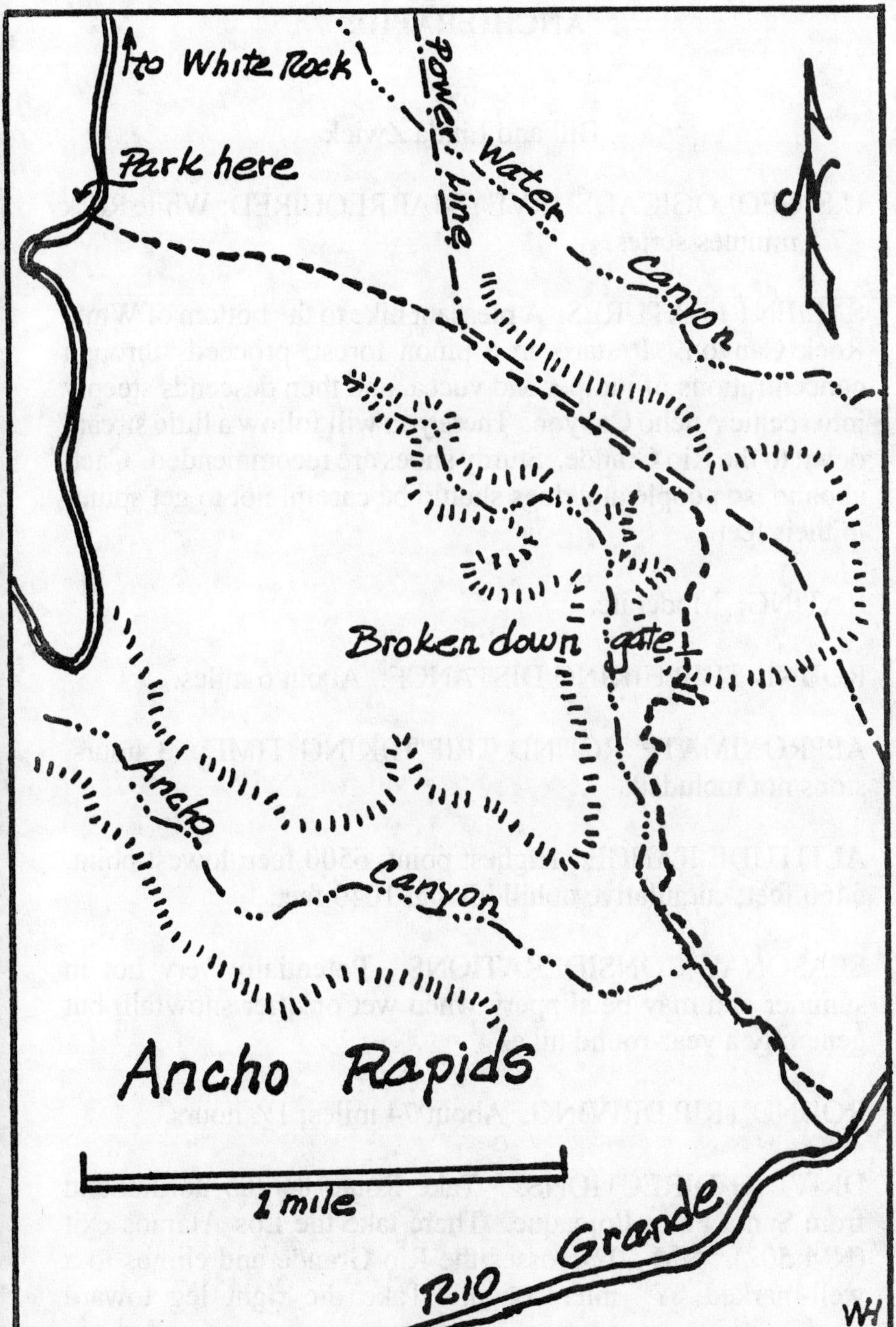

to White Rock

Park here

Power Line

Water Canyon

N

Broken down gate

Ancho

Canyon

Ancho Rapids

1 mile

Rio Grande

WH

ANCHO RAPIDS

by
Bill and Linda Zwick

U.S. GEOLOGICAL SURVEY MAP REQUIRED: White Rock - 7.5 minutes series.

SALIENT FEATURES: A pleasant hike to the bottom of White Rock Canyon. It starts in a piñon forest, proceeds through concentrations of juniper and yucca, and then descends steeply into scenic Ancho Canyon. There you will follow a little stream down to the Rio Grande. Sturdy shoes are recommended. Cacti abound, so people and dogs should be careful not to get spines in their feet.

RATING: Moderate.

ROUND TRIP HIKING DISTANCE: About 6 miles.

APPROXIMATE ROUND TRIP HIKING TIME: 3 hours, stops not included.

ALTITUDE RANGE: Highest point, 6500 feet; lowest point, 5460 feet; cumulative uphill hiking, 1040 feet.

SEASONAL CONSIDERATIONS: Potentially very hot in summer and may be slippery when wet or after snowfall, but generally a year-round hike.

ROUND TRIP DRIVING: About 74 miles; 1½ hours.

DRIVING DIRECTIONS: Take Route 84/285 northbound from Santa Fe to Pojoaque. There take the Los Alamos exit (NM 502). NM 502 crosses the Rio Grande and climbs to a well-marked "Y" intersection. Take the right leg toward

Bandelier and White Rock. About 1.5 miles from the "Y" is a stoplight where the truck route to Los Alamos and the road to the Pajarito Ski Area go right. You drive straight ahead through this light toward White Rock and Bandelier. Five miles from the "Y," you arrive at White Rock's second traffic signal (the intersection with Pajarito Road). Carefully check your odometer reading here and drive on straight through the traffic signal, still heading south. Continue on toward Bandelier National Monument for about 3.4 miles.

As you approach a yellow diamond-shaped sign indicating that the road will turn left (the fifth such sign after White Rock), look for a gate on the left side of the road. There is a graveled parking area and a metal "Notice" sign in front of this gate. The gate is identified as No. 4. You might find it necessary to pull off on the right shoulder of the road (the road is narrow here) to see the gate and the small graveled parking area. Traffic in this area moves rapidly around blind curves, so take appropriate care in pulling into the parking area. (If you have taken a hair-pin curve to the left over an arroyo and then up a moderate hill to find a gate, you've gone too far! If the walking entrance through the fence is a simple opening, you are at the wrong gate and you should go back 0.2 miles toward White Rock.) The large gate will probably be locked due to a recent DOE crackdown on motor vehicle traffic in the area. Pedestrian access is through an entrance to the right of the large gate. This entrance forms a sharp angle to prevent the passage of cattle.

HIKING INSTRUCTIONS: Proceed through the angled pedestrian access. The hike to the rim of the canyon follows a road built for the installation of powerlines in the area. This portion of the hike toward the Rio Grande provides spectacular vistas of the Sangre de Cristo mountains (especially nice in the fall when the aspen are golden) and the return provides nice views of the Jemez Mountains and Bandelier. You will cross under a powerline which heads north and south, and about a mile into the hike the road will converge with another powerline which heads east. Note the radio telescope dish to your right (south) -- this Los Alamos facility is part of an array of radio telescopes stretching from the South Pacific to the continental U.S. Continue walking on the road eastward. Looking down, you might notice large ant hills shimmering in the sunlight -- a result of the ants mining quartz grains to make their homes.

About 1.75 miles from the start of the hike, the road will descend and then begin to rise toward the canyon rim. Shortly after you begin ascending, a road branches off to the right (southeast). Take this spur to its end (approximately 0.5 miles). At this point you are at the rim of Ancho Canyon. Note the broken-down fence and gate which once prevented cattle from descending into the canyon to graze. Bear to your right (toward the sandstone cliff) and you will find a trail winding through rockfall which will then begin a steep traverse to the bottom of the canyon. The trail shows little sign of use, is eroded and rocky in places, but is easy to follow.

At the bottom of the canyon, the trail is mostly obvious, but cairns aid your travel here. When the canyon bottom levels out, you will find a spring-fed stream to your right. It's a nice place to rest after your climb down or before beginning your climb back up. The authors shared this rest spot with a large, but shy, black bear! The river is not far from here and the trail and cairns will take you to the water's edge. If you see the skeleton of a fallen cottonwood on the way to the river, take a closer look. Teeth marks at the bottom end of the trunk will tell you that beavers cut the tree down.

You can explore the bank of the river for varying distances, depending on the water level. Note the dead tamarisk and oak high on the river banks -- a result of the high water level of Cochiti Reservoir several years ago. Rocks and debris washed from Ancho Canyon in flash floods have formed Ancho ("wide"

154

in Spanish) Rapid, the most difficult rapid in White Rock Canyon for the river runners who boat past.

To return, retrace your steps. On the way back up the scree slope, notice the huge cholla next to a large old log at the corner of one of the switchbacks. And pick up a large piece of the pumice which is so light; if you have a camera, get a companion to take a photograph of you as you heft massive rocks with ease.

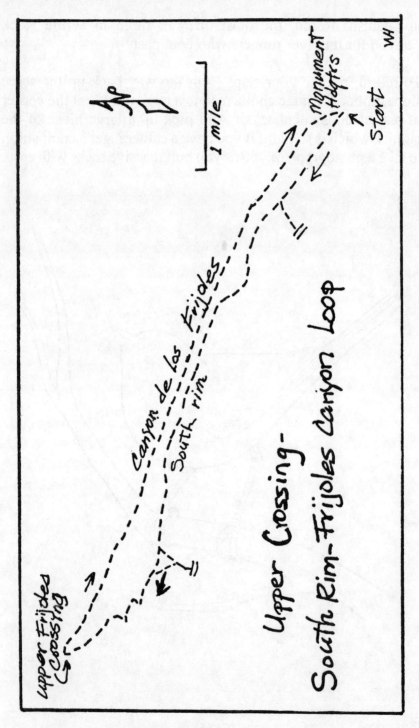

Upper Crossing-
South Rim-Frijoles Canyon Loop

UPPER CROSSING LOOP
SOUTH RIM OF FRIJOLES CANYON
(Bandelier National Monument)

by
Joe Whelan

U.S. GEOLOGICAL SURVEY MAP REQUIRED: Frijoles - 7.5 minute series. You may also consult "Bandelier National Monument, Trails Illustrated," available at Bandelier National Monument Headquarters.

SALIENT FEATURES: The first part of this well-marked loop hike takes you to the southern rim of Frijoles Canyon. You will enjoy views of nearby Indian ruins and distant mountain ranges. On the return, you will hike at the bottom of the narrow canyon, with its sparkling stream, mixed forests and orange tuff cliffs. You may see deer along the trail, if you hike quietly. In the fall, large herds of elk enter this part of the monument to escape hunters in the adjacent Santa Fe National Forest. On the mesa top, the trail passes through two burn areas: the 1977 La Mesa Fire and the Lummis Canyon Burn of 1997. The return trail features 25 stream crossings on flattened logs or flat rocks. In winter, these crossings are usually icy and very slippery, making this part of the loop especially challenging. No dogs are allowed in the Bandelier National Monument.

RATING: Strenuous.

ROUND TRIP HIKING DISTANCE: 13 miles.

APPROXIMATE ROUND TRIP HIKING TIME: 7 hours.

ALTITUDE RANGE: Highest point, 7400 feet; lowest point, 6066 feet; cumulative uphill hiking, 1600 feet.

SEASONAL CONSIDERATIONS: Can be uncomfortably hot in midsummer. In winter, the mesa top is usually lightly snow-covered or muddy, and the stream crossings are icy. Most beautiful during the late fall.

ROUND TRIP DRIVING: 92 miles; 2-2½ hours.

DRIVING DIRECTIONS: From the plaza, drive north on Washington Avenue to Paseo de Peralta. Turn left at the light in front of the pink Scottish Rite Temple. Proceed on Paseo de Peralta to the third stoplight and turn right onto Guadalupe, which merges into US 84/285. Drive north on 84/285 about 15 miles to Pojoaque. Take the Los Alamos exit from the right lane, then turn left under the overpass and proceed west towards Los Alamos on NM 502. NM 502 crosses the Rio Grande and climbs to a well-marked "Y" intersection. Take the right leg, NM 4, toward Bandelier and White Rock. About 1.5 miles from the "Y" is a stoplight. You drive straight ahead toward White Rock and Bandelier. The entrance to Bandelier is about 12.5 miles from the "Y." There is an entrance fee ($10 per car in 1999, good for 7 days, $10 per night for camping). Drive to the Visitors Center and across the bridge over the Rio Frijoles, turn left, and park in the area designated for back country hikers.

HIKING INSTRUCTIONS: From the back country hikers' parking area across the bridge from the Visitors Center, walk back up the paved road past the bridge about 50 yards to a posted map and sign indicating the trails to Yapashi Pueblo and Frijolito Ruin. Take the trail behind the sign about 100 feet to a junction and second sign. Follow the sign for the Yapashi Pueblo Trail to the right (northwest) for a quarter of a mile to another junction and sign, where you will turn left onto the uphill switchback Yapashi Pueblo Trail and follow it to the top of Frijoles Canyon's south rim. On this portion of the trail there are good view of the ruins in and on the north side of Frijoles Canyon. From the top of the rim you can see the Ceremonial

158

Cave and the long ladders leading up to it, directly across the canyon.

Once on the rim there will be 5 trail junctions before you return to the bottom of Frijoles Canyon. At all 5 of these junctions take the trail to your right. At the first four junctions the signs will point toward the Upper Crossing; at the fifth junction follow the sign toward Ponderosa Campground, descending in this last mile to the signs in the bottom of the canyon. Here again you will go to your right toward the Visitor's Center.

Before you start downstream you might enjoy having lunch at a clearing a few feet further along the Ponderosa Campground trail. Go about 50 feet along the trail, cross the creek on a log bridge to the small clearing where the trail begins to climb out of the canyon. This area is usually sunny even in winter and has several large rocks to rest on while you take a break.

After this detour to the clearing, cross back over the creek to the Upper Crossing signpost. Return to the Visitors Center by following the sign at Upper Crossing to the Park Headquarters (6 miles) downstream. This return trail through the narrow canyon bottom and along the stream is bordered by steep, colorful rock formations and is heavily wooded. There are no junctions along the 6 miles of return trail, but there are 25 stream crossings, most of them with primitive bridges. At the Ceremonial Cave ruins, about one mile from the Visitors Center, the trail widens to a nature trail and finally reaches the paved picnic grounds road and back country hikers' parking area.

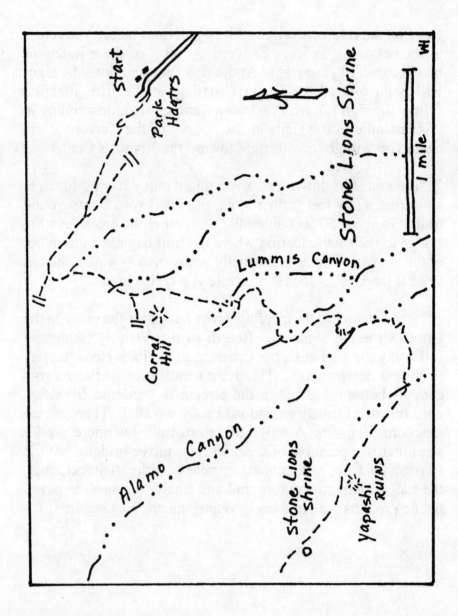

STONE LIONS SHRINE
(Bandelier National Monument)

by
Mickey Bogert

U.S. GEOLOGICAL SURVEY MAP REQUIRED: Frijoles - 7.5 minute series.

SALIENT FEATURES: This is a challenging walk to an ancient shrine showing signs of current use by Indians from the nearby pueblos. It is a strenuous hike because of the climbs in and out of several beautiful canyons, especially Alamo.

The walks across the mesa tops are easy, on good trails, with views of the Sangre de Cristo and Jemez Mountains. Vegetation is mostly piñon-juniper with some ponderosa pine. Just before the Stone Lions Shrine is Yapashi Pueblo, a large, unexcavated pueblo ruin. Note: It is unlawful to remove anything from the National Monument, especially Indian artifacts. No dogs are allowed in the National Monument. Carry plenty of water.

RATING: Strenuous.

ROUND TRIP HIKING DISTANCE: 13 miles.

APPROXIMATE ROUND TRIP HIKING TIME: 8 hours.

ALTITUDE RANGE: Highest point, 6660 feet; lowest point, 6066 feet; cumulative uphill hiking, 2700 feet.

SEASONAL CONSIDERATIONS: Can be uncomfortably hot in summer.

ROUND TRIP DRIVING: 92 miles; approximately 2-2½ hours.

161

DRIVING DIRECTIONS: From the plaza, drive north on Washington Avenue to Paseo de Peralta. Turn left at the light in front of the pink Scottish Rite Temple. Proceed on Paseo de Peralta to the third stoplight, and turn right onto Guadalupe, which merges into US 84/285. Drive north on 84/285 about 15 miles to Pojoaque. Take the Los Alamos exit from the right lane, swing left under the overpass, and proceed west toward Los Alamos. NM 502 crosses the Rio Grande and climbs to a well-marked "Y" intersection about 28 miles from Santa Fe. Take the right leg, NM 4, toward Bandelier and White Rock. About 1.5 miles from the "Y" is a stoplight where the truck route to Los Alamos and the road to the Pajarito Ski Area go right. You drive straight ahead through this light toward White Rock and Bandelier. The entrance to Bandelier is beyond White Rock, about 12.5 miles from the "Y." There is an entrance fee. Drive to the Visitors Center and across the bridge over the Rio Frijoles, turn left, and park in the area designated for back country hikers.

HIKING INSTRUCTIONS: From the parking area, walk back up the paved road, past the bridge for a few hundred feet where you will see a sign on your left which will identify the trail to Yapashi Pueblo and Frijolito Ruin. Turn left (southwest) onto this trail. The Yapashi Pueblo Trail soon branches from the Frijolito Ruin Trail and heads northwest (right). This is a fairly gradual climb and affords good views of the ruins in Frijoles Canyon. When you reach the top of the mesa you can see Ceremonial Cave, with the long ladders leading up to it, directly across the canyon. A few yards further on is a junction (1 mile from the Visitors Center). At this junction, follow the sign pointing left (south) to Stone Lions via Yapashi Pueblo, 5.0 miles.

Continue on the Stone Lions Trail, crossing Lummis Canyon (identified by a sign) and the two tributary canyons on each side of it, and then on to the rim of Alamo Canyon.

162

For most of this distance the vegetation is varied: juniper, piñon pine and some ponderosa, or yellow, pine, as well as yucca and cactus. The previous canyon crossings are semi-shaded and fairly easy, so Alamo Canyon comes as a shock, as well as a spectacular surprise. There are beautiful views, but no shade, and there is a very steep switchback trail down a precipitous cliff. It is essential to carry sufficient water, for it requires a great deal of effort to descend 500 feet in 0.3 miles and make a similar ascent on the other side. And you must do it again, in reverse, on the way back.

The canyon bottom does have trees, and a stream during certain times of the year. Do not drink the water. The trail goes downstream for several hundred yards before crossing and starting steeply upwards on the south side of the canyon. The south rim of the canyon is a good place for a snack break, to enjoy the view, and to gather strength for the next two miles. A half mile farther on is a shallow canyon, a tributary of Alamo, about 80 feet deep. The vegetation south of Alamo is quite different: more arid in appearance, no more ponderosa, and the junipers and piñons are shorter. Cactus is much more abundant.

(From here on, when snow covered, the trail may be difficult to follow.)

One mile beyond the little canyon, in a westerly direction, is Yapashi Pueblo, now a mound of rubble. From here you will have magnificent views of many mountains. To the west, the San Miguel Mountains; south, the Sandias; southeast, the Ortiz and San Pedro Mountains; northwest, the Jemez; and to the northeast, the Sangre de Cristo Mountains. A half mile beyond the Yapashi ruins, on your left, you will see a small enclosure made of piled-up stones. In the middle of this is what is left of the stone lion carvings. Time and the elements have obliterated the heads but the backs and haunches remain. Sometimes there are offerings of deer antlers hanging on the trees in back of the

163

lions but more often antlers are racked around them, almost like a wreath. Most of us who come here sense a special atmosphere about this place. Remember that it is a sacred area, so please respect and enjoy it accordingly. Do not disturb any of the offerings.

(Editor's note: Unfortunately visitors other than Pueblo Indians also started to leave offerings at the shrine, interfering with the religious practices of the Pueblo people. Today, the Indians no longer leave offerings. Offerings left by Wannabe Indians are removed by the Park Service.)

Return to your car over the same trails.

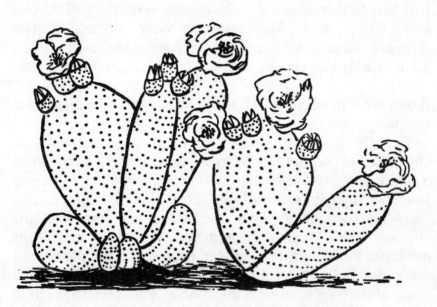

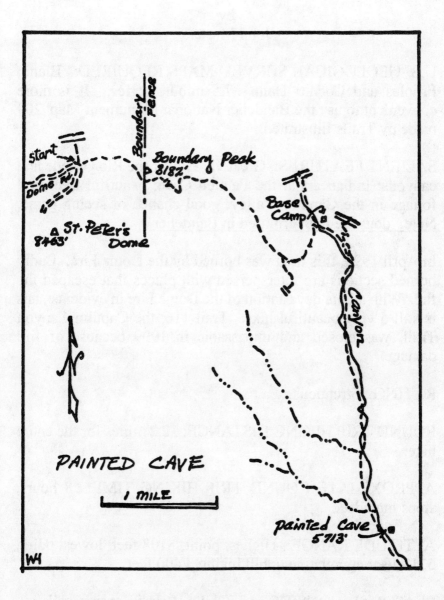

Start

Dome No. 4

△ St. Peter's
8463' Dome

Boundary Fence

Boundary Peak
8182'

Base Camp

Horse Canyon

N

PAINTED CAVE

1 MILE

painted Cave
5713'

WH

PAINTED CAVE

by
John Masters

U.S. GEOLOGICAL SURVEY MAPS REQUIRED: Bland, Frijoles and Cochiti Dam - 7.5 minute series. It is more convenient to use the Bandelier National Monument Map 209 made by Trails Illustrated.

SALIENT FEATURES: Great views over the Rio Grande and canyons; Indian art at the Painted Cave; beautiful trees and foliage in the Capulin Valley; good chance of seeing game. Note: dogs are not permitted in Bandelier.

In April 1996, this area was burned by the Dome Fire. Badly burned sections are interspersed with places that escaped the fire. With all the devastation of the Dome Fire in evidence, this is still a very beautiful hike. Trail 116, the Capulin Canyon Trail, was closed and impassable in 1999 because of fire damage.

RATING: Strenuous.

ROUND TRIP HIKING DISTANCE: 12.2 miles for the entire hike.

APPROXIMATE ROUND TRIP HIKING TIME: 8 hours, stops included.

ALTITUDE RANGE: Highest point, 8108 feet; lowest point, 5713 feet; cumulative uphill hiking, 2400 feet.

SEASONAL CONSIDERATIONS: Best in spring and fall. Forest Road 289 is usually closed in winter and early spring.

Call the Jemez Ranger (505-829-3535) for information about road closings and driving conditions.

ROUND TRIP DRIVING: 97 miles; 3.5 to 4 hours, depending on road conditions.

DRIVING DIRECTIONS: Take Route 84/285 northbound from Santa Fe to Pojoaque. There, take the Los Alamos exit (NM 502) on your right. Stay in the left lane of this road. After a signal, it goes through an underpass and on toward Los Alamos. NM 502 crosses the Rio Grande and climbs to a well-marked "Y" intersection. Take the right branch toward White Rock and Bandelier. About 1.5 miles from the "Y" turn right at a traffic light. You are now on East Jemez Road. After 5.7 miles, your road branches. Do not take the right lane that goes to Los Alamos. Keep straight ahead/slightly left through a series of traffic lights, on past the Los Alamos National Laboratory. In another 5.4 miles you will come to a "T" intersection with Route 4. Turn right here and check your odometer. The road winds and twists sharply. Drive carefully (large trucks use this road). After driving about 6 miles on Route 4, you will come to Forest Road 289.

Turn left here onto 289. You have 11 more miles to go to reach the trailhead. After 2 miles on FR 289 you will cross a cattle guard. Shortly after several roads branch off FR 289. Stay on FR 289, following signs that say "Dome Wilderness." After 7.5 miles on the well-maintained gravel road, you will come to a "T" junction. "Dome Lookout" and "Dome Wilderness" signs direct you to the left onto a narrow, rocky and rutted road, FR 142.

3.5 more miles to go to the trailhead. The last half mile or so can be very rutted and you might consider parking your vehicle before reaching the trailhead. While driving on FR 142, ignore secondary roads going off to the left and right. Park as the road turns sharply right and comes out on a steep edge overlooking the Rio Grande valley. This is St. Peter's Dome Lookout corner and trailhead. In 1999 there were two signs at the trailhead. One sign informs you that the Capulin Trail is temporarily closed. The other sign indicates that Bandelier is 0.8 miles ahead. Your trail, Boundary Peak Trail 427, goes to the right of this sign. You will return on the same trail.

HIKING INSTRUCTIONS: This is a very beautiful walk, especially in fall, from the colors, and in spring, from the rush of water in the Capulin. Look for great cliff formations of tuff as you drop into Capulin Canyon; distant views of Chicoma and Caballo Mountains, and the Truchas Peaks across the whole valley; all three types of juniper -- common, Rocky Mountain and alligator; magnificent stands of ponderosa pine; hoof/paw marks and scats of black bear, deer, elk and wild burro (all these seem to use the area freely); tremendous views over Jemez canyons; fingerling trout in the Capulin; and, always, the half-hidden things -- the wildflowers, small animals, birds.

The walk is all down, then all up. If it's too hot, have a dip in the stream before starting the final ascent.

From the parking area, take Trail 427 heading, at that point, northeast, and for a short distance, uphill. Next, the trail turns east and wends down the side of Boundary Peak. After about one hour the trail approaches a drainage (on its right) and seems to disappear. Cross the drainage, turn sharply right on the other side, and look for the continuation of the trail. In a few minutes you will come to a sign indicating the junction with the Turkey Springs Trail. Put your back to the sign and follow your trail north, down into Capulin Canyon. After about 15 minutes cross the Rio Capulin at a large log building. Continue on the trail downstream to a marked trail junction. A trail goes off to the left to Ponderosa Campground and the Visitor's Center. You continue straight ahead toward Painted Cave.

Proceed on downstream, with several stream crossings (which are great fun in spring) for about another 45 minutes, where you will see the big scooped-out overhang of the Painted Cave to your left. A trail (sign-posted) takes off toward it, crossing the stream. Do not attempt to climb up to the cave itself. Get out your binoculars instead and have a closer look at the pictographs. You will see horned serpents, stars, kachinas, stepped cloud designs, strange animals, a man on horse back ... Many of the paintings were made between A.D. 1300 and 1600. More were added after the arrival of the Spaniards. The Painted Cave has been an important shrine for many centuries and is still a sacred site revered by the Indians from the nearby pueblos.

When you're ready to return, go back the same way you came. Follow the signs that point you to the Dome trailhead. After passing the log cabin, make sure you take the trail that branches off to the left.

Walk away quietly in any direction and taste the freedom of the mountaineer...Climb the mountains and get their good tidings. Nature's peace will flow into you as sunshine flows into trees. The winds will blow their own freshness into you, and the storms their energies, while cares will drop off like autumn leaves.
–John Muir

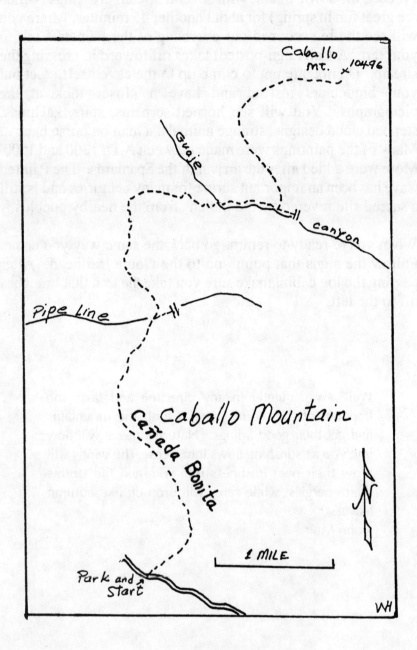

Caballo Mt. x 10496

Guaje

canyon

Pipe Line

Caballo Mountain

Cañada Bonita

1 MILE

N

Park and Start

WH

CANADA BONITA
VALLE DE LOS POSOS OVERLOOK
GUAJE CANYON - CABALLO MOUNTAIN

by
Norbert Sperlich

U.S. GEOLOGICAL SURVEY MAPS REQUIRED: Valle Toledo, and (for the top of Caballo Mountain) Guaje Mountain, 7.5 minute series. On the Valle Toledo map, look in the lower right corner for a road called "Camp May Trail." Just past the ski area (going toward Camp May), a trail goes off in a northerly direction. This is your trail.

SALIENT FEATURES: A hike to the high country near Los Alamos. The first part (easy) takes you to a high meadow and to the rim of the Valles Caldera. For a moderate hike, continue to the edge of Guaje Canyon. For a strenuous hike, cross Guaje Canyon and climb to the top of Caballo Mountain. Great views across the Rio Grande valley! Leave early and bring plenty of water if you plan to do the whole hike.

RATING: Easy - moderate - strenuous, depending on the distance hiked.

ROUND TRIP HIKING DISTANCE: Cañada Bonita, - about 4 miles; Valle de los Posos Overlook - close to 6 miles; edge of Guaje Canyon - about 8 miles; Caballo Mountain - 14 miles.

APPROXIMATE ROUND TRIP HIKING TIMES: To Valle de los Posos Overlook about 3 hours; to edge of Guaje Canyon 4 hours or more; to Caballo Mountain 8 hours or more, stops not included.

ALTITUDE RANGE: Easy hike - highest point 9650 feet, lowest point 9220 feet, total vertical ascent about 650 feet.

171

Moderate hike - same highest and lowest points, total vertical ascent about 1000 feet. Strenuous hike- lowest point 8,600 feet, highest point 10,496 feet, total vertical ascent about 3300 feet.

SEASONAL CONSIDERATIONS: Not a winter hike. Trails might be clear of snow from May to October. Cañada Bonita is especially beautiful in the fall, when the aspens are golden.

ROUND TRIP DRIVING: About 86 miles, 2 hours.

DRIVING DIRECTIONS: Take Route 84/285 northbound from Santa Fe to Pojoaque. There, take the Los Alamos exit (NM 502) on your right. Stay in the left lane of this road. After a signal it goes under an overpass and on toward Los Alamos. NM 502 crosses the Rio Grande and climbs to a well-marked "Y" intersection. Take the right branch toward White Rock and Bandelier. About 1.5 miles past the "Y" turn right at a traffic light onto East Jemez Road. Some 5.7 miles later your road branches. Do not take the right lane: that goes to Los Alamos. Keep straight ahead (slightly left) past 3 traffic lights. Some 1.2 miles past the last intersection look for a sign on the right side of the road pointing to the ski area. Turn right here and drive 4.4 miles on a narrow, winding road. Drive through the parking area, then down a short hill. At the bottom of the hill park in a small parking area on your left.

HIKING INSTRUCTIONS: Across from where you parked, on the other side of the road, a dirt road goes off the main road. It crosses and then follows a little stream. This is your trail. Some 40 yards along this road there is an empty information board and a sign "Guaje Canyon Trail 282, Cañada Bonita 1, Pipeline Road 3". Shortly after the road goes through a gate. You are now hiking in the shadow of enormous aspens and Douglas firs. In about 20 minutes you will reach Cañada Bonita, an open meadow that has not been grazed since Los Alamos was established in 1943. For a while, you are hiking on a narrow trail. It crosses the meadow and goes up a slope, across a ridge, and into the trees again. Next, it merges with the road and starts to go downhill. There is another gate, then comes an intersection where a road goes off to the left. Continue straight ahead, uphill now. In a few minutes, the road forks. The right branch is Pipeline Road. Take the left, less traveled branch. After about 100 yards it will take you to a spot with a view into the Valle de los Posos. The "Valley of the Holes" – the holes are prairie dog burrows – is part of the huge Valles Caldera, the crater-like depression that originated about a million years ago after the eruption and collapse of an enormous magma chamber. Just past the overlook, the road forks again. Take the left fork. It is marked by a sign "Guaje Canyon, Trail 282, Guaje Canyon 2." You are now hiking on the narrow rim of the Valles Caldera. Soon you will reach a place at the edge of steep cliffs where you get another view into the Valle de los Posos. This is a good place for a stop. If you came for an easy hike, turn around here.

The trail continues to meander in a northerly direction, then turns east and starts to drop into Guaje Canyon. It seems to head straight for the edge of a cliff, but then makes a hairpin turn to the left. Before you continue on the trail, step to the edge for a look into and across Guaje Canyon. You will see Caballo Mountain on the other side, and Santa Fe Baldy and Lake Peak in the distance. For a moderate hike, this is a good place to turn around.

Those with time and energy to spare will now head down the steep trail into Guaje Canyon. After reaching the canyon bottom, follow the trail downstream for about 10 minutes. One is tempted to hike further along the stream, but, alas, there is a fork in the trail. In the fall of '98 it was not marked. The left branch of the trail goes up steeply, the right branch leads past a small campsite towards a drainage. You have reached the lowest point of the hike. The highest point is only about 1.5

miles away, but 1900 feet up. Take the left trail. It will take you up and up. After some 25 minutes you will cross a drainage near a spring. Time to catch your breath.

You have an hour or so of steep climbing before the trail comes out on a meadow close to the top of the mountain. There is a sign that tells you to stay on the trail and not to disturb sacred objects. This sign refers to the Agua Piedra Trail, which, in days past, crossed the top of Caballo Mountain and passed through Santa Clara Indian land. Hikers are no longer welcome on Santa Clara land. Therefore, stay on the south side of the summit and don't go into the trees on the very top.

Enjoy the sweeping views across the Rio Grande, with the Sangre de Cristos in the background, the Sandias toward the south, and closer by, Pajarito Mountain and St. Peter's Dome. For better views toward the north, go past the sign and parallel to the edge of the trees on your left. In a few minutes, you will reach a place where the forest forms a corner. At the corner, turn left, still following the edge of the trees. Now the Truchas come into view in the distance.

Return the way you came.

Generations have trod, have trod, have trod;
　And all is seared with trade; bleared, smeared with toil;
　And wears man's smudge and shares man's smell: the soil
Is bare now, nor can foot feel, being shod.
And for all this, nature is never spent;
　There lives the dearest freshness deep down things.
--Gerard Manley Hopkins.

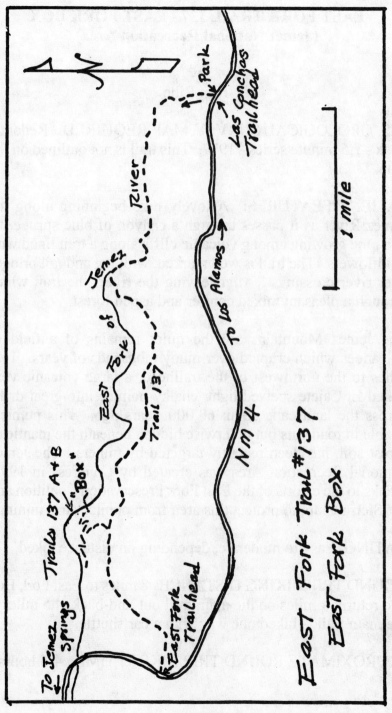

East Fork Trail #137
East Fork Box

EAST FORK TRAIL 137 - EAST FORK BOX
(Jemez National Recreation Area)

by
Tom Ribe

U.S. GEOLOGICAL SURVEY MAP REQUIRED: Redondo Peak - 7.5 minute series - 1977. This trail is not outlined on the map.

SALIENT FEATURES: A lovely hike beginning along the Jemez River as it passes through a canyon of blue spruce, fir and pine growing among volcanic cliffs along a trail lined with wildflowers. The trail is well marked, with log and rail bridges over river crossings. After leaving the river, the trail winds through a pleasant mixed conifer and aspen forest.

The Jemez Mountains are the quiet remains of a field of volcanoes which erupted over many thousands of years. Two miles to the northwest of the trailhead, a large volcanic vent called El Cajete spewed light, chalky pumice into great drifts across the landscape about 60,000 years ago. This pumice, visible in road cuts but otherwise hidden beneath the mantle of forest soil, has been recently targeted by miners. The Jemez National Recreation Area was created by Congress in 1993, thanks to the efforts of the East Fork Preservation Coalition and the Sierra Club, to protect this area from pumice strip mining.

RATING: Easy to moderate, depending on distance hiked.

ROUND TRIP HIKING DISTANCE: 8 miles to East Fork Box and return; 9 miles on the main trail out-and-back; 4.5 miles if the main trail is hiked one way with a car shuttle.

APPROXIMATE ROUND TRIP HIKING TIME: 4-5 hours.

ALTITUDE RANGE: Highest point, 8560 feet; lowest point, 8080 feet on main trail, 8000 feet at East Fork Box; cumulative uphill hiking, 640 feet on main trail, 720 feet to East Fork Box.

SEASONAL CONSIDERATIONS: Spring through fall, depending on snow conditions.

ROUND TRIP DRIVING: 110 miles; about three hours, due to winding roads.

DRIVING DIRECTIONS: Take Route 84/285 northbound from Santa Fe to Pojoaque. There take the Los Alamos exit (NM 502) on your right. After a traffic light, the road goes through an underpass and on toward Los Alamos. NM 502 crosses the Rio Grande and climbs to a well-marked "Y" intersection. Take the right branch toward White Rock and Bandelier. About 1.5 miles from the "Y," turn right at a traffic light. You are now on East Jemez Road. After about 5.7 miles, your road branches. Do not take the right lane that goes to Los Alamos. Keep straight ahead/slightly left through a series of traffic lights and past the Los Alamos National Laboratory. In another 5.4 miles you will come to a "T" intersection with Route 4. This intersection is called the West Gate of Los Alamos. Turn right here and check your odometer. The road winds and twists sharply and the scenery is beautiful, so drive carefully. The trailhead is 13.7 miles from the right turn.

Once in the Jemez Mountains, the road winds up along the Frijoles Canyon watershed until you drop down into the Valle Grande, a huge caldera and grassland surrounded by the Jemez peaks. The road then drops out of the Valle Grande and crosses the Jemez River at Las Conchas Campground. Half a mile farther, the road recrosses the river in an open area where a few houses stand on the left side of the road. Park in the gravel parking area on the right side of the road at the river crossing, directly across the road from a private driveway, and pass

177

through the gate on the East Fork Trail to the north. This trailhead is called "Las Conchas" on the USFS signs.

HIKING DIRECTIONS: Begin hiking to the north following the river on the well-used trail, crossing on several log and rail bridges. The river meanders between steep canyon walls covered with an amazing variety of orange, chartreuse, pale green and black lichens. Desert varnish trails over honeycomb patterns in the rock.

Though the canyon is beautiful, it bears the scars of decades of cattle grazing, which has denuded the streamside of much of its native vegetation, polluted the water, and eliminated many plant and bird species. Look for old beaver gnaw marks on some of the trees. Beaver were once plentiful here before cattle eliminated most of the willow thickets that provided the beavers' food and lodging material. Alert hikers may see dippers (water ouzels) along the stream, along with Steller's jays, western tanagers and Rocky Mountain chickadees.

About two miles from the trailhead, the river leaves the meadow and forest bottom land and plunges in gentle falls into a box canyon where the cliffs fall directly into the water. At this point, at a cattle fence and gate, the river turns at nearly a right angle. The hiking trail leaves the river a few yards before the bend at trail signs noting that Las Conchas Trailhead (where you began) is 2 miles back and East Fork Trailhead is 3 miles farther on, to the left. The trail switches back up the north-facing slope in a 200-foot or so elevation gain to the ridgetop, passing through a wooden gate about one-third of the way up. At the top, Redondo Peak can now be seen directly to the north, with its forested ramparts and montane grasslands gleaming among aspen groves.

After arriving on the ridgetop, the trail continues through a logged forest of mixed conifer, New Mexican locust and aspens.

On the ridgetop, the forest tells the story of logging and fire suppression, which has changed it from open park lands of big trees before 1900 to the thickets of small trees that grow here today. After hiking 20 minutes on the ridgetop, the trail is crossed by a logging road. Shortly thereafter, it merges with a ski trail, the latter coming in from the left and marked by blue diamonds nailed to the trees. On occasion, the trail runs closely parallel to a logging road -- stay on the narrow trail!

Soon you will come to a trail junction marked by a sign. Trail 137 continues straight ahead to reach the East Fork Trailhead in a mile. Another trail (137 A and B) goes off to the right and one-half mile down to the river. This right-hand trail soon branches. The right branch goes to the East Fork Box where the river leaves the box canyon. The trail makes a very steep descent to reach the river and cross a bridge. Head upstream after crossing the bridge to where the river comes out of a wild, rocky canyon. This spot makes an excellent lunch area and turnaround point for the hike. If you wish, follow the river upstream into the canyon (you will get your legs wet!) for 5 more minutes to a popular picnic area.

Rather than descending to the East Fork Box, you might choose instead to continue straight ahead from the junction on the main Trail 137 one more mile to the East Fork Trailhead. There you will find a wooden fence, parking area, outhouses and the highway.

Unless you are doing this hike as a shuttle, return on the main trail. About 20 minutes past the sign for the turnoff to the East Fork Box, the blue diamond ski trail separates from Trail 137 by veering off to the right (there is a lot of downed timber at this fork). Make sure you stay on the better defined hiking trail, to the left, to return to Las Conchas Trailhead and your car.

If your group has more than one car, you could arrange a car shuttle between the two highway trailheads -- Las Conchas and East Fork, which is 3.7 miles farther west on NM 4. This would cut the hiking distance in half.

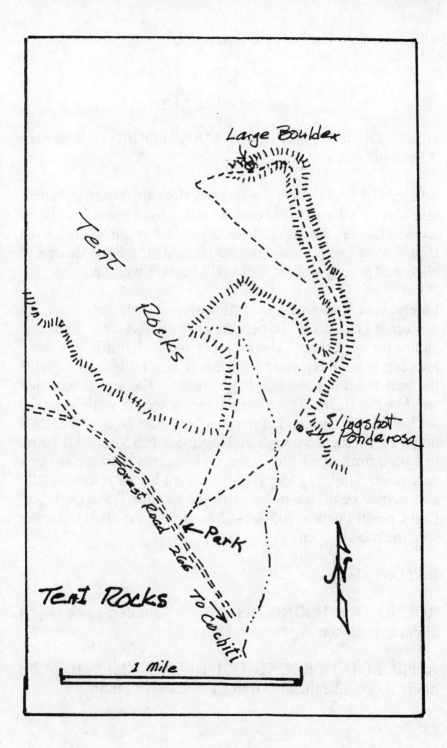

Large Boulder

Tent

Rocks

Slingshot
Ponderosa

Forest Road 266

Park

Tent Rocks

To Cochiti

N

1 Mile

181

TENT ROCKS

by
Alan and Jenny Karp

U.S. GEOLOGICAL SURVEY MAP REQUIRED: Cañada - 7.5 minute series.

SALIENT FEATURES: Fascinating slot canyon and unbelievable tuff rock formations, only 40 miles from Santa Fe. There are wildflowers in season. The canyon is very photogenic; even if you don't bring a camera, the banded striations, shadowed cliffs and gravity-defiant rocks will be ever with you.

Lately Tent Rocks has been "discovered" and the number of visitors is increasing. To beat the crowds, visit early in the day and/or on week days. There is only so much traffic this small area can bear. Keep your dog leashed, don't litter, don't go off the trail and don't come in large groups. The area is administered by the BLM. There is a $5 on-site fee per vehicle, no fee for holders of Golden Eagle or Golden Age cards. Visitation hours are 8 a.m. to 5 p.m. from November 1 to March 31, 7 a.m. to 6 p.m. from April 1 to October 31. Access is controlled by a gate about 5 miles <u>before</u> you reach Tent Rocks. Occasionally access may be closed by order of the Cochiti Tribal governor. Call Cochiti Pueblo (505-465-2244 or 505-465-0121) to make sure the road is open.

RATING: Easy.

ROUND TRIP HIKING DISTANCE: 2 miles; more if you climb to ridge top.

APPROXIMATE ROUND TRIP HIKING TIME: About 2-3 hours if you hike the loop trail <u>and</u> the canyon trail.

ALTITUDE RANGE: Highest point, 6100 feet; lowest point, 5750 feet; cumulative uphill hiking, 350 feet.

SEASONAL CONSIDERATIONS: Spring or fall or early summer morning hours make this an idyllic, short, comfortable hike. Not a winter hike if there has been heavy snowfall.

ROUND TRIP DRIVING: 80 miles; approximately 2 hours.

DRIVING DIRECTIONS: Take I-25 south toward Albuquerque and get off at the Cochiti exit 264. Take the right turn (west) off the exit ramp onto NM 16. In about 8 miles you will come to a "T" intersection. Turn right here onto NM 22 and follow this road for about 2.5 miles. Look for an intersection where you will take a sharp turn left (still NM 22) toward Cochiti Pueblo. Stay on this road for 1.8 miles. To the right of the road you will see a water tower painted like an Indian drum and then a similar but narrower tower. After passing a sign, "←Cochiti Pueblo," you will come to an intersection where a paved road comes in from the right. This road is marked, "266, Tent Rocks." Turn right onto this road.

Soon it becomes a gravel road that takes you to the aforementioned gate. For the next 3 miles you are on Cochiti Pueblo land. No parking is allowed on this stretch. After another 1.8 miles you will come to the well-marked entrance to the Tent Rocks area on your right. The fee station is to the left of the entrance. Turn right and park.

HIKING INSTRUCTIONS: Look for a wide trail that will take you to an information board protected by a roof. Here you will find descriptions and pictures of the area and a map. The map shows two trails. One is a loop trail (also referred to as CAVE LOOP on signposts) that starts and ends at the information board. It is maintained and marked with wooden posts and brown plastic stakes. You can do this loop in an hour or less.

Where the loop trail comes to the entrance of a narrow canyon the canyon trail branches off. This trail is not maintained or marked. In the following both trails are described.

The Loop Trail goes past the information board and, after some 50 yards, branches. Take the left branch and follow the arrows. You will be hiking amidst tent rocks that have lost their "caps". The trail climbs up a slope, with cliffs on your left, then drops into a bowl that is surrounded by sculpted cliffs on three sides. The trail starts to climb again and goes up to the right, past a cave in the cliff wall. The "cave art" in and around the cave is of very recent origin. From here, you have beautiful views to the south. The trail follows the cliffs, then descends steeply through manzanita bushes down to a drainage. A sign post CAVE LOOP points in the direction from which you came. To your left the drainage leads into a narrow canyon. There is a sign CANYON at the entrance. This is the beginning of the Canyon Trail. It will take you into an enchanted world.

Mother Nature's imagination went wild in this stone wonderland. Over the ages, wind and water have sensuously carved out this inspiring miniature canyon, a mini Grand Canyon that envelopes and entices you with its cap rocks and volcanic tuff, ponderosa-lined trail and cheerful wildflowers. It gives you a very special spiritual feeling. The arroyo funnels into this inner sanctuary. As you wind your way up the canyon, the soft curving walls provide you with meditative niches. The sky appears a deeper blue than imaginable and provides a dramatic backdrop for the still-forming tent rocks. Approximately fifteen minutes into the hike, a tall ponderosa and a lone tent rock appear at the base of the left wall of the canyon. The wall bears petroglyphs depicting a serpent, handprints and other symbols.

The canyon narrows into a stone hallway in which at several places you must scramble over rock steps. At one point you will need to crawl on hands and knees under a huge boulder. Some hikers may require a helping hand or a boost. The trail continues to wind, alternating between open and more narrow sections. You will finally arrive at a boulder in a fall of small rocks going up through a narrow passage. Access is difficult here and most hikers will make this the turn-around point of the hike.

Experienced hikers might consider continuing the hike out of the canyon and up to the top of the ridge that runs parallel to the canyon. Getting up there will take some 15 to 20 minutes on one of several steep trails. First you need to get past the boulder that blocks the way. Next you will see the trunk of a fallen ponderosa on the left. Parallel to the trunk a trail starts to climb out of the canyon. It ascends along a small, steep ridge where footing is poor. About half way up, the trail makes a little switch to the left. At this point a hard-to-see branch of the trail continues straight ahead and <u>down</u> into the drainage, past a small ponderosa tree. This branch is the easiest way to get to the top. Go down this steep trail, past the ponderosa and into the drainage, then go up the drainage. In about 3 minutes the trail goes left and leaves the drainage. For a short while it follows the edge of the canyon, then it goes away from the canyon and up. Just before you reach the top of the ridge, a branch of the trail goes off to the left. Take this branch to a high point of the ridge and on to where the ridge ends in a cliff. From here, you see the Tent Rocks area nearby as well as the slot canyon below; to the east is the familiar shape of Tetilla Peak above Cochiti Lake, to the north are the Sangre de Cristo Mountains, and to the south, Sandia Peak.

Return the way you came. Once you leave the canyon keep on going in the drainage until you come to an arrow that directs you out of the drainage and to the right. You will walk past a large ponderosa on your left, then cross another drainage and arrive back at the parking lot in a few minutes.

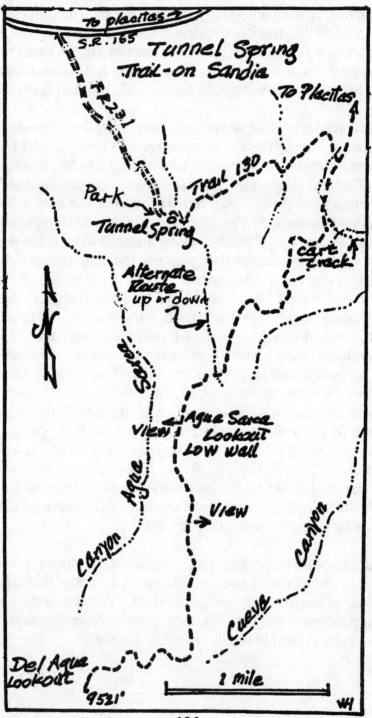

To placitas →

S.R. 165

FR 2331

Tunnel Spring
Trail - on Sandia

To Placitas

Trail 190

Park

Tunnel Spring

cart track

Alternate
Route
up or down

Agua
Sara
Canyon

VIEW

Agua Sara
Lookout
Low Wall

VIEW

Cueva
Canyon

Del Aqua
Lookout

9521'

1 mile

WH

TUNNEL SPRING TRAIL TO DEL AGUA OVERLOOK
(In the Sandia Mountains)

by
Polly Robertson, Norma McCallan and Norbert Sperlich

U.S. GEOLOGICAL SURVEY MAP REQUIRED: Instead of the Placitas - 7.5 minute series, use the "Sandia Mountain Wilderness" map, published by the US Forest Service and sold at the Public Lands Bookstore, 1474 Rodeo Road, in Santa Fe.

SALIENT FEATURES: A hike into the Sandia Mountain Wilderness offering sweeping views. Lovely wildflowers. The walk from Tunnel Spring is all uphill on the north slope of Sandia; but it's ALL downhill returning. No water other than Tunnel Springs at the trailhead.

RATING: Moderate to strenuous

ROUND TRIP HIKING DISTANCE: 16 miles, but can be cut to any length you wish, as it is an "out and back" hike. If you take the alternate route up or down Del Orno Canyon subtract 2 miles.

APPROXIMATE ROUND TRIP HIKING TIME: 7-10 hours.

ALTITUDE RANGE: Highest point, 9640 feet; lowest point, 6400 feet; cumulative uphill hiking, 3240 feet.

SEASONAL CONSIDERATIONS: Best in spring or fall. Snow may linger in the upper reaches in early spring. Summer is hot.

ROUND TRIP DRIVING: 108 miles; about 2½ hours.

DRIVING DIRECTIONS: Take I-25 south toward Albuquerque. About 47 miles from Santa Fe, take Exit 242 towards Placitas. Make note of your odometer reading at the highway and go 5.2 miles east toward Placitas. After passing a street sign, "Puesta del Sol," on your right, look for the next dirt road to your right, marked "Tunnel Springs Road," with a group of mail and newspaper boxes. There is a small sign (FR 231) a few yards up this bumpy dirt road. Turn right here and drive 1.5 miles past several houses, bearing left if in doubt. You will pass the spring on your right gushing through a pipe behind a stone wall. The large parking area with toilet facilities is immediately beyond. Many people fill their water jugs at the spring.

HIKING INSTRUCTIONS: Trail 130 (North Crest Trail) starts next to an information board with a map. Crest Trail signs give the distance to Agua Sarca Overlook as 5 miles, Del Agua Overlook 8 miles and Sandia Crest 11 miles. You will start at 6400 feet. Agua Sarca Lookout is at about 7800 feet and Del Agua Lookout at 9640 feet. The time given on the sign to reach these spots is probably exaggerated for most experienced hikers. Trail 130 ultimately reaches Sandia Crest after 11 miles and continues to the southern end of the Sandias. Any part of this distance is a lovely walk.

Close to the trailhead, your trail crosses a drainage. There is a wooden sign, "Sandia Mountain Wilderness," at this point. Here, an unmarked trail goes to the right and steeply up into Del Orno Canyon. You might choose to come down (or go up) on this trail as an alternative. For the main trail, continue straight ahead on Trail 130. To your left, in the distance, you can see Cabezon Peak, a volcanic neck, and closer by, the Jemez Canyon reservoir and the fingerlike mesas of the San Felipe volcanic field. Next to your trail grows Mormon tea, a virtually leafless shrub with jointed stems.

188

Ignore two unmarked trails joining your trail from the left. The trail is a long, gentle traverse going northeasterly (toward Placitas) for about 1 mile, then it bears due south (right) and up Arroyo Colorado. You are hiking on grey limestone, deposited in an ocean 300 million years ago. Look for fossils! After you have followed the drainage for about 10 minutes, the trail levels out. There is a large slab of limestone in the middle of the trail which seems to be a marker for a faint trail coming in from the left. If you come back this way, keep the limestone slab on your right and stay to the left of the upcoming drainage.

The trail starts to climb again. About one hour into the hike, old cart tracks cross the trail at right angles. Five minutes later, another track approaches the trail from the left, runs parallel to the trail, then veers left again. Stay on the narrow trail to the right of this track. To the east, the Ortiz and San Pedro Mountains are coming into view now. Soon the trail turns west and takes you to the rim of Del Orno Canyon. Looking down the canyon, you can see your car. In the distance, to the west, appears Mount Taylor; to the north are the Jemez Mountains with Redondo Peak prominent.

For a while you will hike below the vertical cliffs that form the east rim of Del Orno Canyon. About 3.5 miles from the start of the hike, just before you come to the head of the canyon (where your trail crosses a drainage and turns sharply right), you will notice an unmarked trail that drops down to the right into the canyon. This is the start of the shorter alternative route down the canyon which will save you about 2 miles. Note this junction since you may want to return on it and it may be difficult to find on the way down.

About ten minutes after passing this trail junction, you will reach the east rim of Agua Sarca Canyon at the overlook, where there is a low stone wall on the right, overlooking a steep escarpment with expansive views to the west. It takes something under two hours to reach this point. This overlook makes an excellent place to stop for a break.

The trail now moves away from the edge, then returns briefly to the rim of Agua Sarca Canyon about half an hour further on. This overlook also offers great views. Soon the vegetation changes as piñon and juniper give way to dense scrub oak. Near some rock outcrops, where there is a sign for the Peñasco Blanco Trail (barely visible heading off to the left of the main trail), you can follow a narrow path and wiggle through the brush for a few feet to end up on a large flat rock which offers a great spot for lunch and a good turnaround point if you don't want to hike the entire distance. This "picnic rock" offers striking views to the east and is generally protected from the winds that often sweep across the Sandias.

Keep on going straight ahead and up through the oak thicket. In late May, you should see lots of flowers along this section of the hike; the oak bushes will have leafed out and the gorgeous Fendler bushes should be in bloom. About half an hour past this trail junction, the trail returns briefly to the rim again, then turns left at a stone wall and keeps climbing in a southerly direction. The air is getting thinner and the oak bushes smaller, and you will have magnificent views to the north. In another half hour, the trail approaches the rim once more, leaves the oak behind, and goes into the fir trees. The trail makes a hairpin turn to the right and soon runs alongside the rocky rim, with great views to the west. There is no sign marking the Del Agua overlook; however, a stone bench close to the trail must be the place. Strong hikers can reach this point in four hours.

You may return to your car by the same route or take the shorter route previously mentioned. The shortcut saves you about 2 miles or one hour of hiking time. The trail descending through Del Orno Canyon is steep, a bit of a scramble, and rough in spots with a lot of loose rock, making for poor footing. Caution should be exercised while descending. Don't use this trail during or after heavy rains. It is bad enough in dry weather! It is somewhat easier to ascend than descend due to the loose rocks, so a more pleasing way to do this alternative route is to go up Del Orno and return via the standard trail.

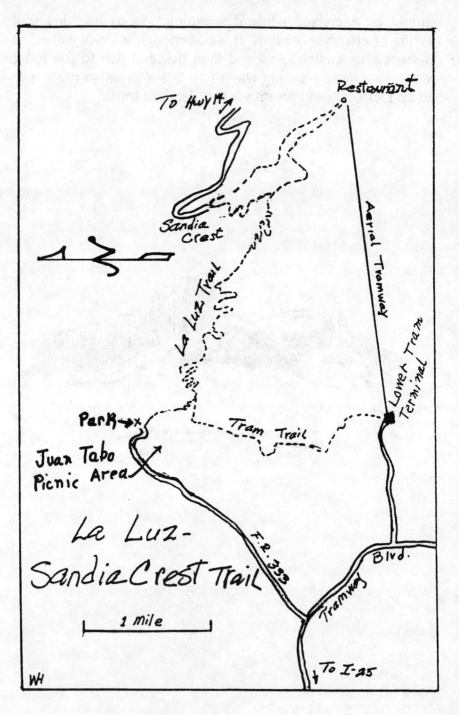

To Hwy 14

Restaurant

Sandia Crest

Aerial Tramway

La Luz Trail

Lower Tram Terminal

Park→x

Tram Trail

Juan Tabo Picnic Area

La Luz-
Sandia Crest Trail

F.R. 333

Tramway Blvd.

1 mile

To I-25

WH

192

LA LUZ - SANDIA CREST TRAIL

by
Lionel Soracco

U.S. GEOLOGICAL SURVEY MAPS REQUIRED: Sandia Crest - 7.5 minute series

SALIENT FEATURES: The La Luz trail (Trail 137) is one of the most interesting in northern New Mexico thanks to its range of vegetation zones and varied landscape features. You begin in the high desert with a wealth of cactus, Engelmann oak, Apache plume, Indian paintbrush and more. As you climb you'll see the vegetation change, greening as you enter the higher canyon areas. The trail rises through sheltered oases with cooling streams, climbing through deep canyons between sheer granite walls hundreds of feet high, finally reaching the high altitude spruce and fir. Except for the first few miles (the "desert" zone) most of the trail is shaded.

Along the way you'll enjoy innumerable dramatic views of northern Albuquerque framed by the canyon walls, of towering granite cliffs and spires and of cool bands of trees in the canyon bottoms. Great photo ops all the way.

The entire trail passes through an area which was returned to the Sandia Pueblo in 1999. The Pueblo has promised to keep the trail open to the public, but STAY ON THE TRAIL, respecting the Indian lands.

RATING: Strenuous. This hike is long with considerable elevation gain. Take two or three quarts of liquid: it can be warm and by summer there may be no running streams on the way up. There are drinking fountains at the top.

APPROXIMATE ROUND TRIP HIKING TIME: Early each August there is a La Luz Run, starting about a mile or so below the parking lot. The great Indian runner, Al Waquie, of the Jemez Pueblo, set the record years ago, reaching Sandia Crest in 1 hour and 11 minutes. Mere mortals, even starting at the trailhead, should expect to take 4 to 5 hours up (we're told Mr. Waquie made it from there in 56 minutes!), and around 3 hours to get back, plus time out for breaks and lunch. Ten hours for the entire hike is not excessive.

Note: A tram shuttles between a point south of the La Luz trailhead at the bottom and at the end of the La Luz Trail at the top. The lower tramway terminal is joined by trail to the La Luz trail (see map). If you only want a one-way hike, park your car at the lower tram terminal, hike over to the La Luz Trail, follow it to the upper tram terminal and take the tram back to your car. Or, take the tram up and hike down to your car. The tram doesn't run every day so check in advance by phoning 505-856-7325 for times and rates. When running, trams leave every 30 minutes and the time up or back is 15 minutes.

ROUND TRIP HIKING DISTANCE: 14 miles to Sandia Crest, 15.6 miles to the upper tram terminal.

ALTITUDE RANGE: Highest point 10,600 feet at Sandia Crest, 10,200 at the top of the La Luz Trail (where the tramway ends). Lowest point 7,036 feet at the trailhead. Cumulative uphill hiking about 3800 feet.

SEASONAL CONSIDERATIONS: Hiking can begin in May, as soon as the snows have melted from the upper regions (call the Sandia Ranger Station, 505-281-3304, for a status report). After the middle of June it may be too hot for a pleasant hike. Monsoon thunderstorms with accompanying lightning make it hazardous during July, August and early September. From mid-September through early November it may be hiked until the first snows fall, after which icy conditions make the upper trail hazardous. Early October is a particularly good time since the air is cool and fall colors abound. In all cases a very early start is recommended to take advantage of cooler morning temperatures and shade from the lower sun during the ascent.

ROUND TRIP DRIVING: The round trip distance from the Santa Fe Plaza to the trailhead is 115 miles. Allow one hour each way.

DRIVING DIRECTIONS: The trail begins in the foothills of the Sandia mountains above northeast Albuquerque. Take I-25 traveling south towards Albuquerque. After driving about 48 miles exit at the Tramway off-ramp (Exit 234, just past the Sandia Casino). After exiting, turn left (east) onto Tramway (NM 556) and proceed 4.2 miles. As Tramway starts to curve rightwards (south) you will see Forest Road 333 to your left. Exit onto FR 333 and follow it for about 2.5 miles to the La Luz parking area at the end of FR 333A (upper end of the Juan Tabo Picnic Area). This is a fee area: $3 per car ($1.50 with a Golden Eagle or Golden Age pass). There is a bathroom on the lot. (NOTE: If you're doing a one-way hike, don't turn onto FR 333. Follow Tramway as it turns south. You'll soon come to a stop, where a sign indicates the tram terminal is to your left.)

HIKING INSTRUCTIONS: The La Luz Trail 137 begins on the uphill side of the parking lot. Immediately you enter the Sandia Mountain Wilderness. Juniper, cactus, Apache plume, mountain mahogany, cholla, live oak, piñon, cottonwoods in the draws, thistles with magenta blossoms, prickly pear cactus and more greet the eye. After about 45 minutes you'll cross a large arroyo. The trail forks with signs indicating straight ahead for the La Luz Trail and right (Trail 82) for the tramway station. Stay on the La Luz trail. The first Gambel oak appears. The TV towers atop Sandia Crest are regularly in view.

195

In another 45 minutes or so take a look back towards Albuquerque, noting how the vegetation density increases as you rise from the barren plane. Soon you'll pass over a ridge separating two major canyons, then continue up the new canyon high above the bottom. You may hear water running below. Before long you'll reach a shaded cove, with a stream. A good spot for a break.

Another hour or so brings you to a lookout point, with massive granite walls and spires to your left and across the canyon. The trail next descends across a cliff face on your left and into the new canyon. Here you'll find a lovely, sheltered rest stop with cliffs on either side. You're just two miles from the top. A sign warns that ice and snow may make the higher trail impassable (a possible problem from late fall to early spring). Continuing, you pass to the opposite side of the canyon and cross a number of ancient rock slides. High above you, just below the Sandia Crest, you'll see limestone strata and, beneath your feet, you'll start to see grey limestone rocks along the trail. Look back towards Albuquerque, which is now visible only in part through a gateway of massive, granite cliffs.

Shortly after crossing the last rock slide you'll move into forest and rise in a series of short, steep switchbacks through aspen to a saddle, where the trail forks. The right fork is the La Luz Trail, which leads you to the tramway terminal and a restaurant ("High Finance", 505-243-9742) in about 45 minutes of fairly level walking. The view to your right is dramatic, as the canyon is very deep. You may spot a tramcar or two crossing this canyon, suspended thousands of feet above ground. The left fork involves a bit more climbing (400 feet higher). It brings you to Sandia Crest after a half mile and includes a surprise concrete stairway with 36 steps. At the crest is a curio shop, restrooms and snacks (but no restaurant). A trail joins Sandia Crest and the tramway terminal. The way back is the same as the way up, with more time to enjoy the views.

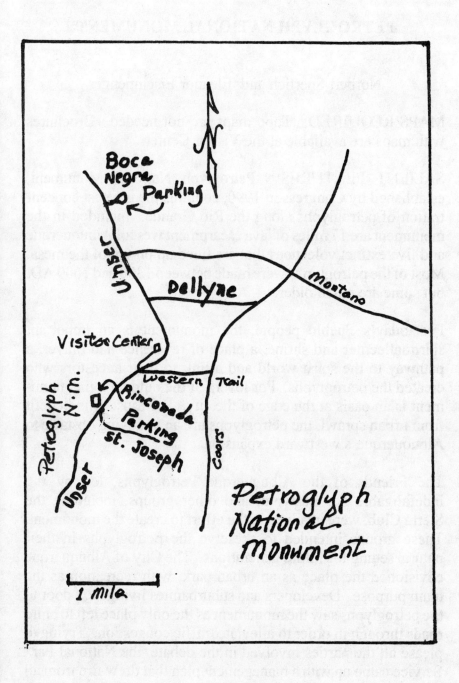

N

Boca
Negra
Parking

Unser

Montano

Dellyne

Visitor Center

Western Trail

Petroglyph N.M.

Rinconada
Parking
St. Joseph

Coors

Unser

Petroglyph
National
Monument

1 mile

PETROGLYPH NATIONAL MONUMENT

by
Norbert Sperlich and Eleanor Eisenmenger

MAPS REQUIRED: Topo maps are not needed. Brochures with maps are available at the Visitor Center.

SALIENT FEATURES: Petroglyph National Monument, established by Congress in 1990, contains the greatest concentration of petroglyphs along the Rio Grande. Included in the monument are 17 miles of lava escarpment west of Albuquerque and five extinct volcanoes that are lined up on top of the mesa. Most of the petroglyphs were made between 1300 and 1600 AD, but some are much older.

For today's Pueblo people, the monument is an important spiritual center and shrine, a place of reverence and prayer, a pathway to the spirit world and a link to their ancestors who created the petroglyphs. For lovers of the outdoors, the monument is an oasis at the edge of the city. For those who benefit from urban sprawl, the petroglyphs are an annoying obstacle to Albuquerque's westward expansion.

The Friends of the Albuquerque Petroglyphs, led by the indefatigable Ike Eastvold, and other groups, including the Sierra Club, were involved in the effort to create the monument. These groups intended to preserve the petroglyphs in their natural setting for future generations. The City of Albuquerque envisioned the place as an urban park, with recreation as the main purpose. Developers and suburbanites living next door to the petroglyphs saw the monument as the only place left to build roads through in order to alleviate traffic congestion. Trying to please all the parties involved in the debate, the National Park Service came up with a management plan that drew fire from all sides. The controversy surrounding the monument reached a peak when the City of Albuquerque asked Congress to withdraw land from the monument to allow the extension of Paseo del Norte. This was done in 1998, but at the time of this writing, the road construction project was on hold.

Beleaguered and threatened as it is, with housing developments coming right up to its eastern and northern boundaries, the monument is still a wonderful place to visit, not just once, but many times. Ranger-guided tours are available on summer weekends. Call the Visitor Center (505-899-0205, ext. 335) for more information. Bring binoculars to watch wildlife and to look at petroglyphs that are far from the trails. Note: Dogs are not allowed in the areas described below.

RATING: Easy.

ROUND TRIP HIKING DISTANCES AND TIMES: Boca Negra Canyon, about 1 mile, one hour or more. Rinconada Canyon, 2-3 miles, 2 hours or more. Piedras Marcadas, about 2 miles, 2 hours or more. Distances are short, but there is much to see, and you don't want to rush.

ALTITUDE RANGE: Lowest point, about 5200 feet; highest point, about 5300 feet. The Mesa Point Trail in Boca Negra Canyon is the only trail with a notable elevation gain (some 100 feet).

SEASONAL CONSIDERATIONS: The monument is open year round, with many visitors coming during October's Balloon Fiesta. Late fall and winter are great times to visit because the light is perfect for viewing the petroglyphs, temperatures are warmer compared with Santa Fe, and there are fewer visitors. Mornings are much quieter than afternoons, and chances for seeing wildlife are better, too. If you come during the warmer months, bring water, wear a hat and look out for rattlesnakes. Hiking boots are always a good idea.

ROUND TRIP DRIVING: About 140 miles from Santa Fe to the Visitor Center, 2.5 hours or more.

DRIVING DIRECTIONS: From Santa Fe drive south to Albuquerque on I-25. In Albuquerque, take exit 228, Montgomery-Montaño, and turn right at the traffic light onto Montaño Road. Keep on going straight on Montaño Road, across the Rio Grande, past the intersections with North Coors and Taylor Ranch Road, to the intersection with Unser Boulevard. Turn left onto Unser. Go south on Unser past the Dellyne intersection, around a bend, and on to the intersection with Western Trail Road, where you take a right to the Visitor Center. Hours are 8 - 5 daily except Thanksgiving, Christmas and New Year's Day. Summer hours are 8-6. The Visitor Center has rest rooms, maps, pamphlets and books with information about the area.

To get to the hiking trails requires more driving. Driving descriptions are included in the following hiking instructions.

HIKING INSTRUCTIONS:

1. BOCA NEGRA CANYON: This site gives quick access to short, self-guiding trails. Trailside signs explain petroglyphs and other features. Water, rest rooms and picnic tables are available. Parking fee is $1 on weekdays, $2 on weekends. Come early to avoid the crowds.

From the Visitor Center, drive north on Unser, past the Dellyne and Montaño intersections. As you drive into the Boca Negra Canyon, look for a sign on your right that directs you to the site. Turn right and drive to the pay station and the first parking lot. From there the Mesa Point Trail, quite steep in places but paved most of the way, will take you to the mesa top in about 20 minutes, past many petroglyphs. The view from up there is striking: you are right at the edge of housing developments.

Worlds in collision - urban sprawl held in check by the magic of the petroglyphs!

Two shorter trails start at the next parking area. Among the highlights of the Macaw and the Cliff Base Trails are the petroglyphs of a parrot and a mysterious star being.

2. RINCONADA CANYON: This easy hike takes you away from the road and the suburbs into a secluded area where you can truly appreciate the petroglyphs in their natural setting. A pamphlet with a map of Rinconada is available at the Visitor Center. The parking lot at the entrance to the canyon is open from 8 - 5.

From the Visitor Center drive south on Unser for 0.5 miles, then turn right at a traffic light (intersection with St. Joseph's Road). Park in the designated area. Don't leave valuables in your vehicle. Thieves know about this place! As you start walking the sandy trail that follows the escarpment, you will notice countless boulders riddled by bullets. Was this once a war zone? No, just a place for target practice. And trash dumping. Reverence for nature and respect for other cultures are not key ingredients of our civilization. This is one of the more embarrassing insights you will gain from your visit here.

Further away from the road, there are fewer shot-up rocks and more petroglyphs. Don't touch them or climb on them, they are fragile. Stay on the trail, don't trample the rattlesnakes. If you get tired of the petroglyphs, look out for the rabbits, squirrels, quail and other wildlife. The vegetation of the high desert, mostly shrubs and grasses, is quite different from what we have in Santa Fe. There are no shade trees.

As you approach the head of the canyon, you will encounter the last large group of petroglyphs. By now, your mind has calmed down, your eyes have learned to recognize subtle designs on the

201

rocks, and the urge to rush from one roadside attraction to the next has vanished. Enjoy the feeling! This is what you came here for.

Retrace your steps, or continue on along the southern escarpment toward Unser. Looking back once in a while, you will catch glimpses of the volcanoes on the mesa top. Before you reach Unser, turn left (north) and go back to your car.

3. PIEDRAS MARCADAS CANYON: The northernmost part of the monument, with suburbs on two sides, holds a treasure trove of petroglyphs in a setting somewhat like Rinconada Canyon. Extension of Paseo del Norte would cut this area off from the rest of the monument. In the spring of 1999 Piedras Marcadas was undeveloped and the access was hidden behind a housing development. Ask for a map and driving directions at the Visitor Center.

When you pass from the closely spaced houses of the suburb into the open canyon, you know that you have entered a parallel universe. Be extra careful not to disturb this special place. Follow the sandy trail that runs along the escarpment of the lava mesa. Many petroglyphs are to be found in little side canyons, on south-facing boulders. You will see depictions of masked beings, birds, animals, stars, hands and many other things. You might also notice grinding slicks (stones with a smooth surface where grains or herbs were ground). Here and there, you will startle a rabbit or quail that was hiding between the rocks. Notice the many bird and animal tracks that crisscross the sand. Before long, you will forget how close you are to the city. Follow the escarpment for a while, then return the way you came.

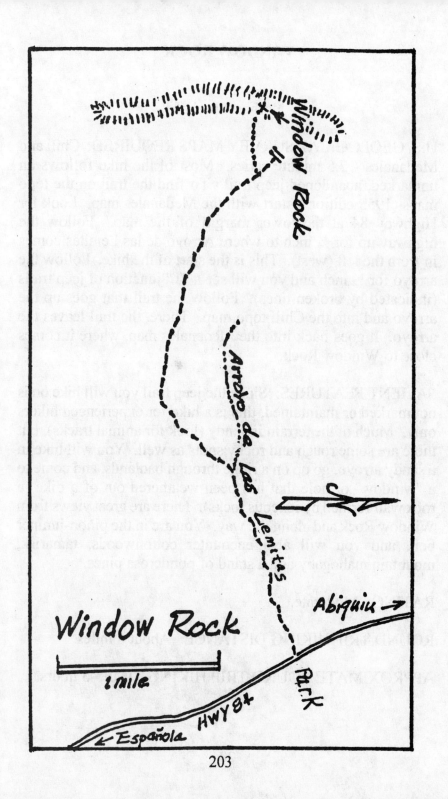

Window Rock

Window Rock

Arroyo de Las Lemitas

Abiquiu →

Park

Window Rock

½ mile

HWY 84

← Española

WINDOW ROCK

by
Norbert Sperlich

U.S. GEOLOGICAL SURVEY MAPS REQUIRED: Chili and Medanales - 7.5 minute series. Most of the hike follows an unmarked, abandoned jeep trail. To find the trail on the topo maps (1953 edition), start with the Medanales map. Look for Highway 84 at the lower margin of the map. Follow the highway up for ¾ inch to where Arroyo de las Lemitas comes in from the left (west). This is the start of the hike. Follow the arroyo for ½ inch and you will see a "T" junction of jeep trails (indicated by broken lines). Follow the trail that goes up the arroyo and into the Chili topo map. There, the trail leaves the arroyo. It goes back into the Medanales map, where it comes close to Window Rock.

SALIENT FEATURES: Since the jeep trail you will hike on is not marked or maintained, this is a hike for experienced hikers only. Much of the terrain is sandy (look for animal tracks), but there are some rough and rocky spots as well. You will hike in a sandy arroyo, go up on a ridge through badlands, and come to a "window" or hole that has been weathered out of a dike (a rock wall formed by igneous rocks). There are great views from Window Rock and along the way. You are in the piñon-juniper belt, and you will also encounter cottonwoods, tamarisk, mountain mahogany and a stand of ponderosa pines.

RATING: Moderate.

ROUND TRIP HIKING DISTANCE: About 8 miles.

APPROXIMATE ROUND TRIP HIKING TIME: 5 hours.

ALTITUDE RANGE: Highest point, 6463 feet; lowest point, 5800 feet; cumulative uphill hiking, about 1000 feet.

SEASONAL CONSIDERATIONS: All seasons, but not recommended in hot weather. If you go in summer, take extra water.

ROUND TRIP DRIVING: 70 miles; 1½ hours or more.

DRIVING DIRECTIONS: Take US 84/285 northbound from Santa Fe to Española. At the first signal light in Española, turn left and cross the Rio Grande. At the next light, turn right. Get in the left lane as you approach the third light and turn left. You are still on US 84/285. About 6 miles north of Española, Route 285 separates from Route 84. Keep going straight on Route 84. Look for the green mile posts on the right side of the road. Slow down when you pass mile post 200. About 0.1 miles after this post look for a grey, barn-like building (made from corrugated sheet metal) on your right. Some 40 yards past this building, a power line crosses the highway, and a paved private driveway goes off to the right. Go just past this driveway and park your car on the side of the highway.

HIKING INSTRUCTIONS: Cross the highway. On the west side of the highway is a fence marked "Property Boundary, National Forest." Cross the fence and go down into a sandy arroyo which comes in from the west. Follow the car tracks that run parallel to the arroyo along its right (north) side. If the tracks are gone, follow the arroyo, staying on its right side. Disregard a jeep trail that goes off to the right. Some 7 minutes or so into the hike, you should see a freestanding, orange-brown rock ahead of you on the right side of the arroyo. In another 5 minutes or so you will be close to this rock. In front of the rock is a rectangular, green water tank and a well. The car tracks (your "trail") pass the tank on the left and go in and out of the arroyo. There are cottonwoods, elm trees and tamarisks along your way, and sandy hills with piñon and juniper along the sides of the arroyo. Here and there, you will encounter light grey rocks, formed by sand particles that have been cemented together. Often, the surface of these rocks is covered with balls or nodules consisting of cemented sand. These balls come in different sizes: peppercorns, peas, tennis balls and larger.

A little over a mile into the hike (it seems longer because of the sandy terrain) the arroyo starts to narrow down. Just where it makes a turn to the right, look for a jeep trail that goes out of the arroyo and uphill on your left. This is your trail to Window Rock.

The trail climbs to the top of a ridge and follows the ridge line. Here and there, the trail is blocked by mounds of dirt. You are surrounded by badlands dotted with juniper bushes and mountain mahogany. There are more of the grey sandstone formations sculpted by the elements. About 20 minutes after leaving the arroyo, you come to a high point on the ridge, with splendid views in all directions. Ahead of you are the Jemez Mountains; to the east you will see the Sangre de Cristo Range, with the flat-topped Black Mesa in the foreground. As you continue your hike, the ridge widens and levels out. Soon, it narrows again and the trail goes steeply uphill. Here, the ground is covered with loose rocks and the going is rough until you reach level ground again. Ahead of you, to the left, you will see a ridge that is crested by a dark rock wall, sticking out like a spine.

Look for a hole in the rocks. That's Window Rock! For about three quarters of a mile, the jeep trail goes gently downhill, taking you to a flat, treeless area. This is a reservoir where water collects after heavy rains. Window Rock is to your left. Here you leave the jeep trail and go toward Window Rock. Just below the ridge, there is a sandy bank with tall ponderosa pines. This is a great spot for a break before ascending the ridge.

Look for a drainage coming down to the left of Window Rock. Climb up on the rock-strewn slope to the left of this drainage. As you near the top of the ridge, bear to the right and onto a trail leading to the other side of the dike and to the window. You can take great pictures looking through the window toward the east, especially if you have a wide-angle lens. Caution should be taken if you climb up on the dike. It is only 6 feet wide. Do not attempt to cross over the top of the window. Enjoy the views and the solitude, then return the way you came.

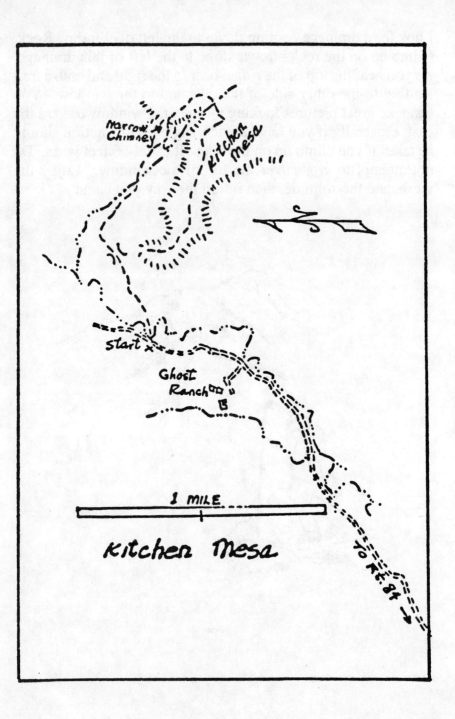

Narrow
Chimney

Kitchen
Mesa

Start

Ghost
Ranch

1 MILE

Kitchen Mesa

To Rte. 84

KITCHEN MESA

by
Norma McCallan

U.S. GEOLOGICAL SURVEY MAP REQUIRED: Ghost Ranch - 7.5 minute series - 1953, photo-revised 1979. This trail does not show on the topo map.

SALIENT FEATURES: All-season access and hiking possibilities, striking vistas, interesting geological features, the best display of red rock in northern New Mexico. The origin of the name Kitchen Mesa is unknown. The director of Ghost Ranch suggested it might be due to the fact that it overlooks the dining/kitchen area of the ranch. Owned by the Presbyterian Church, Ghost Ranch is used by many organizations and groups for conferences and retreats. Staff is friendly and knowledgeable about the area.

RATING: Moderate

ROUND TRIP HIKING DISTANCE: About 5 miles.

APPROXIMATE ROUND TRIP HIKING TIME: 2½ hours.

ALTITUDE RANGE: Highest point, 7077 feet; lowest point, 6500 feet; cumulative uphill hiking, 600 feet.

SEASONAL CONSIDERATIONS: Spring and fall are the most pleasant. Winter might be OK if there has not been a recent heavy snowfall or rainstorm in the area. Summer will be hot; try to get an early start in the cool of the morning. Note: trail is very slick when wet!

ROUND TRIP DRIVING: 122 miles; approximately 2 hours 45 minutes.

DRIVING DIRECTIONS: Take Route 84/285 northbound from Santa Fe to Española (approximately 23.5 miles). At the first traffic light in Española turn left and cross the Rio Grande. At the next light, turn right and continue on Route 84/285. Get into the left lane as you approach the third light. Turn left, still on Route 84/285. Stay on Route 84 (straight ahead) where Routes 84 and 285 separate about 6 miles north of Española. Continue north through the village of Abiquiu. When you come to the Abiquiu Dam turnoff (Hwy 96), note your odometer reading. Continue north on US 84 for about 6 miles where you will see, on the right, a wooden sign for Ghost Ranch. Turn here and drive up the dirt road. Note the historic-looking log cabin on the right; it was actually built for the set of the movie, "City Slickers." At 1.1 miles the road forks; stay left and stop at the Ghost Ranch Office to sign in for your hike. The office is generally open 8-5 everyday; a small library and museum next door has more restricted hours. Continue up this road, turning left 0.2 miles further, toward "Teepee Village" and "Trails to Kitchen Mesa & Box Canyon." After another 0.3 miles, you will reach a parking area with a sign which says "No vehicles allowed beyond this point." Park here. There is a water faucet on the right to fill your canteens.

HIKING INSTRUCTIONS: Follow the dirt road a few yards down a short hill and you will see a sign pointing right for Kitchen Mesa. Follow the trail across a shallow stream and up the far bank. You will start to see green painted coffee cans nailed upside down on small posts; these markers continue intermittently the whole length of the trail. The trail follows the river bank a short distance, then joins an old dirt road going up the hill to the right, through the deep red Chinle formation soils of the valley floor. After 5 to 10 minutes of walking, the trail takes you up to the top of a low, but steep, ridge and down on the other side. You can now see, to your right, the small box canyon stretching southeast, which the trail follows, ascending by degrees to the mesa top at the far end.

After meandering along the base of some wonderfully sculpted Entrada sandstone cliffs, the trail crosses an arroyo and starts going up the rocky talus slope of the canyon wall. The trail is steep from here to the top, so proceed slowly and watch your footing. The loose clay soils can be quite difficult to cross when muddy. About halfway up, you will begin having to traverse around or over large boulders. There are several dead-end paths branching off to the right of the main trail in this section, so keep your eye out for the green coffee cans and a few faded arrows painted on the rocks which denote the actual trail.

Just before you reach the top, you will find yourself directly in front of a sheer cliff. Look to the left and you will see a slot in the rocks. You will need to scramble up this narrow passage. The first part is the most difficult. There are adequate foot and hand holds if you look around for them; however, you will need to hoist a small child or your dog up the steepest section, and some adults may want help from their hiking companions. It may not be possible to get very heavy dogs up this vertical rock; the author was unable to hoist her 125-pound Rottweiler up here, even with the help of a friend.

When you reach the top, note carefully where the passage is, since the slot is not easy to see from the top.

The trail now veers right, crosses an arroyo, and goes steeply up on easily ascended sandstone ledges to the top of the mesa. The trail markers are farther apart here, but visible if you look for them. Once up, you can easily see the trail heading north, to your right, along a flat peninsula to the chalky white, lunar landscape at its end. This porous, hollow-sounding substance is called the Todilto Formation and is gypsum deposited by a lake that evaporated millions of years ago. Roam around this point and enjoy the magnificent views, but don't get too close to the edge since the gypsum is crumbly and the cliffs below it are sheer.

Walk back a few hundred yards to the beginning of the vegetation, find a comfortable rock outcropping under a wind-sculpted juniper, take out your picnic lunch and feast your senses. All is silence, sky and magnificent rock formations. Ghost Ranch, surrounded by green fields, sits right under the cliffs. The ridge immediately to the north of it is Mesa Montosa and the further ridge to the northwest is Mesa de los Viejos (see the Rim Vista/ Salazar Trail hike, page 215). Abiquiu Reservoir spreads out to the west and Cerro Pedernal (see the Pedernal hike, page 227) is the prominent flat-topped peak on the southwest horizon. The multi-colored bluffs all around you expose geologic history, from the reddish purple Chinle Formation muds at the base to the tree-topped Dakota sandstone at the highest points. At your feet may be patches of cryptogamic soils, a crusted brown substance made up of mosses and lichens which take many years to form and are easily destroyed. Try not to step on them. The destruction of cryptogams is the most significant factor in the erosion of desert soils. You may see the grey-green leaves and small white trumpet-shaped flowers of Bigelow's sand abronia, or tufted sand verbena, a rare plant which grows only on Todilto gypsum soils.

If you have time and want to immerse yourself longer in the red rock, turn south and wander along the relatively flat mesa top, following the undulating edge of the cliffs for a mile or so to the southern terminus of this remarkable plateau. Just be careful not to get too close to the edge since the rocks could be crumbly!

Return the way you came. Some hikers find the descent difficult because they feel more exposed and footing is more precarious. In any case, proceed very slowly, and always with great care. Take time to enjoy the rich hues of the twisted juniper stumps as you return along the ridge, and, when descending the trail back down the canyon, look for a few stately Douglas firs nestled in the coolest, shadiest nooks of the rocky walls. Don't forget to sign out at the Ghost Ranch Office.

<u>Note</u>: If you want to spend more time hiking in the area, you can take the short well-marked trail to Box Canyon, which starts at the same trailhead. Follow the signs along the streambed to a picturesque box canyon with steep walls and lush vegetation, whose subdued lighting reminds one of a mysterious grotto. Ghost Ranch also provides a written description, available at the office for 25 cents, of the short Chimney Rock Trail, just north of the Ranch, with much useful geological information.

Two miles north of Ghost Ranch on the paved highway is the Ghost Ranch Living Museum. This museum, with its many wild animal exhibits and descriptions of the area, would be worth a visit. However, as of October, 1999 the museum was closed and its future being evaluated. For up to date information, call the Canjilon Ranger Station, 505-684-2489.

Let children walk with Nature, let them see the beautiful blendings and communions of death and life, their joyous inseparable unity, as taught in woods and meadow, plains and mountains and streams of our blessed star, and they will learn that death is stingless indeed, and as beautiful as life... All is divine harmony.
–John Muir

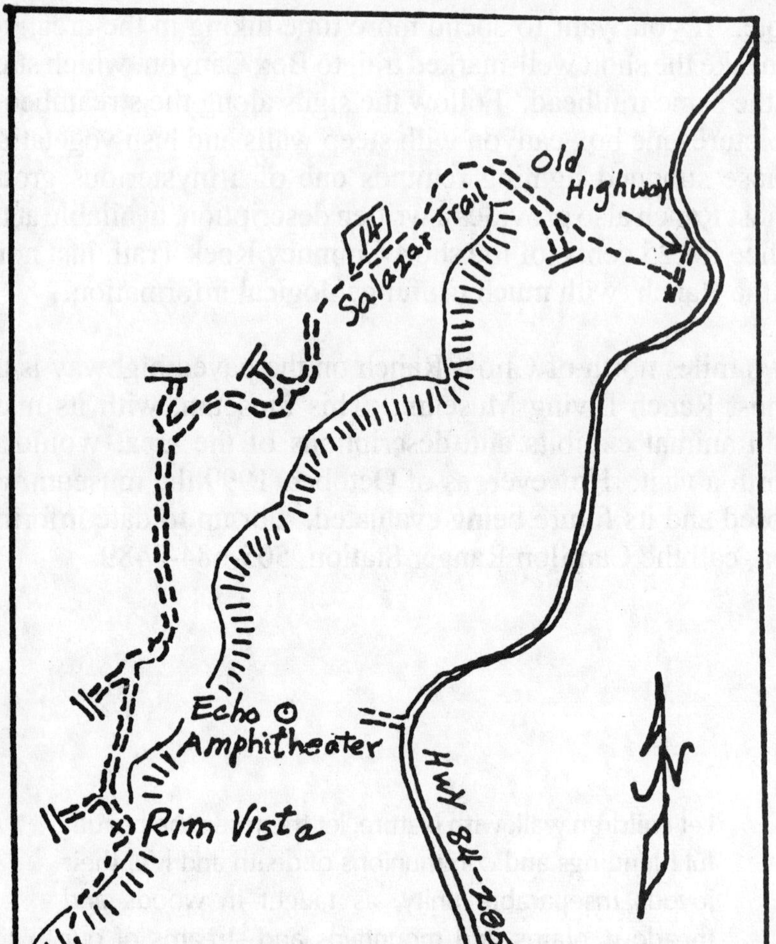

Old Highway

14

Salazar Trail

Echo ⊙ Amphitheater

× Rim Vista

Hwy 84-285

15

Park →

151

To Abiquiu

1 mile

Rim Vista/Salazar
Trails

RIM VISTA TRAIL - SALAZAR TRAIL

by
Norma McCallan

U.S. GEOLOGICAL SURVEY MAPS REQUIRED: Alire, Canjilon, Echo Amphitheatre - 7.5 minute series. These trails do not show on the topo maps. The Carson National Forest map shows both trails and most of the connecting roads.

SALIENT FEATURES: This hike is on two trails connected by a section of a Forest Service road. The southern segment (Rim Vista Trail) offers great views of red rock cliffs and the Ghost Ranch valley. The mesa-top connecting segment of the hike has expansive mountain views. The northern segment (Salazar Trail) takes you through a lovely forested canyon. Can be hiked one-way in its entirety with a short car shuttle, or either trail can be hiked up to the Forest Service road with a return on the same route. The hike description proceeds from south to north (Rim Vista Trail to mesa top to Salazar Trail.

RATING: Easy to moderate.

HIKING DISTANCE: About 7.5 miles entire length (one way); Rim Vista Trail and return, about 4.5 miles round trip; Salazar Trail and return, about 5 miles round trip.

APPROXIMATE HIKING TIME: Entire length (one way), 5 hours; Rim Vista Trail and return, 2½ hours; Salazar Trail and return, 3 hours.

ALTITUDE RANGE: Highest point, 7900 feet; lowest point (Rim Vista trailhead), 6200 feet; cumulative uphill hiking, 1700 feet.

215

SEASONAL CONSIDERATIONS: Best in spring or fall. Summer can be very hot. In winter there may be snow on the mesa top and on the Salazar Trail. After heavy rains or in early spring during snow melt, the dirt road into the Rim Vista Trailhead could be impassable.

ROUND TRIP DRIVING: Approximately 130 miles to Rim Vista Trailhead, 140 miles to Salazar Trailhead; 3-3½ hours.

DRIVING DIRECTIONS: From the plaza, drive north on Washington Avenue, left on Paseo de Peralta. At the third stoplight turn right onto Guadalupe, which merges into US 84/285, continuing north to Española (approximately 25 miles). At the first traffic light in Española turn left and cross the Rio Grande. At the next light, turn right and continue on Route 84/285. Get into the left lane as you approach the third light. Turn left, still on Route 84/285. Stay on Route 84 (straight ahead) where Routes 84 and 285 separate about 6 miles north of Española. Continue north past the Abiquiu Dam turnoff (Hwy 96); you will start to see the striking red sandstone cliffs ahead which are the setting of the hike. Two miles after you pass the dirt road to Ghost Ranch, you will pass the Ghost Ranch Living Museum. Slow down; in one mile you will see a small BLM sign on the right pointing to Forest Road 151 to Rio Chama on the left. This road goes to the Christ in the Desert Monastery and closer by, to the trailhead for the Rim Vista Trail. If you want to go up on this trail and come back the same way turn left onto Forest Road 151. Skip the next paragraph, then read on.

If you will be hiking south to north on the entire hike (as in the hiking instructions below) and want to do a car shuttle, note Forest Road 151, but continue driving north on Highway 84 past the Echo Amphitheatre Campground. At 5.3 miles beyond the FR 151 turnoff, immediately after a long guardrail on the left, you will see a small shrine in the rocks to your left. Although no road is visible, turn left at the end of the guardrail and you will see a section of the old highway (now a dirt track) and a sign, "Virgin Maria," by the shrine. Turn left again immediately and go about 0.2 miles down the old highway to a Forest Service sign on the right for Trail 14, the Salazar Trail. Park in the grass. This is the trailhead for the Salazar Trail. If you reach an old bridge, you have gone too far. Leave one car here and return in a second car on Highway 84 to the earlier turnoff to Forest Road 151.

Turn onto FR 151 and go 0.7 miles. Here at the crest of a saddle you will see a narrow dirt road going right, signed, "Rim Vista Trail." Follow this road and, where it forks, stay right. In 0.3 miles you will reach the end of the road and the trailhead for both the Rim Vista Trail 15 and the one-way hike. You will see a sign: "Trail 15 - Rim Vista 2.3 miles." Park here.

HIKING INSTRUCTIONS: Proceed up the well-trodden trail, which slowly wends its way uphill toward the cliff face to the north, passing through piñon-juniper forest with lots of Indian paintbrush, Perky Sue and blue penstemon. In about 15 minutes, you will start to see blue diamond trail signs. These blue diamond markers continue the entire length of the hike. Shortly before you reach the cliffs, at a partial clearing in the heavy piñon-juniper forest, the trail makes a sharp right. The trail is fainter here and you may fear you have lost the trail, but look to the right and you will see a blue diamond marker ahead as well as a blaze in a tall piñon near the turn. Just before the trail makes a sharp left to go up the cliffs, you will pass a large rock. This is a nice shady spot for a rest before ascending in the full sun.

The trail is now steep but well-graded. Almost immediately you will be rewarded by great views of Abiquiu Lake and the whole Ghost Ranch valley. Near the top, where you pass a small stone embankment, the trail once made a sharp left then angled gently up to the top. A fallen tree now obstructs this, and the Forest

217

Service has marked with blue diamonds a shorter but steeper route to the right.

Once on the top, veer right for a few steps and you will reach a dirt road with a large brown sign facing away from you which says, "Carson National Forest Rim Vista Overlooking Ghost Ranch and Abiquiu Dam - 2.3 miles to FS Rd 151" (which of course is where you have come from). Find a comfortable seat on the rocks at the edge of the cliffs and feast your eyes on the magnificent vista: Pedernal and Chicoma Peaks are prominent to the southwest, Highway 84 snakes south, the red rock cliffs surrounding Ghost Ranch are to the southeast and beyond them in the far distance are the peaks of the Sangre de Cristos. Peace and solitude reign, broken only by the caws of the ravens cruising in the thermals and, far below, an occasional car on the highway. If your destination is Rim Vista, you have reached it and you can simply return the way you came.

If you are hiking the entire one-way trip, you now head north on the dirt road, avoiding a dirt track to the left. In a few yards you will come to a "T" intersection. The Forest Service signs facing away from you on the right say "131 - South Rim 3" and "Rim Vista, 131A, left." Turn right and continue to follow the blue diamonds. Now you are hiking on a high, open, sagebrush-covered plateau called Mesa de los Viejos (Old Ones' Mesa). In the distance are the snowy ridge of the Canjilon Peaks and, further still, the high peaks at the southern end of the San Juans. The dirt road heads roughly north; after rain or snow it can be quite muddy. Soon you will see a white barn slightly to the left of your route which stays prominent for a long time. You will pass a small Forest Service sign (again facing away) indicating you are on Route 131. Stay straight here where a dirt track comes in from the left. This is also signed "Route 131." In a few yards the trail starts curving to the right and is joined by a lane on the left. Stay on the main trail. Soon you will cross a cattleguard and briefly find yourself back in piñon-juniper forest.

Later, at a point where the dirt road starts to veer left, look for a blue diamond marker on a small piñon to the right and a brown sign noting 131T6, Trail 14, with an arrow pointing right. Turn right here and follow this faint track east. Happily, the blue diamonds continue to mark your way. Along this section, the trail stays just to the left of a narrow band of forest which follows along the edge of the cliffs. You can walk out to the edge at almost any point to take a break while you enjoy the views and watch the ravens play.

After about a mile, you will come to another "T" intersection with a sign indicating Trail 14 to the right and a blue diamond just ahead on your right. Go right on a dirt road which circles northeast and in another quarter of a mile you will reach a brown sign noting "Trail Ahead." Ignore the ruts to the right. You will soon come upon a muddy cow pond. Here at this pond is where you reach the Salazar Trail. It would be your turn-around point if you had arrived from the north and were doing the Salazar Trail only.

Keep to the left around the pond. You will see a trail sign right after the pond and a series of large cairns which mark the trail as it moves down the floor of an emerging canyon. In less than half a mile, the trail leaves the canyon floor and proceeds along a bench on the south side of the canyon. The vegetation is quite different here from that on the mesa top or the Rim Vista Trail; you are walking amidst stately ponderosa pines and scrub oaks and the temperature is 5-10 degrees cooler.

In another half mile or more, the trail becomes an old, unused, very rocky dirt road and the side canyon you have been following comes out into the main canyon. The road makes a sharp right to follow the main canyon south. In about a quarter of a mile from the right turn, you will pass a cairn on your left, then in a few more yards come to a cairn on your right, just where the road is becoming less steep and rocky and more grassy. There may be a blue diamond on a tree on the right above the cairn. Here, the trail leaves the road and turns left into the woods. (If you are using the Forest Service map, you will note that only the trail, and not this old road, is shown.) If you look to the left you can spot several more cairns among the trees. Follow the faint but discernible trail as it heads slowly down toward the canyon floor, then more steeply into an arroyo at the bottom. After crossing the arroyo and going up its steep bank, the trail veers right across a smaller arroyo. It then heads south through an open, sagebrush-covered meadow and in no time at all arrives at the old highway where you parked your first car.

We must be refreshed by the sight of inexhaustible vigor . . .
The wilderness with its living and its decaying trees,
The thundercloud and the rain . . .
Some life pasturing freely where we never wander.
–Thoreau

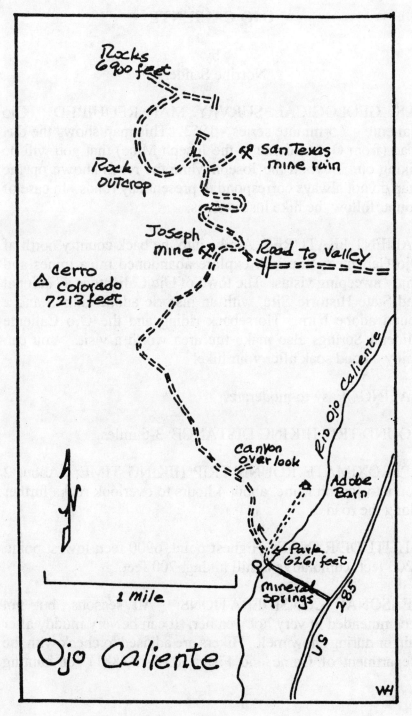

Rocks
6900 feet

San Texas
mine ruin

Rock
Outcrop

Joseph
mine

Road to Valley

Cerro
Colorado
7213 feet

Rio Ojo Caliente

Canyon
overlook

Adobe
Barn

Park
6261 feet

N

1 Mile

mineral
springs

US 285

Ojo Caliente

WH

221

OJO CALIENTE

by
Norrine Sanders

U.S. GEOLOGICAL SURVEY MAP REQUIRED: Ojo Caliente - 7.5 minute series - 1953. This map shows the dirt road (from Ojo Caliente to the Joseph Mine) that you will be hiking on. Beyond the Joseph Mine the roads shown on the map do not always correspond to present day roads. In case of doubt, follow the hike instructions.

SALIENT FEATURES: A hike into the back country north of Ojo Caliente. You will explore abandoned mica mines and enjoy sweeping vistas. The town of Ojo Caliente is a National and State Historic Site, with an historic adobe church and a round adobe barn. Horseback riding and the Ojo Caliente Mineral Springs also make the area worth a visit. You can enjoy a good soak after your hike!

RATING: Easy to moderate.

ROUND TRIP HIKING DISTANCE: 3-6 miles.

APPROXIMATE ROUND TRIP HIKING TIME: About 2 hours to Joseph Mine, about 4 hours to overlook rocks further along the road.

ALTITUDE RANGE: Highest point, 6900 feet; lowest point, 6200 feet; cumulative uphill hiking, 700 feet.

SEASONAL CONSIDERATIONS: All seasons, but not recommended in very hot weather. It can be very muddy after rain or during snow melt. Hikers are advised to check with the Department of Game and Fish (505-841-8881) for hunting

regulations in the area during the fall; the hike area is o
land.

ROUND TRIP DRIVING: 100 miles; 2 hours.

DRIVING DIRECTIONS: Take Route 84/285 northbound from
Santa Fe to Española. At the first traffic light in Española turn
left and cross the Rio Grande. At the next light, turn right and
continue on Route 84/285. Get into the left lane as you approach the third light. Turn left, still on Route 84/285, and drive
north 6.3 miles to where Route 285 separates from Route 84.
Take the right turn here. Continue north on 285 about 17 miles
to the village of Ojo Caliente. The Ojo Caliente Post Office is
on your left; just past it is the left turn to the mineral springs.
Drive toward the springs, making a right turn just after you cross
the river, and park in the large parking area under the cottonwood trees. The road ahead of you goes to the Round Barn,
about a quarter-mile away and worth a visit.

HIKING INSTRUCTIONS: From your car, go back a few yards
on the road you drove in on and look for a dirt road that goes up
to the right (northwest) between two hills. This is your trail. To
the right of this road is a brown TRAIL sign. For a short
distance, this trail, recently established by the BLM, coincides
with the dirt road you will be hiking on. Later on, it goes its
separate way, then crosses the road again. Ignore all trail signs
and stay on the road. In case of doubt, follow the hike description.

Take the road uphill. In a few minutes, a road comes in from
the left (from the water tower above the spa). Ignore it. Some
five minutes later the terrain levels out and then the road starts
to descend. You will come to an intersection where the BLM
trail goes off to the left and a faint jeep trail goes off to the right.
The latter takes you to a nearby picturesque canyon with a steep

drop to the Ojo Caliente valley. This would make a short side trip of 15 minutes or so.

To get to the Joseph Mine, stay on the main road which goes straight ahead toward the rounded shape of Cerro Colorado. In about 15 minutes, the road approaches and passes a ridge on your right and then turns to the right and northeast. Cerro Colorado is now on your left. Ignore trail signs that mark the BLM trail and stay on the road. For a while, the road has two tracks that run parallel to each other and then merge again. When the road crosses a drainage, it briefly divides into two tracks again. Next, the road starts to climb and the tailing piles of the Joseph Mine come in view on your left. The ground is strewn with glittering mica. The road levels out as you reach the mine pit on your left. There are three mine shafts in the rock wall of the pit. Mica mines were operated commercially until the 1960s.

Continuing on the road, you will soon come to a fork. Ignore the trail marker pointing to the right fork. The right fork of the road goes down into the valley. Take the left fork, which goes up and skirts the mine pit on the left. Look for a way to get to the three shafts. On a hot summer day, they offer a cool place for a break. You could make this the endpoint of the hike and spend some time exploring the vicinity.

For a longer hike continue up on the road. Soon it tops out and goes down into a canyon (Cañada Pueblo). At the bottom of the canyon, on your left, you will notice another mine shaft. This one is propped up with wooden beams and not safe to enter. Some 30 yards past this shaft, the road curves left and climbs out of the canyon. In a few minutes, you will come to a fork. The right branch, which goes straight ahead and down into a side canyon, would take you to the San Texas mine with more remnants of mining activity. A side trip to this mine adds 15 minutes or more to the hike.

If you want to enjoy sweeping views of distant mountain ranges, take the left fork of the road. In about 2 minutes you will come to another fork and again take the left branch. In about 10 more minutes, you will reach an outcrop of stone on the left which makes a good spot for lunch and a turnaround point of the hike. You have now hiked about 2.5 miles.

You may want to extend the hike by another mile by following the road up to an even more spectacular outcrop about half a mile from the first. There is a very steep pitch up to these rocks but the views of the high mountains to the north and east are excellent.

Return by the same route. At the bottom of the steep pitch, the main road turns right. It is an easy mistake to go straight ahead on a faint road here.

A mineral bath makes a nice finish to this hike.

Few are altogether deaf to the preaching of pine trees.
Their sermons on the mountains go to our hearts; and
if people in general could be got into the woods, even
for once, to hear the trees speak for themselves, all
difficulties in the way of forest preservation would
vanish.
–John Muir

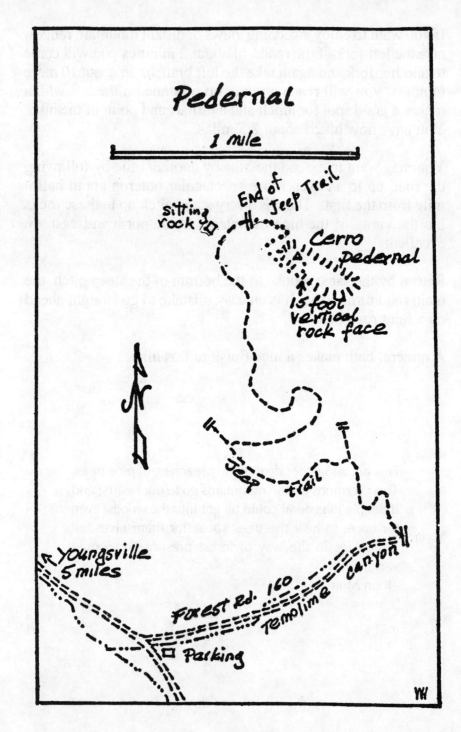

Pedernal

1 mile

sitting rock

End of the Jeep Trail

Cerro Pedernal

15 foot vertical rock face

N

Jeep Trail

Youngsville 5 miles

Forest Rd. 160

Temolime Canyon

Parking

PEDERNAL

by
John Muchmore and Norbert Sperlich

U.S. GEOLOGICAL SURVEY MAPS REQUIRED:
Youngsville and Cañones - 7.5 minute series. Note: the Santa Fe National Forest map shows none of the roads or trails you will use.

SALIENT FEATURES: Cerro Pedernal (commonly referred to as simply "Pedernal") is a landmark well known throughout north-central New Mexico. Its truncated pyramid shape is visible from Taos to Cuba and from Chama to Española. The mountain has appeared in works by famous (and less well-known) American artists. From its summit, you will enjoy sweeping views in all directions.

Cerro Pedernal is Spanish for "Flint Hill." Flint (a variety of quartz) can be found on the lower slopes of the mountain at about 8500 feet. For more than 10,000 years, Indians have used the flint from Cerro Pedernal to make arrowheads and tools.

Much of the hike is on unmarked jeep roads; the last part is very steep with only a faint trail. This hike is not suitable for inexperienced hikers and <u>not</u> recommended for solo hiking. The last part of the hike is steep and rocky, and can be dangerous unless you are confident of your ability to climb up and down a vertical 15-foot rock face (dogs will not be able to negotiate this rock face). Sturdy boots with good traction are required. This is dry country, so carry sufficient water and be prepared for wind, cold and rain.

RATING: Moderate in miles, strenuous due to steep climbs.

ROUND TRIP HIKING DISTANCE: Approximately 9 miles.

APPROXIMATE ROUND TRIP HIKING TIME: 6-7 hours, including ample time for stops.

ALTITUDE RANGE: Highest point, 9862 feet; lowest point, 8000 feet; cumulative uphill hiking, 1862 feet.

SEASONAL CONSIDERATIONS: Not safe when snow hides the jeep roads and makes the rocks slippery. The best time to visit is in the spring, fall and early winter. A favorite area for elk and deer hunters.

ROUND TRIP DRIVING: 146 miles; approximately 3½ hours.

DRIVING DIRECTIONS: Take Route 84/285 northbound from Santa Fe to Española. At the first traffic light in Española turn left and cross the Rio Grande. At the next light, turn right and continue on Route 84/285. Get into the left lane as you approach the third light. Turn left, still on Route 84/285. Stay on Route 84 (straight ahead) where Routes 84 and 285 separate about 6 miles north of Española. Continue north through the village of Abiquiu until you reach the Abiquiu Dam turnoff. There, turn left onto Highway 96. Take your mileage at this intersection. Continue approximately 11 miles to the outskirts of Youngsville. As you approach a "Youngsville" sign, look for a gravel road that comes in on your left. This is Forest Road 100 (Rito Encino Road). Turn left onto the gravel road and follow this road for about 5.5 miles, until you see a dirt road branch off to the left. Turn left onto this road and park your car in the meadow immediately after the turnoff. You are now on Forest Road 160, the Temolime Canyon jeep road. The road is not marked at the turnoff. However, a sign "160" appears some 100 yards along the road. The Temolime Canyon road is on the Youngsville and Cañones topo maps.

HIKING INSTRUCTIONS: Follow Forest Road 160 up Temolime Canyon for about 1 mile (20 minutes or more) to a fork in the road. Forest Road 160 effectively ends as further passage is blocked by dirt berms. Follow the main road that goes to the left (north). (This road appears on the topo maps as a broken line. On the Cañones map, look for the second "m" in the word "Temolime." That is where the road starts.) Ignore an abandoned logging road that branches right. In a few minutes, you will cross a drainage where the road turns to the left and starts climbing. Soon the road turns to the right (north) again and it appears to head toward the eastern end of the Pedernal summit ridge. Some 5 minutes after crossing the drainage, you may notice a block of flint to your right, with an old "2" spray-painted on it. All around, and especially to the left of the road, are pieces of flint on the ground.

In a few more minutes, you will come to a fork in the road. The road that goes straight ahead (toward the summit) was blocked with a pile of dirt in 1998. Continue on the travelled road that goes off to the LEFT, in a westerly direction. Look at your watch. About 15 minutes after taking the left fork, as you are going uphill, you will notice a drainage on your left, where Gambel oaks are growing. Just before your road is about to cross the drainage and make a turn to the left, look to your right. A road comes in sharply behind you on the right. There should be a cairn marking this intersection.

Take the rocky road that comes in from the right. It is not on the Youngsville topo map, but its approximate location is shown on the sketch map in this book. At first, you will climb steeply in an easterly direction. Then the road turns north, toward the summit ridge. It crosses a drainage and starts climbing again, turning to the left, away from the summit. This is obviously not the shortest way to get to the top—but it's the easiest! After briefly heading south, the road turns right to almost level ground. In a few minutes, you will come to the first of a series of meadows. From the last intersection you have now hiked some 25 minutes or more.

229

For a while, the road heads toward the center of the summit ridge, then turns left and runs parallel to the ridge. In the meadows, the jeep tracks are less distinct but still visible. Follow the jeep tracks past the western end of the summit ridge to a level spot between two pine trees with a nice sitting rock. You have now hiked 40 minutes or more since the last intersection. Ahead of you, the terrain starts to descend, opening up splendid vistas over valleys, mesas and mountain ranges. Take a break and enjoy the views.

It will take another hour or so of strenuous hiking to reach the summit. Look to your right. A talus slope, studded with scrub oak and piñon, rises up to the lower end of the basalt ridge that forms the summit. Walk several hundred feet up to the end of the jeep tracks. Turn right and head up toward the narrow end of the ridge, veering a little to its left. You should shortly see cairns marking a faint path which becomes more discernible as you get higher. This zigzag trail ends at a layer of boulders which you must cross with care. When you reach the vertical basalt cliffs, note where you crossed the boulder field for your return trip. Go to the right and follow a faint trail that runs along the base of the cliffs. After about 10-15 minutes of hiking the trail passes between the cliff wall on the left and a large juniper tree on the right. (If you come to a cave in the rocks on your left, you have gone too far. Go back and look for the juniper tree.) Follow the trail 10 yards past the juniper tree. Stop and look. To the right of the trail, there might be a cairn, and to your left, leaning against the rock wall, might be a log pole. There is a very faint, white arrow painted on the rock face. The cliff on your left is somewhat broken up, providing hand and foot holds. This is the place to climb up, or to call it a day if it looks too scary to you. The first 15 feet are nearly vertical, but then you will come to a rough trail that goes up to your right, leading to the top of the ridge. Watch for loose rocks! When you come to the flat top, look for cairns. They will tell you where to start your descent on the way back. Any other way down is dangerous. Continue left on the ridge to its western end. This is the highest point of Pedernal.

After you have enjoyed the spectacular views, you might want to go to the other end of the ridge, where the views are toward the east. Then find the cairn that marks the descent and start your way down to the base of the cliffs. Proceed very slowly down the steep, gravelly slopes: loose rocks abound. It helps to have one of the more able members of the party go down the final 15 vertical feet first so he/she can help direct the rest in finding footholds. Once at the base, you will be tempted to head straight down to the jeep trail in the meadow below. However, to stay out of harm's way, avoid loose rocks on a very steep slope and cause less erosion, return to the meadow the same way you came up, along the zigzag trail to the jeep road, and retrace your route back to your car.

The cleanness of the ground suggests Nature taking pains like a housewife, the rock pavements seem as if carefully swept and dusted and polished every day. No wonder one feels a magic exhilaration when these pavements are touched.
–John Muir

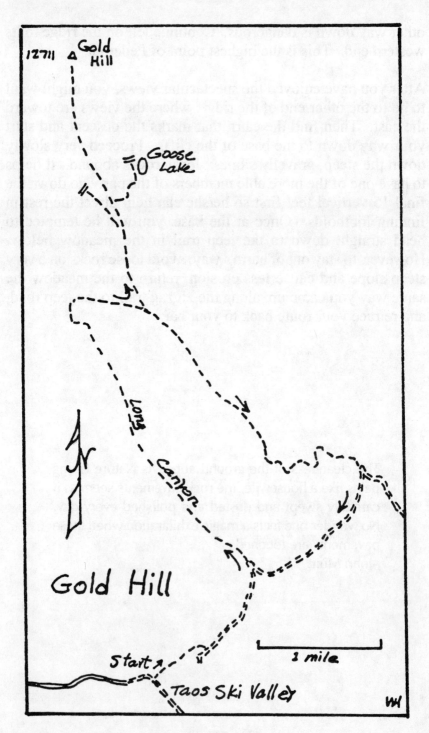

Gold Hill

12711 △ Gold Hill

○ Goose Lake

Long Canyon

N

Gold Hill

Start ↗

1 mile

Taos Ski Valley

WH

GOLD HILL

by
John Jasper

U.S. GEOLOGICAL SURVEY MAPS REQUIRED: Wheeler Peak and Red River - 7.5 minute series. Also recommended is the US Forest Service Map of the Carson National Forest.

SALIENT FEATURES: Spectacular views of highest peaks, including Wheeler; alpine flowers in summer and golden aspen in fall. An interesting loop trip via Long Canyon and Gold Hill Trails above Taos.

RATING: Strenuous.

ROUND TRIP HIKING DISTANCE: 10 miles.

APPROXIMATE ROUND TRIP HIKING TIME: 6+ hours.

ALTITUDE RANGE: Highest point, 12,711 feet; lowest point, 9300 feet; cumulative uphill hiking, 3411 feet.

SEASONAL CONSIDERATIONS: Not a winter hike. Parts of the trail may be snow-covered through June, and snowfall comes early in the autumn this far north and this high. Get an early start, since you do not want to be above timberline during summer's afternoon thunderstorms.

ROUND TRIP DRIVING: 184 miles; approximately 4½ hours.

DRIVING DIRECTIONS: From Santa Fe, take US 84/285 northbound to Española. Do not take the left turn when 84 turns, but continue straight through Española on NM 68 to Taos. After taking you through the center of Taos and approaching an Allsups store, the road forks. Take the left branch toward

Questa. North of Taos the highway is called NM 522. Some 3.5 miles later you come to the junction with NM 150. Turn right onto NM 150 and drive to the Taos Ski Valley, where the road ends. Drive to the highest public parking lot and park. You will see a Forest Service map and sign describing the area.

HIKING INSTRUCTIONS: From the upper parking lot at Taos ski area, look for the Wheeler Peak Wilderness sign and registration board. The trailhead has a great wooden map that details most of the major hikes in the area. Follow the Bull of the Woods trail uphill and eastward. In several minutes the trail forks. Take the left fork, which continues to climb steeply alongside the creek. See if you can pick out the bramble berries, aster, yarrow, hare bells and blue gentian growing along the trail.

In 10 minutes and 450 feet of climbing through the forest you reach a solitary arrow pointing left into the deep woods. Follow the arrow and in several minutes cross the feeder stream exiting from Long Canyon. Several minutes further brings you to a sign that declares "Long Canyon Trail 63". Turn left onto Trail 63. The trail climbs consistently through spruce and fir woods complete with Spanish moss. Rowan bushes dot the dense streamside vegetation. You pass the remains of a wooden gate, now defunct, that crosses the trail.

After an hour of climbing from the junction with Trail 63 the trail takes an obvious rightward traverse up and out of Long Canyon. By now you will have climbed about 2100 feet from the trailhead. Soon the trail takes an abrupt switchback to the right as it continues to climb out of Long Canyon toward the high open ridgetop. After ten minutes of hiking from the switchback you arrive at an open meadow with long views toward Kachina and Lake Fork peaks to the south. You first pass a rock cairn, and in several more minutes a wooden sign indicating National Recreation Trail, Long Canyon and Gold

Hill. Follow the sign arrow toward Gold Hill by turning left and heading north up towards an open grassy alpine meadow.

The trail follows a well-furrowed course with several rock cairns. Your trail intersects the trail to Goose Lake. Continue northward. Looking northward up the hill to what you think must be Gold Hill, the panorama unfolds. Check the sky for any indications of lightning. This exposed ridge is not friendly in poor weather.

The trail swings on up to the edge of the ridge and for the first time you can see off to the east and northeast. You can see Goose Lake far below. The hill you've been looking at as you have climbed, probably thinking it is Gold Hill, is a little 12,000 foot bump to the south of Gold Hill. The trail contours around the southwest side of this bump and continues its steady climb to the real Gold Hill. On the summit of Gold Hill was once a USGS brass cap, but it appears that a cairn has been built over the cap. To the north you can see scars on the mountains from the Questa molybdenum mine, and beyond that, the Latir Peaks.

Return down the trail the same way you came up. When you reach the big meadow in the saddle and the sign at the intersection of Long Canyon Trail and Gold Hill Trail, stay straight instead of turning right. You want to take this alternate route back, down the Gold Hill Trail to intersect Bull of the Woods Road and then back to the ski valley. It's easy to lose this trail at first because it's hard to see in the meadow. The trail heads down in an east-southeasterly direction. Look around the meadow for the trail leading into the trees. It is not cairned. As you head easterly, you should come to a little knoll with a dead log lying across your line of travel; you should then be able to see the trail approaching from your left and heading down into the trees. Turn right onto it. Looking left, you can see the trail clearly going uphill to the old fallen log cabin.

At the right time of year, from the point where the return trail enters the woods all the way down to Bull of the Woods Pasture, this is an excellent mushrooming area. Through the end of June, you may encounter big snow drifts in the trees. The trail is blazed but you must be very observant if the trail is snow-covered. The trail winds in and out of the trees and there are some spectacular views.

About 3 miles (an hour and a half) from Gold Hill, you intersect Bull of the Woods Road in Bull of the Woods Pasture. There is a nice pond which makes a good break spot. Head downhill on the road. (Uphill, the road goes to Bull of the Woods Mountain and the Wheeler Peak Ridge Trail.) The road has been closed for some years and is reverting to a trail since it has had no vehicular traffic. A little stream runs down the valley to your left. You'll note across the valley signs of mining activity: tailing piles and some stripped timber. After almost a mile, the road turns sharply left. Here is a small trail marker, a post with a very small sign saying "Twining" with an arrow pointing down a trail. Leave the road and follow the trail, which is well-defined with a small canyon to the left.

Soon you will find yourself at the intersection of the Long Canyon Trail and the trail you came up on from the ski valley, which makes a sharp right turn, downhill, with a small sign saying "Twining." Proceed down the trail you came up on, back to the parking lot.

> God has cared for these trees, saved them from
> drought, disease, avalanches, and a thousand strain-
> ing, leveling tempests and floods; but he cannot save
> them from fools—only Uncle Sam can do that.
> –John Muir

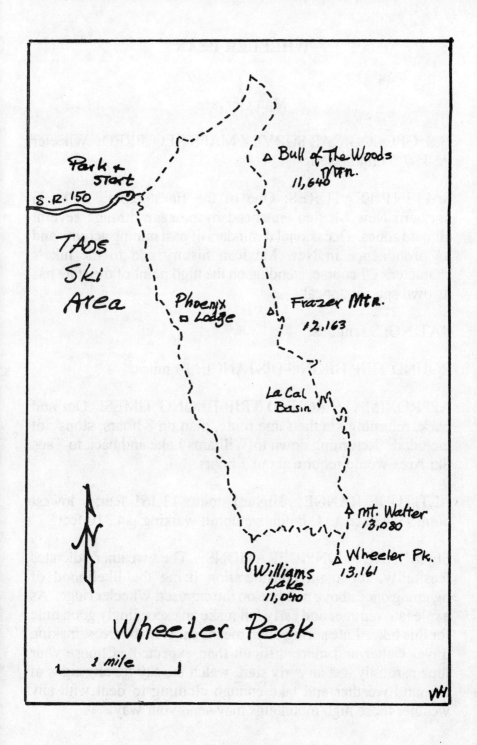

Park +
Start

S.R. 150

TAOS
Ski
Area

Phoenix
Lodge

△ Bull of The Woods
Mtn.
11,640

△ Frazer Mtn.
12,163

La Cal
Basin

N

Williams
Lake
11,040

Mt. Walter
13,080

△ Wheeler Pk.
13,161

Wheeler Peak

1 mile

VH

WHEELER PEAK

by
Matt Gervase

U.S. GEOLOGICAL SURVEY MAPS REQUIRED: Wheeler Peak, 7.5 minute series.

SALIENT FEATURES: One of the finest alpine walks in northern New Mexico enhanced by passage through several climate zones. Occasional reminders of past mining activity and its prominence in New Mexican history add to the hike's character. Of course, standing on the high point of the state has its own special appeal.

RATING: Strenuous.

ROUND TRIP HIKING DISTANCE: 14 miles.

APPROXIMATE ROUND TRIP HIKING TIMES: Out and back, returning via the same route, plan on 8 hours, stops not included. Returning down to Williams Lake and back to Taos Ski Area would require about 7 hours.

ALTITUDE RANGE: Highest point: 13,161 feet; lowest point: 9,430 feet. Cumulative uphill walking: 4,310 feet.

SEASONAL CONSIDERATIONS: The weather dictates feasibility, the main consideration being the likelihood of lightning once above tree line on the exposed Wheeler ridge. As a rule late summer and early fall make an exceedingly good time for this hike. Late spring often means snow in the trees, making travel wetter and more difficult than expected. Choose your time carefully, get an early start, watch the sky for any signs of inbound weather and take enough clothing to deal with any weather these high mountains may send your way.

ROUND TRIP DRIVING: 184 miles, approximately 4.5 hours. From Santa Fe, take US 84/285 north to Española. Continue through Española on NM 68 to Taos. After taking you through the center of Taos and approaching an Allsups store, the road forks. Take the left branch toward Questa. North of Taos the highway is called NM 522. Some 3.5 miles later you come to the junction with NM 150, marked by a traffic light and sign indicating Taos Ski Area. Turn right onto NM 150 and follow it to the highest parking lot adjacent to the main entrance at the Taos Ski Area.

HIKING INSTRUCTIONS: From the upper ski area parking lot of the Taos Ski Area, at about 9,430 feet, walk to the wooden registration sign declaring Wheeler Peak Wilderness. Look for the Bull of the Woods trail sign indicating Bull of the Woods 1.8 miles and Wheeler Peak trail. Take this trail. After 15 minutes of ascent from the parking lot cross a small stream, then proceed rightwards (northeast) alongside a small feeder stream coming in from the right.

In several minutes you reach an intersection of three trails, the first left turn goes to Long Canyon, the second left is marked by a wooden sign stating "Bull of the Woods." Follow Bull of the Woods trail. In roughly an hour of hiking the trail climbs out of the canyon, with remnants of now defunct mines dotting the area. A wooden sign indicating Wheeler Peak Trail 90, La Cal, marks the Bull of the Woods pasture. Take the right fork at the sign, passing a small 20 foot pond on your left.

At an altitude of about 10,880 feet you can appreciate you have only 2,260 feet of ascent left. The trail ascends a southwestward traverse, with the first views of Kachina Peak and the Taos Ski Area ahead. In 30 minutes from the Bull of the Woods junction a wood barricade crosses the trail that continues uphill. On a clear day, which it should be for this hike, take a well-deserved look backward over your left shoulder. If you look closely you can pick out Fishers Peak outside of Trinidad, Colorado, the Latir Mountains to the north and the area comprising Philmont Scout Ranch to the east.

The trail breaks out above tree line and continues south. The trail contours around Frazer Mountain on a low shoulder, then descends eastward into La Cal basin, by now an obvious low point in the trees. In a little over 2 hours of continuous hiking, you reach La Cal Basin at 11,800 feet. Note the protected campsites alongside the stream and plan for a return visit. Shortly after crossing the stream, the trail makes an obvious rightward turn to the south and continues to climb out of the protection of the densely forested basin. Once the treeline is again reached, the trail is clearly etched into the hillside, ascending eastward toward the ridge.

Take heed, the ridge from here to Wheeler Peak is exposed to weather. You are a long way from protection if the weather turns sour. Attempt this hike in good weather without the threat of lightning.

From La Cal basin, another hour of hiking deposits you at the low saddle between 13,133 foot Mount Walter and Wheeler Peak, 13,161 feet. Note this saddle at about 13,080 feet. If you look closely down the scree slope to the west you will see the intermittent outline of a return trail leading to Williams Lake and ultimately the Taos Ski Area parking lot where you began. Continue along the ridge for another 15 minutes and attain the high point of New Mexico. Thus far you have climbed about 4,030 feet in 4 hours from the parking lot.

The return presents two options; reverse the hike or return down the scree slope from the 13,080 foot saddle between Wheeler Peak and Mount Walter. If you consider the descent to Williams Lake, take note of the 1,800 feet of steep descent. Ski poles can help take the load from the knees on the descent.

The climb up from Williams Lake takes about 1 hour 40 minutes. On the other hand, you can expect to reach the lake in about half that time descending. The steep scree route follows the path of least resistance down to a defined trail returning to Williams Lake. The return to trees marks the approach to the lake.

At the lake at 11,080 feet the trail takes an obvious right turn near the wooden outhouse situated in the trees to your right. From here the trail, by now well used and hard to lose, descends in 1.9 miles to the Taos Ski Area, Phoenix Lodge. Along the way appreciate the steep avalanche chutes coming down from the high ridge to the east that you just hiked across. The avalanche debris is a vivid reminder of winter. Once at the Phoenix Lodge, look for a trail sign that indicates 1.6 miles back to the Taos Ski Valley base. Thirty minutes of fast hiking along Rubezahl, a beginners trail, takes you back to the parking lot at Taos Ski Valley base.

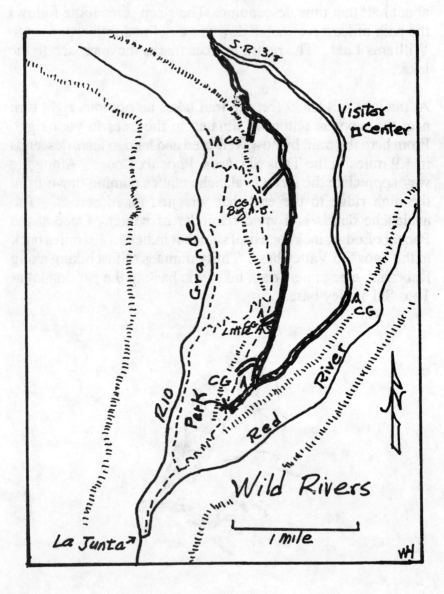

S.R. 318

Visitor Center

A CG

CG B

Rio Grande

A CG

Little

CG

Rio

Lower Park

Red River

Wild Rivers

N

1 mile

La Junta

WH

WILD RIVERS RECREATION AREA

by
Norbert Sperlich

U.S. GEOLOGICAL SURVEY MAP REQUIRED: Guadalupe Mountain - 7.5 minute series. See also trail map on Wild Rivers brochure, available at the Visitor Center.

SALIENT FEATURES: The Wild Rivers Recreation Area is north of Taos and west of Questa, where the Red River joins the Rio Grande, and both rivers have cut deep canyons into the Taos Plateau. Sage brush, juniper and piñon give the plateau its austere character. In the distance, long extinct volcanoes rise above the plain. To the east the towering ridges of the Sangre de Cristo Mountains form a dramatic backdrop, marred only by the highly visible waste piles of the Molycorp Mine! Descending to the bottom of the Rio Grande canyon, one encounters lush riparian vegetation and towering ponderosa pines.

The area is managed by the BLM and features a Visitor Center staffed from Memorial Day through Labor Day, several campgrounds and picnic areas, and many hiking trails. Fees are charged for parking and camping. Pets must be kept on a leash and are not allowed on Big Arsenic Trail or in fresh-water springs. Wild Rivers' telephone number is 505-770-1600.

While a day hike to the rivers will give you a good introduction to the area, spending a night or two at one of the camp sites will make your stay more memorable. Wear hiking boots and carry plenty of water when the weather is warm. Watch out for poison ivy (very common near the springs) and rattlesnakes (hard to find).

RATING: Moderate.

243

ROUND TRIP HIKING DISTANCE: About 9 miles for the longest hike described here (La Junta Overlook to La Junta to Big Arsenic Springs and back the same way). This hike gives you the most time at the bottom of the gorge. For a shorter hike, return by way of Little Arsenic or Big Arsenic Springs Trail and Rinconada Loop Trail, as indicated in the hike description. Just to go down to the river and back is about two miles on steep trails.

APPROXIMATE ROUND TRIP HIKING TIME: 5 to 6 hours or less, depending on route taken.

ALTITUDE RANGE: Highest point, about 7400 feet; lowest point, about 6600 feet; cumulative uphill hiking, about 1500 feet for the longest hike described, about 800 feet to go down to the river and back.

SEASONAL CONSIDERATIONS: The area is open year round, but access may be difficult in winter. Snow is possible from November to March. Thunderstorms are common in July and August. Summer afternoons in the canyon can be very hot.

ROUND TRIP DRIVING: About 220 miles from Santa Fe. Driving time close to five hours. A long, but very beautiful drive. Start early!

DRIVING DIRECTIONS: From Santa Fe, take Highway 84/285 northbound to Española. Do not take the left turn where 84 turns, but continue straight through Española on NM 68 to Taos. After taking you through the center of Taos and approaching an Allsups store, the road forks. Take the left branch toward Questa. North of Taos the highway is called NM 522. Some 3.5 miles later you come to a signal (at the intersection with NM 150). Continue straight ahead on NM 522 toward Questa. At the intersection in Questa continue straight ahead. Some 2.5 miles past the stop light in Questa, look for a sign "Wild Rivers" and turn left onto Road 378. This road takes you through the community of Cerro and to the entrance of the recreation area. About 1.7 miles past the entrance, you will pass the turnoff (on your left) to the Guadalupe Mountain trail. 3.8 miles further the road forks, with the left branch going to the Visitor Center. Stay on the right branch, unless you're going to the Visitor Center. In about 0.4 miles, you will approach a turnout on the right that takes you to Chawalauna ("Hole in the Rock"), an overlook that offers a first glimpse into the canyon of the Rio Grande. Down below, you can see the camp sites of Big Arsenic Springs. Return to your car and continue south for 1.9 miles, past the turnoffs to Big Arsenic Springs, Little Arsenic Springs and Montoso camp sites, to the turnoff to La Junta on your right. A short dirt road takes you to a parking area with a pay station and rest rooms. Park your car and pay your fee: $3 per day to park, $7 per night to camp.

HIKING INSTRUCTIONS: Follow the sign to the overlook on a paved trail, along a rock wall and down a few steps to the trail head. Awesome views of La Junta (where the two rivers meet 800 feet below). A sign indicates La Junta 1.2 miles, Little Arsenic Springs 1.7 miles. The first part of the descent is the steepest, involving metal stairs at one point and many switchbacks further down. The trail is rough when it crosses boulder fields or loose gravel. After hiking for about 25 minutes, you will come to a trail intersection. Continue straight ahead for another 10 minutes to La Junta. This is a great place to hang out for a while. Several shelters offer shade and a trail takes you right down to the water where the two rivers come together. Large boulders, carved and polished by the water, will remind you of modern sculptures, and there is always a cool breeze blowing at this place. A trail leads to the Red River, across a bridge and up to the Cebolla Mesa campground. You might want to explore that trail some other time.

For now, retrace your steps back some 0.4 miles to the trail intersection and take the trail to the left to Little and Big Arsenic Springs. The trail goes down to the river, then climbs up above a boulder field. Soon it reaches the Little Arsenic Springs camp sites in the shade of huge ponderosas. Next, it climbs away from the trees and intersects a trail that goes up to the rim of the canyon.

If you need to keep your hike short, you could go up to the rim at this point and be back at the car in less than one hour. Once you reach the rim, look for the Rinconada Loop Trail, which will take you back to La Junta overlook, if you follow it in a southerly direction. The trail is marked with brown plastic stakes and coincides (at times) with dirt roads. If you can't find a trail sign right away, follow the nearest dirt road until you come to a trail marker. If in doubt, follow the dirt road to the paved road and go south on the paved road to the La Junta turnoff and your car.

More likely you will ignore the trail that goes up to the rim and continue on toward Little and Big Arsenic Springs. Your trail soon descends toward the river again and crosses a creek that comes from Little Arsenic Springs. ("Arsenic" is a misnomer, by the way. There is no arsenic in any of the springs that you will encounter.) Next, a branch of the trail goes down to the left to a shelter at the river's edge. Stay on the main trail. Up to this point, the river was running its course fairly quietly, but from here on upstream, its path is blocked by many boulders. If you happen to be here during spring runoff (May/June), you might experience the river at the peak of its power.

The trail climbs up above another boulder field to a level area with sage brush, where the Big Arsenic Springs trail comes down from the canyon rim. Again, you have the choice to go up to the edge of the canyon and return to your car in a little over an hour's time. As mentioned in the previous exit description,

246

you would have to find the Rinconada Loop Trail and follow it south to La Junta Overlook. You would miss the beautiful setting of Big Arsenic Springs, though, which is less than half a mile away. Onward to the springs, then.

The trail drops down again and crosses the creek that comes from the first spring. Huge ponderosas and lush vegetation (lots of poison ivy, too) make you feel that you have arrived at an oasis. Take a little side trail that follows the creek right down to the river. What a lovely spot to eat your lunch. The river makes a bend at this point and the views are grand.

You have hiked about 2.5 hours to reach this place, short stops included. If you feel inspired to explore more and have another hour to spare, go up to the main trail and continue on past an outhouse and up some switchbacks. Once you reach level ground again, walk some 60 yards on the trail to where a smaller trail goes off to the left. It leads to a group of boulders with petroglyphs. Petroglyphs are fragile. We trust you will not touch them or climb on them.

Back to the main trail. It goes past another spring and down to a shelter, then crosses the creek from the spring on a wooden bridge. Soon you reach the last shelter, overlooking a wild stretch of the river. Some day you have to come back here and spend the night!

This is as far as the trail goes. Time to go back. The longest and most beautiful way to return would be to retrace your steps. For a shorter return trip, take either the Big or the Little Arsenic Springs Trail up to the rim and then go south on the Rinconada Loop Trail, as described earlier.

Pamphlets available at the Visitor Center will inform you about other trails, including a hike to the top of Guadalupe Mountain, a nearby volcano.

GLOSSARY

by Bill Chudd

Arroyo - A usually dry gully, at times containing a stream. After a rainstorm, or when there is a storm in nearby mountains, a dry arroyo may suddenly become a raging waterway.

Basalt - A dark igneous rock of volcanic origin, sometimes black and columnar.

Blaze - A mark on a tree made by chopping off a piece of bark. Blazes marking trails in the Santa Fe area generally consist of a short cut, with a longer cut below.

Blowhole - A hole through which gas or air can escape. Several deep pits in the Santa Fe area are commonly called blowholes, although they may or may not be the remains of ancient volcanic gas vents.

Borrego - A young lamb.

Cairn - A heap of stones; specifically, a pile of stones placed as a landmark, or to indicate a specific site or trail.

Caja del Rio - Box of the river. The Caja del Rio Canyon, popularly called Diablo Canyon, is a narrow, not a box, canyon.

Caldera - A large volcanic crater.

Camino - Road.

Cañada - Canyon, ravine.

Cerro - Hill.

Chamisa - The rabbitbrush, a ubiquitous grey-green bush whose odorous yellow flowers dominate the fall landscape of northern New Mexico.

Cholla - A tall spiny branching cactus with cylindrical stems.

Cryptogamic soil - A crusted, brown, fragile soil made up of mosses and lichens which takes many years to form.

Diablo Canyon - Devil Canyon (see Caja del Rio).

Divide - A ridge between two drainage areas.

Draw - A basin or ravine through which water drains.

Flume - An artificial channel, such as an inclined chute or trough, through which water is carried for irrigation or other purposes.

Frijoles - Beans (one of the crops cultivated by the ancient Indians in Frijoles Canyon).

Mesa - Spanish for "table." A small, high plateau with steep sides.

Moki stairway - Hand and toe holes dug by ancient Indians for scaling cliffs.

Petroglyph - A design cut or chipped into a rock face. Many interesting Indian petroglyphs may be seen in the Santa Fe area.

Piñon - The pinyon pine tree.

Puerto Nambé - Spanish for "Gateway to the Nambé."

Rio - River.

Rito - A small stream.

Saddle - A ridge between two peaks. Sometimes used loosely for any point where a trail or road tops a ridge.

Sangre de Cristo - Blood of Christ. The local mountain range was so named for the red color it reflects during some sunsets.

Santa Fe - Holy Faith. The full name of the city is "La Villa Real de la Santa Fé de San Francisco de Asis" - The Royal Village of the Holy Faith of St. Francis of Assisi.

Scat - Excrement, animal droppings.

Scramble - To climb or descend using hands as well as feet.

Scree - Same as talus.

Talus - A sloping bank of rocks at the base of a cliff.

Tarn - A high mountain lake or pond.

Tetilla - A small teat. Tetilla Peak was a landmark on the old Royal Road from Mexico, signaling the final approach to Santa Fe.

Tuff - A porous volcanic rock formed from compacted ash.

Viga - An exposed roof beam. (Originally a beam with which grapes or olives were pressed.)

Yucca - A plant of the lily family with sharply pointed, sword-shaped leaves.

USEFUL ADDRESSES AND PHONE NUMBERS

Santa Fe Group of the Sierra Club, 621 Old Santa Fe Trail, Suite 10, Santa Fe, NM, 87501. 505-983-2703

NM State Police Department, in case of emergency: 505-827-9000

Bureau of Land Management (BLM), 1474 Rodeo Rd., Santa Fe. 505-438-7400

National Forest Service, 1474 Rodeo Rd., Santa Fe. 505-438-7840

National Park Service, 1100 Old Santa Fe Trail, Santa Fe. 505-988-6011

NM Department of Game and Fish. 505-827-7911

NM State Park & Recreation Division, 2040 S Pacheco, Santa Fe. 505-827-7173

Bandelier National Monument. 505-672-0343

Pecos National Historical Park. 505-757-6032

Petroglyph National Monument Visitor Center. 505-899-0205, ext. 335

Española Ranger Station. 505-753-7331 or 505-438-7801

Jemez Ranger Station. 505-829-3535

Las Vegas Ranger Station. 505-425-3534

Pecos Ranger Station. 505-757-6121

Sandia Ranger Station. 505-281-3304

Tres Piedras Ranger Station. 505-758-8678

Pecos Valley Medical Center, on Highway 50 in Pecos. 505-757-6482

St. Vincent Hospital, 455 St. Michael's Dr., Santa Fe. 505-983-3361

St. John's College Search and Rescue, Santa Fe. 505-984-6135

Española Hospital, 1010 Spruce St., Española. 505-753-7111

251

Los Alamos Medical Center, 3917 West Rd., Los Alamos.
505-662-4201
Holy Cross Hospital, 1397 Weimer Road, Taos. 505-758-8883
St. Joseph Medical Center, 601 Dr. Martin Luther King Jr. Ave.
NE, Albuquerque. 505-727-8000

Map Sources:
Public Lands Interpretive Association, 1474 Rodeo Road, Santa
Fe. 505-345-9498
Travel Bug, Montezuma & Guadalupe, Santa Fe. 505-988-4226

Some other local environmental organizations:
Concerned Citizens for Nuclear Safety, 107 Cienega, Santa Fe.
505-986-1973
Forest Guardians, 1411 Second St., Santa Fe. 505-988-9126
Forest Trust, 80 E. San Francisco, Santa Fe. 505-983-8992
National Audubon Society, Upper Canyon Rd., Santa Fe.
505-983-4609
Nature Conservancy, The; 212 E. Marcy St. Suite 200, Santa Fe.
505-988-3867
NM Environmental Law Center, 1405 Luisa St., Suite 5,
Santa Fe. 505-989-9022
Quivira Coalition, 551 Cordova Rd. Santa Fe. 505-820-2544
Trust for Public Land, 418 Montezuma, Santa Fe.
505-988-5922

SUGGESTED READING

HIKING:

Evans, Harry. 50 Hikes in New Mexico. 3rd rev. ed. Pico Rivera, CA: Gem Guides Book Company, 1995.

Hill, Mike. Guide to Hiking Areas of New Mexico. Albuquerque, NM: UNM Press, 1995.

Hoard, Dorothy. A Guide to Bandelier National Monument. 3rd ed. Los Alamos, NM: Los Alamos Historical Society, 1989.

Hoard, Dorothy. Los Alamos Outdoors. 2nd ed., Los Alamos, NM: Los Alamos Historical Society, 1993.

Julyan, Bob. New Mexico's Wilderness Areas. Westcliffe, CO: Westcliffe, 1999.

Julyan, Bob. Best Hikes with Children in New Mexico. Seattle, WA: The Mountaineers Books, 1994.

Martin, Craig. 75 Hikes in New Mexico. Seattle, WA: Mountaineers Books, 1995.

Matthews, Kay. Hiking Trails of the Sandia and Manzano Mountains. Rev. ed. Santa Fe, NM: Acequia Madre Press, 1995.

Matthews, Kay. Hiking the Mountain Trails of Santa Fe, a Guide to Trails, People, Places and Events. Santa Fe, NM: Acequia Madre Press, 1995.

Matthews, Kay. Hiking the Wilderness, a Backpacking Guide to the Wheeler Peak, Pecos and San Pedro Parks Wilderness Areas. Santa Fe, NM: Acequia Madre Press, 1992.

Maurer, Stephen. Trail Guide to Pecos Wilderness, Santa Fe National Forest. Albuquerque, NM: Southwest Natural & Cultural Heritage Association, Revised edition, 1995.

Maurer, Stephen. Visitors Guide to Sandia Mountains. Albuquerque, NM: SWNCA, 1994.

Parent, Laurence. Hiking New Mexico. Helena, MT: Falcon Press, 1998.

Pettit, Roland and Hoard, Dorothy. Exploring the Jemez Country. 2nd edition, Los Alamos, NM: Los Alamos Historical Society, 1990.

Sprenger, Joanne M. Trail Guide to the Las Vegas Area: The Sangre de Cristo Range of Northeastern New Mexico. Las Vegas, NM: 1987.

Ungnade, Herbert E. Guide to the New Mexico Mountains. 2nd rev. ed. Albuquerque, NM: UNM Press, 1972.

WILDLIFE:

Bull, John, and Bull, Edith. Birds of North America, Western Region: The Quick Identification Guide for All Bird-watchers. New York, NY: Macmillan, 1996.

Cockrum, E. Lendell. Mammals of the Southwestern United States and Northwestern Mexico. Tucson, AZ: Treasure Chest Publications, 1992.

Cunningham, Richard L. 50 Common Birds of the Southwest. Globe, AZ: Southwest Parks & Monuments Association. 1990.

Findley, James S. The Natural History of New Mexican Mammals. Albuquerque, NM: UNM, 1987.

Hanson, Jonathan & Roseann. <u>50 Common Reptiles & Amphibians of the Southwest</u>. Globe, AZ: SWPMA, 1997.

MacCarter, Jane S. <u>New Mexico Wildlife Viewing Guide</u>. Helena, MT: Falcon Press, 1994.

Peterson, Roger Tory. <u>A Field Guide to Animal Tracks</u>. 2nd ed. The Peterson Field Guide Series. Boston, MA: Houghton Mifflin, 1998.

Peterson, Roger Tory. <u>A Field Guide to Western Birds</u>. 4th ed. The Peterson Field Guide Series. Boston, MA: Houghton Mifflin, 1998.

Sheldon, Ian. <u>Animal Tracks of Arizona and New Mexico</u>. Renton, WA: Lone Pine Publishing, 1998.

Zimmerman, Dale et al, editors. <u>New Mexico Bird Finding Guide</u>. Rev. ed., NM Ornithological Society, 1997.

GEOLOGY:

Baldwin, Brewster, and Kottlowski, Frank E. <u>Santa Fe: Scenic Trips to the Geologic Past, No. 1</u>. 2nd ed. Socorro, NM: New Mexico Bureau of Mines and Mineral Resources, 1968.

Christiansen, Paige W., and Kottlowski, Frank E. <u>Mosaic of New Mexico's Scenery, Rocks and History: Scenic Trips to the Geologic Past, No. 8</u>. 3rd ed. Socorro, NM: New Mexico Bureau of Mines & Mineral Resources, 1972.

Chronic, Halka. <u>Roadside Geology of New Mexico</u>. Missoula, MT: Mountain Press, 1987.

Kues, Barry S. Fossils of New Mexico. New Mexico Natural History Series. Albuquerque, NM: UNM Press, 1982.

Montgomery, Arthur, and Sutherland, Patrick K. Trail Guide to the Geology of the Upper Pecos: Scenic Trips to the Geologic Past, No. 6. 3rd ed. Socorro, NM: New Mexico Bureau of Mines & Mineral Resources, 1975

Muehlberger, W.R. and Sally. Española - Chama - Taos: A Climb Through Time. Scenic Trips to the Geologic Past, No. 13. Socorro, NM: NM Bureau of Mines and Mineral Resources, 1982.

MUSHROOMS:

Arora, David. Mushrooms Demystified. Berkeley, CA: Ten Speed Press, 1990.

Smith, Alexander H. A Field Guide to Western Mushrooms. Ann Arbor, MI: University of Michigan, 1975.

TREES AND SHRUBS

Bowers, Janice E. Shrubs & Trees of the Southwest Deserts. Tucson, AZ: SWPMA, 1993.

Brown, Lauren and Elliot, Charles. Audubon Nature Guide: Grasslands. New York, NY: Random House, 1985.

Elmore, Francis H., and Janish, Jeanne R. Shrubs and Trees of the Southwest Uplands. 2nd ed. Popular Series, No. 19. Tucson, AZ: SWPMA, 1976.

Lamb, Samuel H. Woody Plants of the Southwest. Santa Fe, NM: The Sunstone Press, 1977.

Little, Elbert L. National Audubon Society Field Guide to North American Trees, Western Region. New York, NY: Knopf, 1988.

Whitney, Stephen. Western Forests. The Audubon Society Nature Guides. New York, NY: Knopf, 1997.

WILDFLOWERS:

Arnberger, Leslie P. Flowers of the Southwest Mountains. Rev. ed. Globe, AZ: SWPMA, 1983.

Dodge, Natt N.et al. Flowers of the Southwest Deserts. Rev. ed. Tucson, AZ: SWPMA, 1985.

Foxx, Teralene S., and Hoard, Dorothy. Flowering Plants of the Southwest Woodlands, including Bandelier National Monument. Los Alamos, NM: Otowi Crossing Press, 1984.

Houghton Mifflin staff. Rocky Mountain Wildflowers. The Peterson Field Guide Series. Boston, MA: Houghton Mifflin Co., 1998

Ivey, Robert DeWitt. Flowering Plants of New Mexico. 3rd ed,. Albuquerque, NM: (Self-published), 1995.

Niehaus, Theodore F., et al. A Field Guide to Southwestern and Texas Wildflowers. The Peterson Field Guide Series. Boston, MA: Houghton Mifflin, 1984.

Patraw, Pauline M. Flowers of the Southwest Mesas. Popular Series, No. 5. Globe, AZ: SWPMA, 1977.

Spellenberg, Richard. The Audubon Society Field Guide to North American Wildflowers, Western Region. New York, NY: Knopf, 1979.

257

Tierney, Gail D. and Hughes, Phyllis. Roadside Plants of Northern New Mexico. Santa Fe, NM: Lightning Tree Press, 1983.

MISCELLANEOUS:

Auerbach, Paul. Medicine for the Outdoors. 3rd edition. Boston, MA: Lyons Press, 1999.

DeBuys, William. Enchantment and Exploitation: the Life and Hard Times of a New Mexico Mountain Range. Albuquerque, NM: UNM Press, 1985.

Drake, Bill. Map of the Mountains of Santa Fe. Santa Fe, NM: Drake Mountain Maps,1996 (rev).

Fleming, June. Staying Found, Complete Map and Compass Land Book. Seattle, WA: Mountaineers Books, 1994.

Julyan, Robert. Place Names of New Mexico. 2nd ed. Albuquerque, NM: UNM Press, 1998.

Kjellstrom, Bjorn. Be Expert with Map and Compass: The Orienteering Handbook. Rev. ed. New York, NY: Macmillan, 1976.

McMahon, James A. Audubon Nature Guide: Deserts. New York, NY: Random House, 1985.

Wilkerson, James A., ed. Medicine for Mountaineering and Other Wilderness Activities. 4th ed. Seattle, WA: Mountaineers Books, 1992.

Note: Some of the books listed above may be out of print, but will probably be available from local libraries.

INDEX OF HIKES

Ancho Rapids 152
Apache Canyon Loop 66
Aspen Vista to Tesuque Peak 47
Atalaya Mountain 8
Bayo Canyon 146
Beatty's Cabin/Pecos Falls 89
Borrego/Bear Wallow/Winsor Triangle 33
Brazos Cabin 113
Buckman Mesa/Otowi Peak 140
Caballo Mountain 171
Cañada Bonita 171
Cerro Pedernal 227
Chamisa Trail 24
Diablo Canyon to Rio Grande 136
Dockwiller Trail 93
East Fork Trail 137/East Fork Box 176
El Porvenir Canyon 107
Glorieta Baldy (via Apache Canyon)................... 66
Glorieta Baldy (via Glorieta Baptist Center) 74
Glorieta Ghost Town 79
Gold Hill 233
Guaje Canyon 171
Hermit Peak/El Porvenir Canyon 107
Hidden Lake 118
Holy Ghost Creek/Spirit Lake 84
Hyde Memorial Park Circle 28
Jicarita Peak 127
Kitchen Mesa 209
La Junta Circuit 42
Lake Katherine 61
La Luz - Sandia Crest Trail 193
La Vega 54
Nambé Lake 51

Ojo Caliente	222
Otowi Peak	140
Otowi Ruins/Bayo Canyon	146
Painted Cave	166
Pecos Baldy Lake/Pecos Baldy Peak	102
Pecos Falls	89
Pedernal	227
Petroglyph National Monument	198
Rail Trail	13
Rancho Viejo	37
Rim Vista Trail/Salazar Trail	215
St. John's College Area	3
Salazar Trail	215
Santa Barbara West Fork	123
Santa Fe Baldy	58
Spirit Lake	84
Stewart Lake	97
Stone Lions Shrine	161
Tent Rocks	182
Tesuque Creek	20
Tetilla Peak	133
Trampas Lakes/Hidden Lake	118
Tunnel Spring Trail to Del Agua	187
Upper Crossing/South Rim	157
Valle de los Posos Overlook	171
Wheeler Peak	238
Wild Rivers Recreation Area	243
Window Rock	204

Membership

☐ **Yes**, I want to help safeguard our nation's precious natural heritage. My check is enclosed.

Name _____

Address _____

City _____

State _____ ZIP _____

email _____

☐ Check enclosed, made payable to Sierra Club

☐ Mastercard ☐ Visa Exp Date ____/____

Cardholder Name _____

Card Number _____

Contributions, gifts and dues to the Sierra Club are not tax deductible; they support our effective, citizen-based advocacy and lobbying efforts. Your dues include $7.50 for a subscription to *Sierra* magazine and $1.00 for your Chapter newsletter.

MEMBERSHIP CATEGORIES

	INDIVIDUAL	JOINT
INTRODUCTORY	☐ $25	
REGULAR	☐ $35	☐ $43
SUPPORTING	☐ $60	☐ $68
CONTRIBUTING	☐ $120	☐ $128
LIFE	☐ $1000	☐ $1250
SENIOR	☐ $19	☐ $27
STUDENT	☐ $19	☐ $27
LIMITED INCOME	☐ $19	☐ $27

F94Q [W   ] -1   **SIERRA CLUB** FOUNDED 1892

Sierra Club
P.O. Box 52968, Boulder, CO, 80322-2968

☐ Yes, I want to join the Sierra Club! My check is enclosed.

Name _____

Address _____

City _____ State _____ Zip _____

Introductory ☐ $25   Phone (Optional) (   )_____

Individual ☐ $35   Joint ☐ $43

Contributions, gifts and dues to the Sierra Club are not tax deductible; they support our effective, citizen-based advocacy and lobbying efforts. Your dues include $7.50 for a subscription to *Sierra* magazine and $1.00 for your Chapter newsletter.

F94Q [W   ] -1   **SIERRA CLUB** FOUNDED 1892

Please mail this to Sierra Club, P.O. Box 52968, Boulder, Colorado, 80322-2968

Membership

☐ **Yes,** I want to help safeguard our nation's precious natural heritage. My check is enclosed.

Name _____

Address _____

City _____

State _____ ZIP _____

email _____

☐ Check enclosed, made payable to Sierra Club

☐ Mastercard ☐ Visa Exp Date ____/____

Cardholder Name _____

Card Number _____

Contributions, gifts and dues to the Sierra Club are not tax deductible; they support our effective, citizen-based advocacy and lobbying efforts. Your dues include $7.50 for a subscription to *Sierra* magazine and $1.00 for your Chapter newsletter.

MEMBERSHIP CATEGORIES

	INDIVIDUAL	JOINT
INTRODUCTORY	☐ $25	
REGULAR	☐ $35	☐ $43
SUPPORTING	☐ $60	☐ $68
CONTRIBUTING	☐ $120	☐ $128
LIFE	☐ $1000	☐ $1250
SENIOR	☐ $19	☐ $27
STUDENT	☐ $19	☐ $27
LIMITED INCOME	☐ $19	☐ $27

F94Q ☐ W ☐ -1 **SIERRA CLUB** FOUNDED 1892

Sierra Club
P.O. Box 52968, Boulder, CO, 80322-2968

☐ Yes, I want to join the Sierra Club! My check is enclosed.

Name _____

Address _____

City _____ State _____ Zip _____

Introductory ☐ $25   Phone (Optional) ( )_____

Individual ☐ $35   Joint ☐ $43

F94Q ☐ W ☐ -1   **SIERRA CLUB** FOUNDED 1892

Contributions, gifts and dues to the Sierra Club are not tax deductible; they support our effective, citizen-based advocacy and lobbying efforts. Your dues include $7.50 for a subscription to *Sierra* magazine and $1.00 for your Chapter newsletter.

Please mail this to Sierra Club, P.O. Box 52968, Boulder, Colorado, 80322-2968